Life Lessons from a
UFO C⋏tcher®

An Autobiographical Manga

Life Lessons from a UFO Catcher: An Autobiographical Manga
Season 1

Story and characters by Kenny Loui
Art by Yamawe

Published by UFO Comics
Editor: Kenny Loui

Printed in the United States
First Printing: June 2023

Copyright © 2023 Kenny Loui & Yamawe

Originally published as single issues in *Life Lessons from a UFO Catcher* #1-3... however, this compilation contains additional bonus scenes, "BGM-enhanced" stories, and an epilogue! Yay!

The stories herein are based on the author's personal experiences. However, the names, appearances, and other identifying details of individuals and places have been changed to protect the privacy of the innocent and not-so-innocent... because the author is a nice guy that way. Details of certain events have also been modified for the reasons mentioned above. Therefore, any resemblance to actual persons, living or dead (or ascended... a reference for any *Stargate SG-1* fans out there), or actual events is purely coincidental. However, the lessons the author learned and the many mistakes he made to learn them are real... as real as Cheryl Lynn's 1978 hit single, "Got to Be Real."

Take these lessons to heart so you don't make the same mistakes the author made in life... unless you want to, but he highly advises against it. Although the author has made some good life decisions, too, like writing this nifty manga for you to read to your heart's content. Enjoy, 楽しんで！

ISBN: 979-8-9867300-1-1 (paperback)
ISBN: 979-8-9867300-2-8 (e-book)

Cover art by Yamawe
Cover design by Kenny Loui

CONTENTS

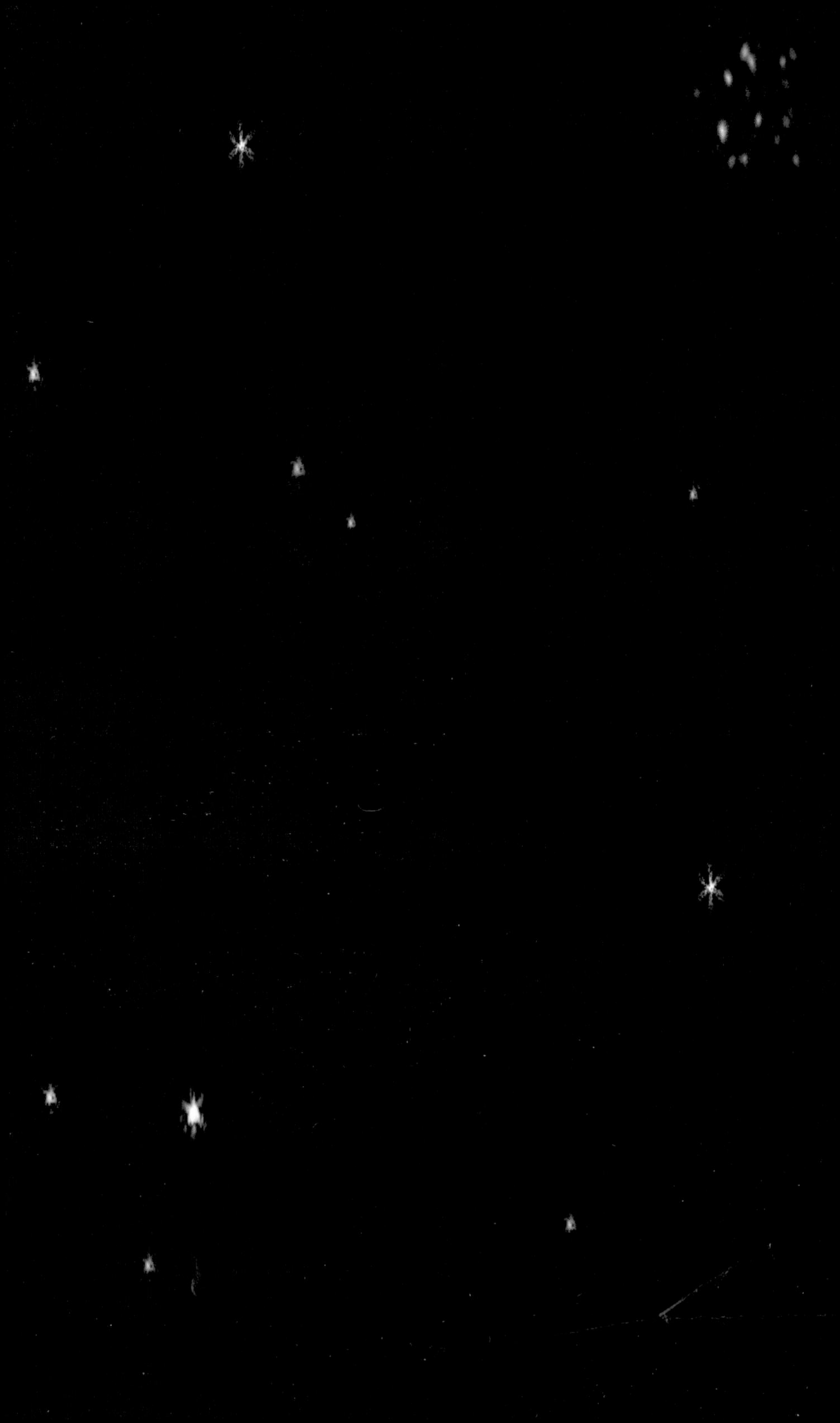

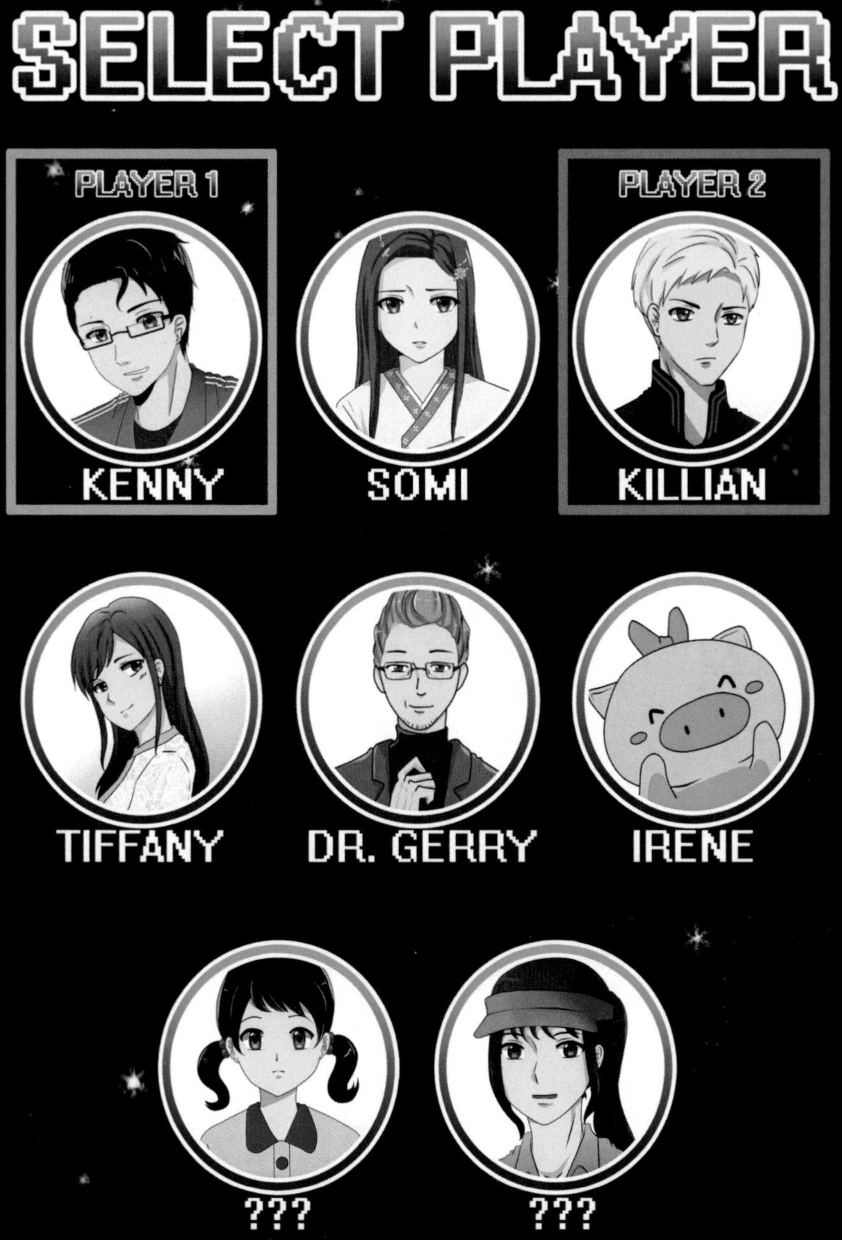
SELECT PLAYER
PLAYER 1
KENNY
SOMI
PLAYER 2
KILLIAN
TIFFANY
DR. GERRY
IRENE
???
???

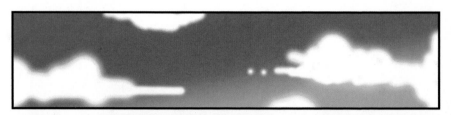

MY NAME IS...

KENNY LOUI.

6

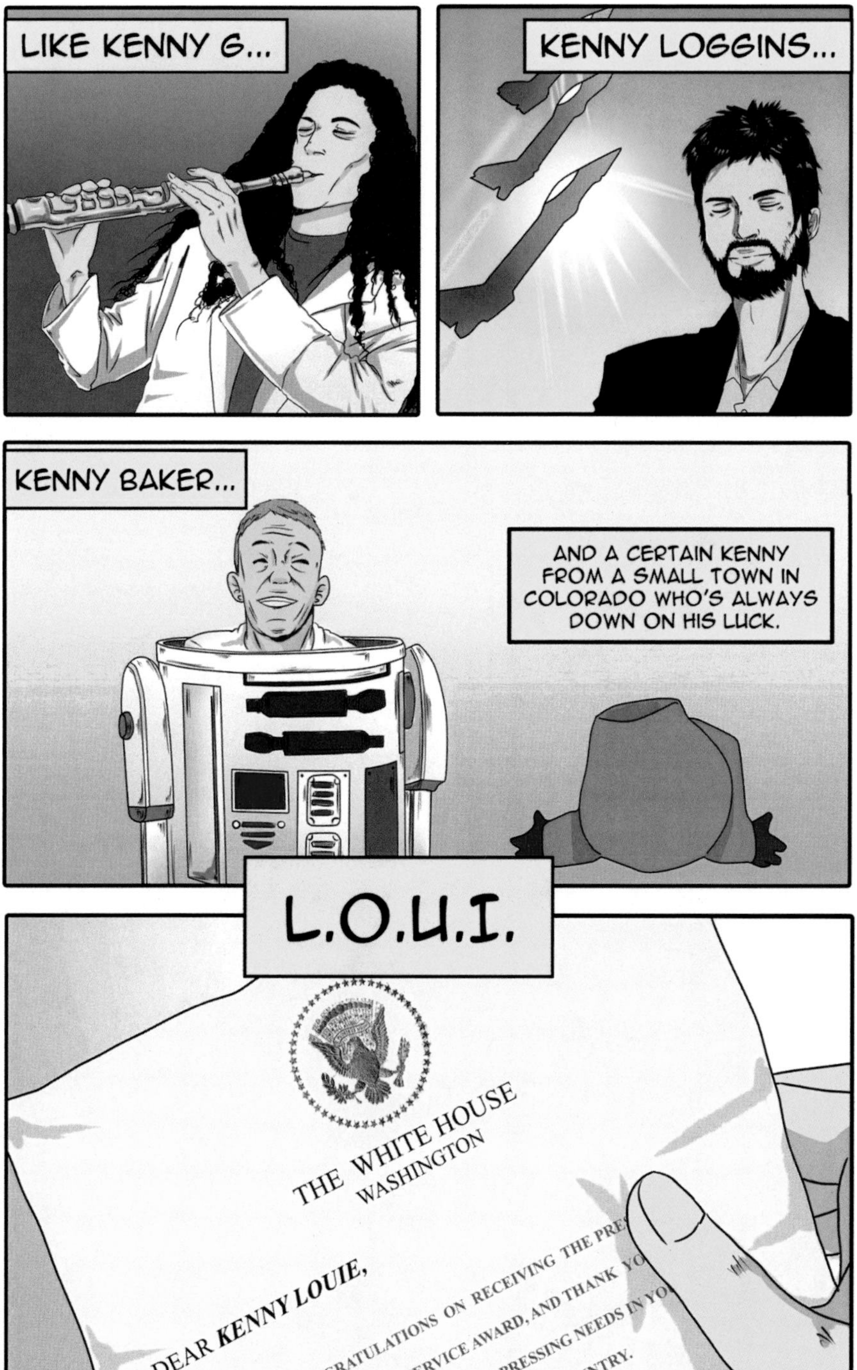
LIKE KENNY G...
KENNY LOGGINS...
KENNY BAKER...
AND A CERTAIN KENNY FROM A SMALL TOWN IN COLORADO WHO'S ALWAYS DOWN ON HIS LUCK.
L.O.U.I.
THE WHITE HOUSE
WASHINGTON
DEAR KENNY LOUIE,
NGRATULATIONS ON RECEIVING THE PRES
SERVICE AWARD, AND THANK YO
T PRESSING NEEDS IN YO
UNTRY.

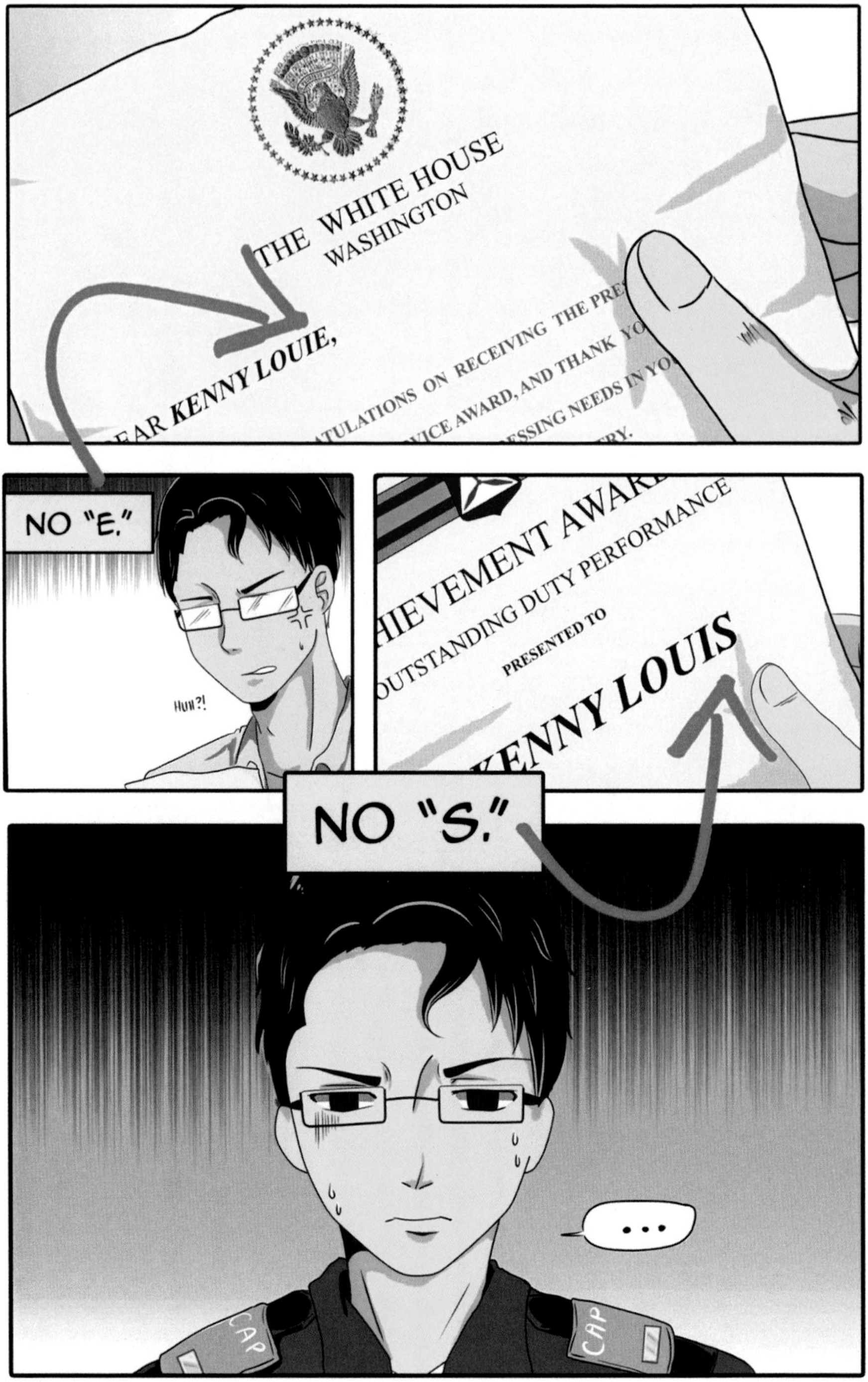
THE WHITE HOUSE
WASHINGTON
KENNY LOUIE,
NO "E."
HUH?!
OUTSTANDING DUTY PERFORMANCE
PRESENTED TO
KENNY LOUIS
NO "S."
...
CAP
CAP

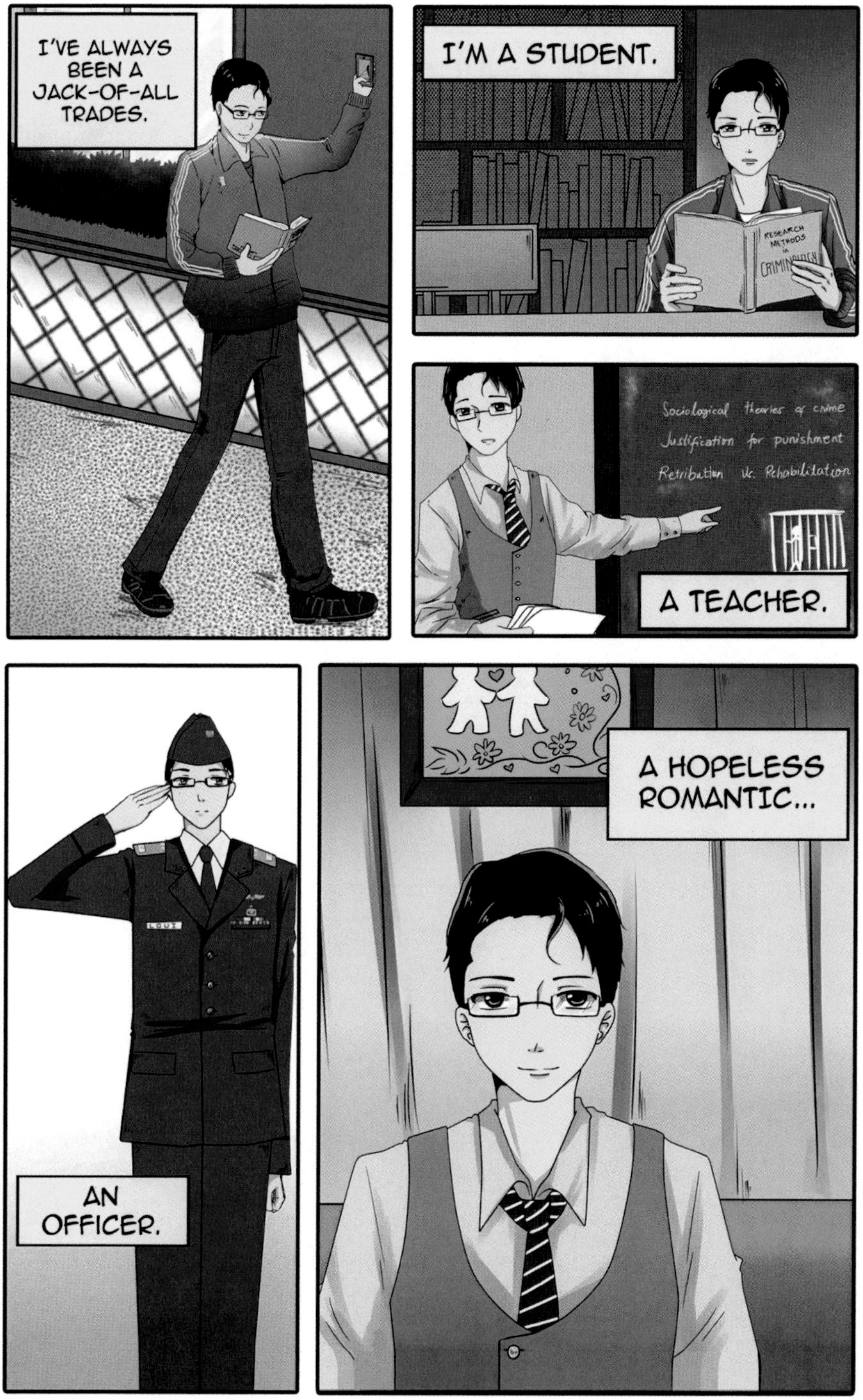
I'VE ALWAYS BEEN A JACK-OF-ALL TRADES.
I'M A STUDENT.
RESEARCH METHODS in
Sociological theories of crime
Justification for punishment
Retribution vs. Rehabilitation
A TEACHER.
AN OFFICER.
A HOPELESS ROMANTIC...

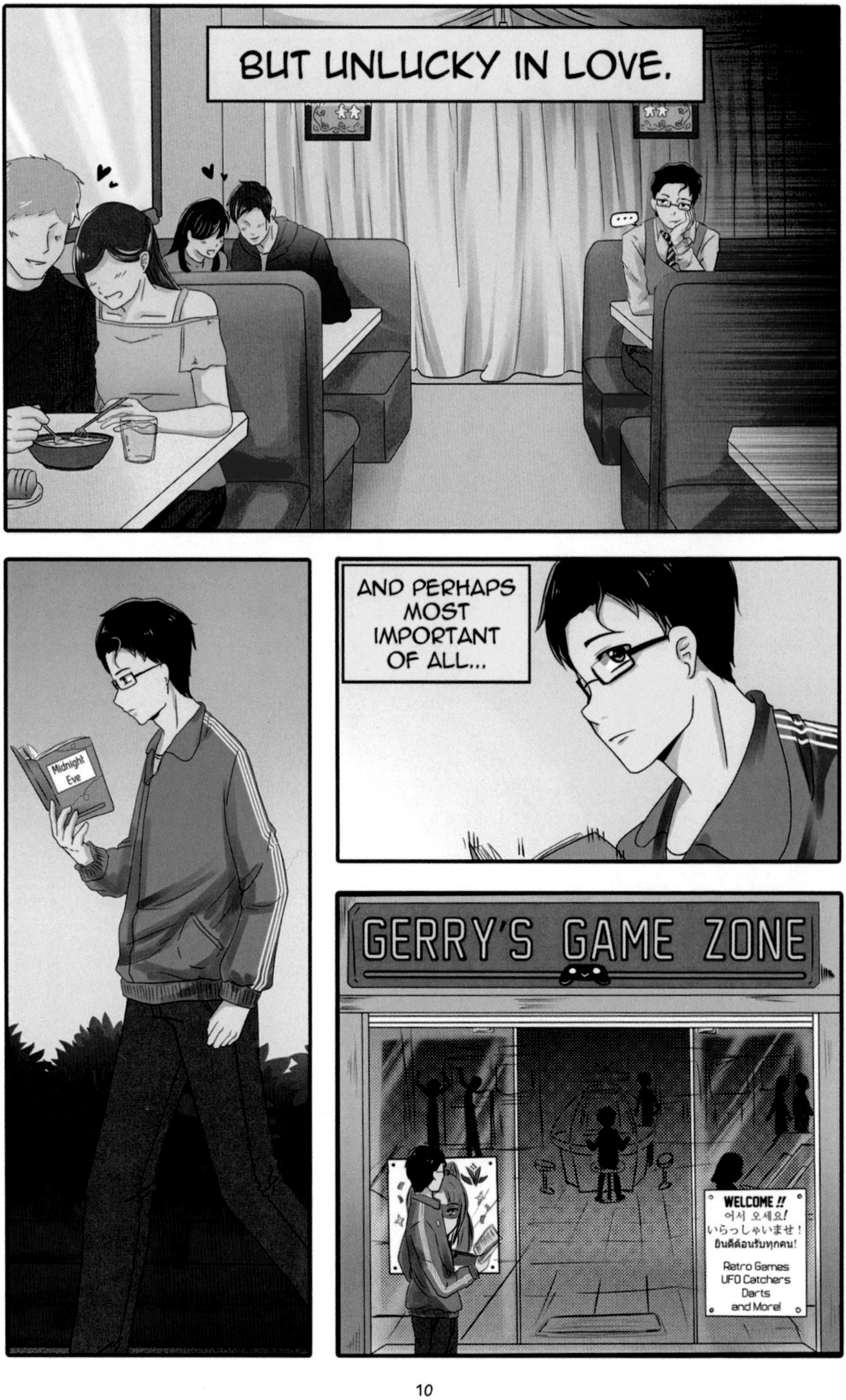
BUT UNLUCKY IN LOVE.
...
Midnight Eve
AND PERHAPS MOST IMPORTANT OF ALL...
GERRY'S GAME ZONE
WELCOME !!
어서 오세요!
いらっしゃいませ！
ยินดีต้อนรับทุกคน!
Retro Games
UFO Catchers
Darts
and More!

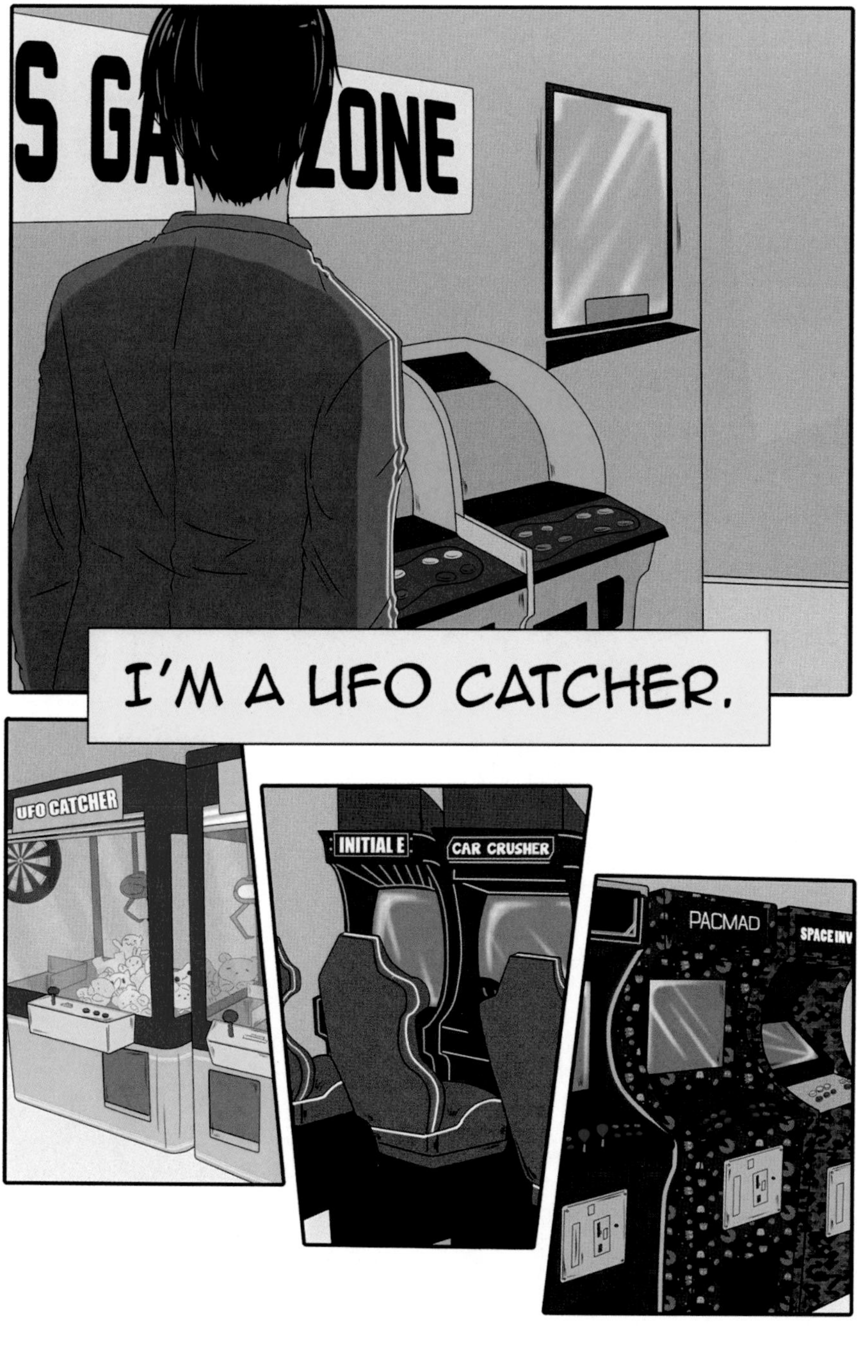
S GA ZONE
I'M A UFO CATCHER.
UFO CATCHER
INITIAL E
CAR CRUSHER
PACMAD
SPACE INV

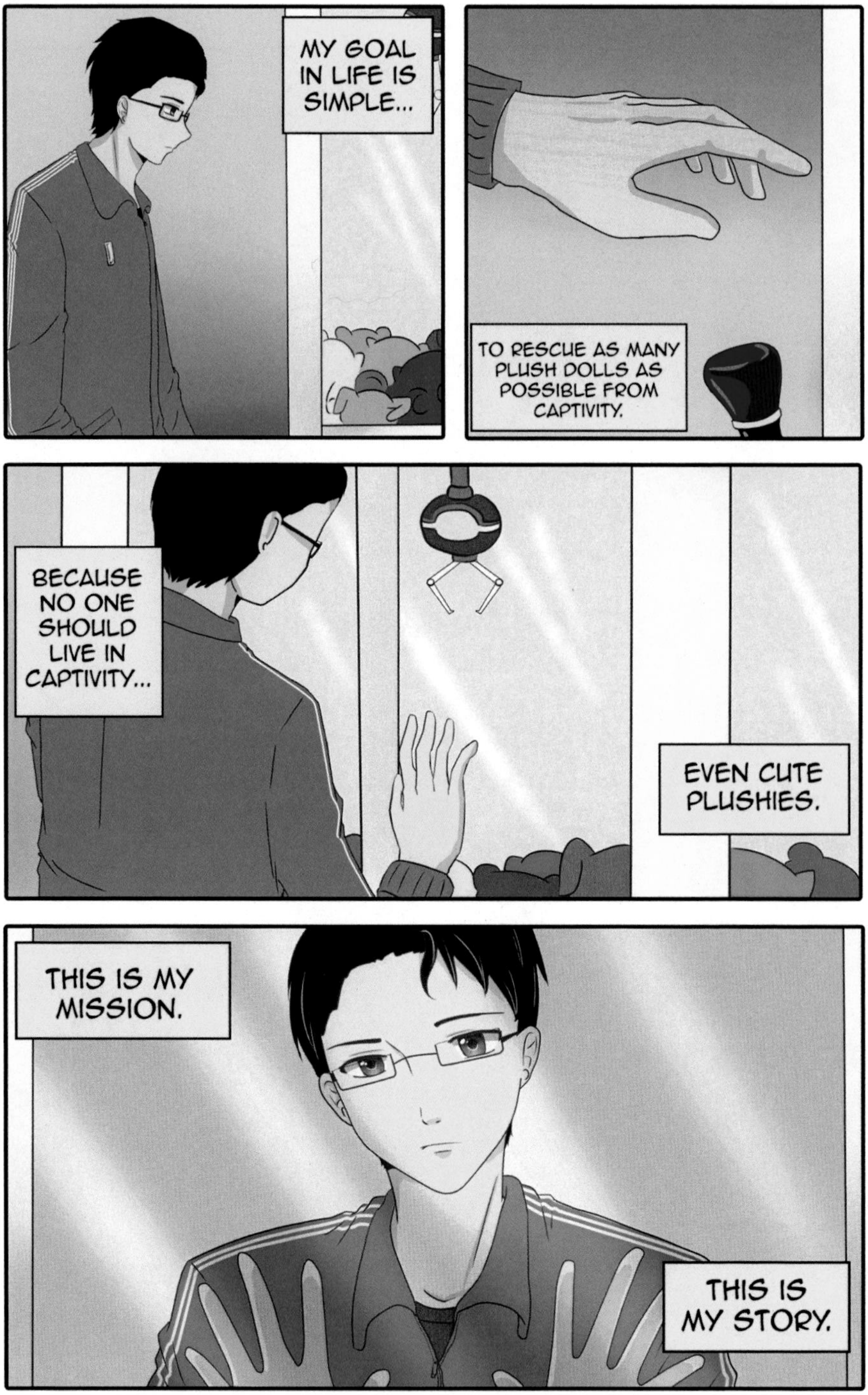
MY GOAL IN LIFE IS SIMPLE...
TO RESCUE AS MANY PLUSH DOLLS AS POSSIBLE FROM CAPTIVITY.
BECAUSE NO ONE SHOULD LIVE IN CAPTIVITY...
EVEN CUTE PLUSHIES.
THIS IS MY MISSION.
THIS IS MY STORY.

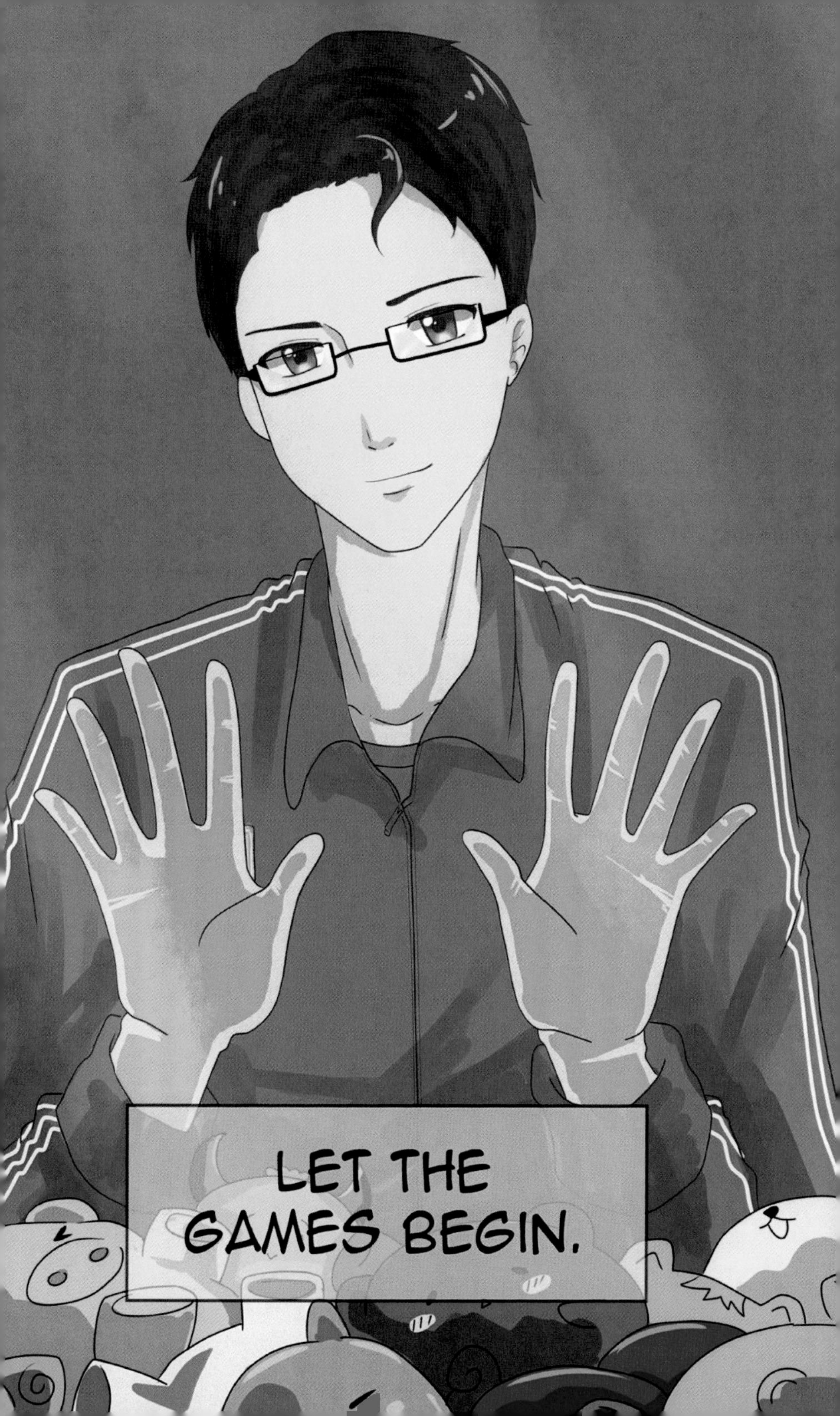
LET THE
GAMES BEGIN.

Life Lessons from a UFO Catcher®

An Autobiographical Manga

Story by
KENNY LOUI

Art by
YAMAWE

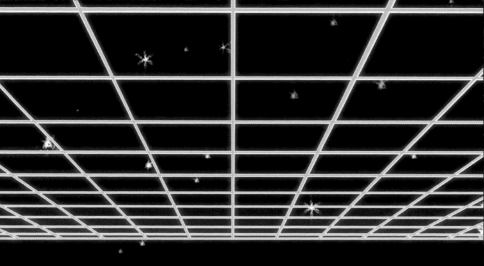

Episode 1:
Look Before You Buy

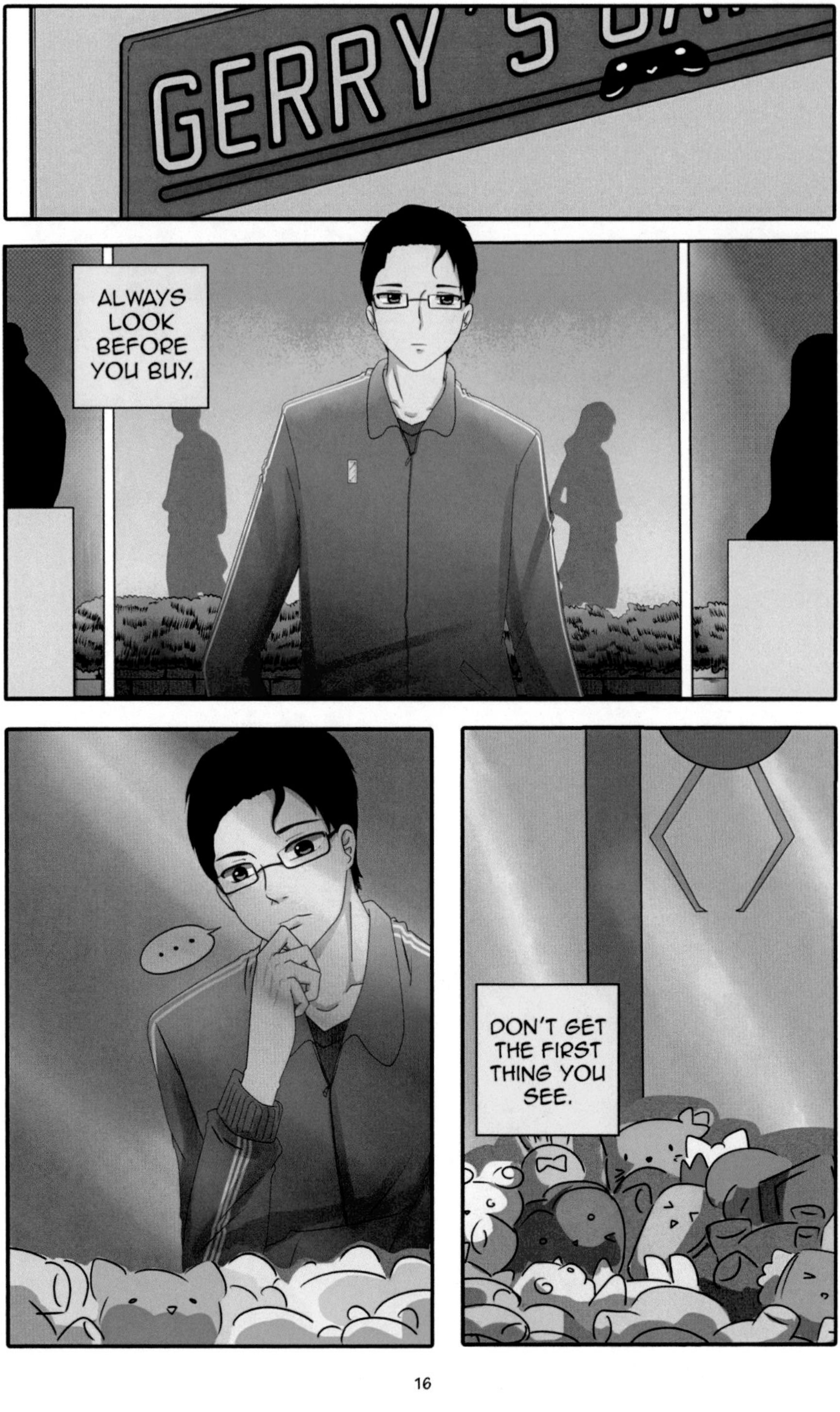
GERRY'S
ALWAYS LOOK BEFORE YOU BUY.
...
DON'T GET THE FIRST THING YOU SEE.

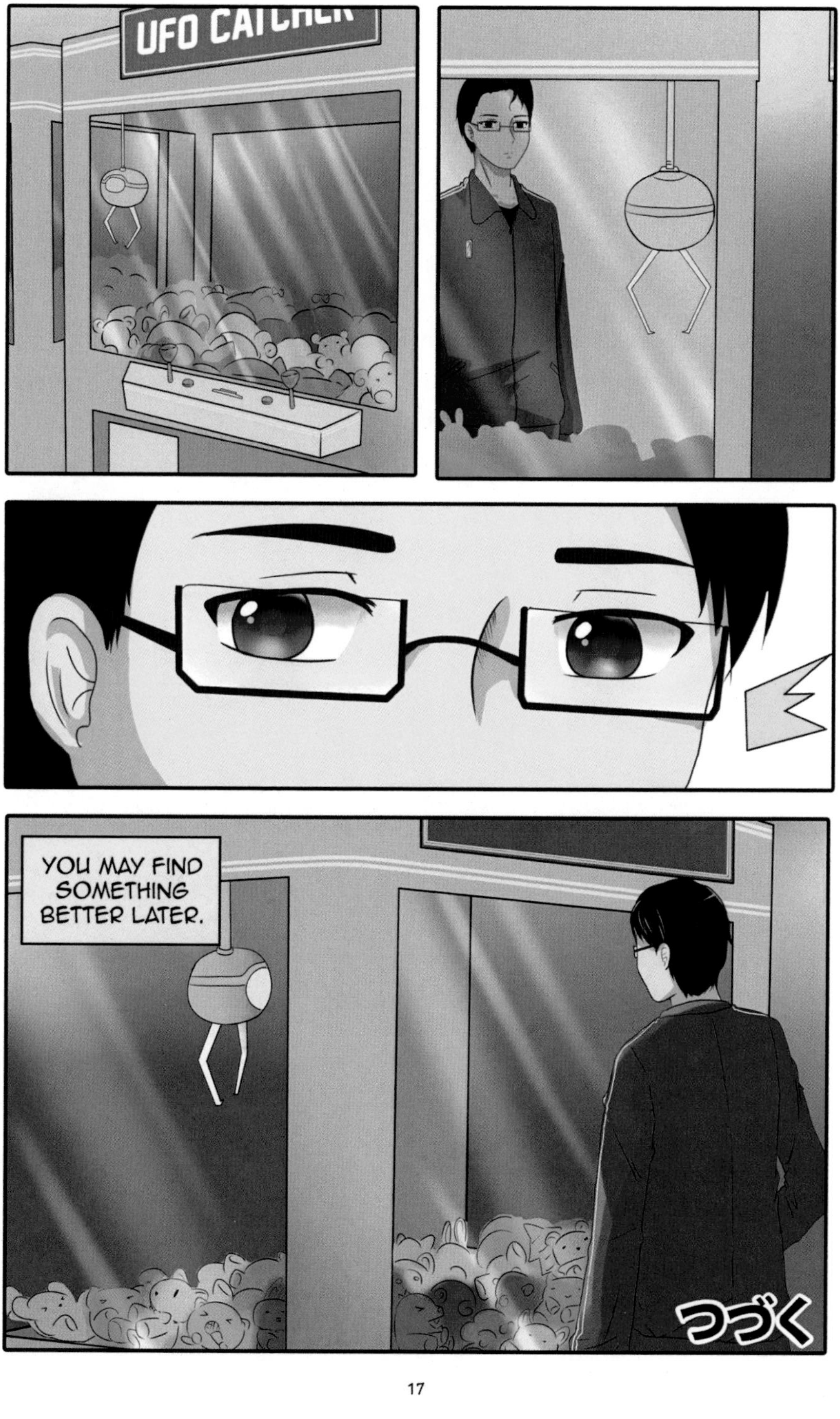
UFO CATCHER
YOU MAY FIND SOMETHING BETTER LATER.
つづく

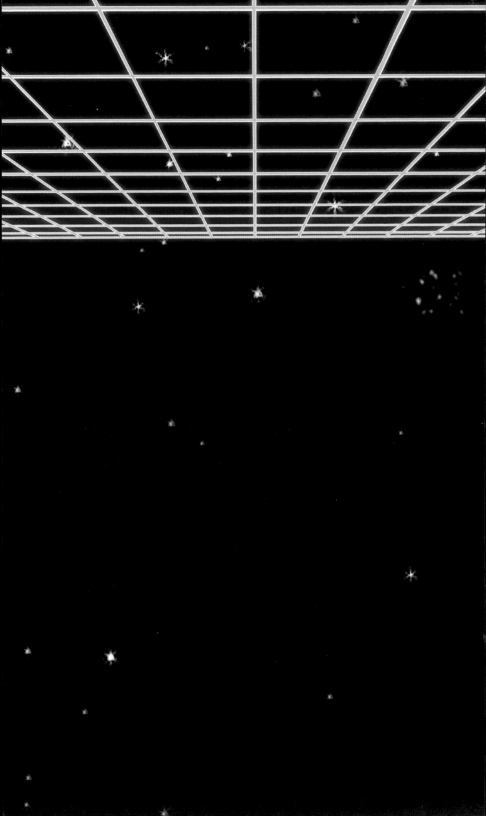

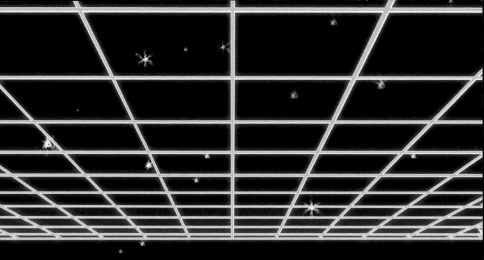

Episode 2:

Always Have A Plan

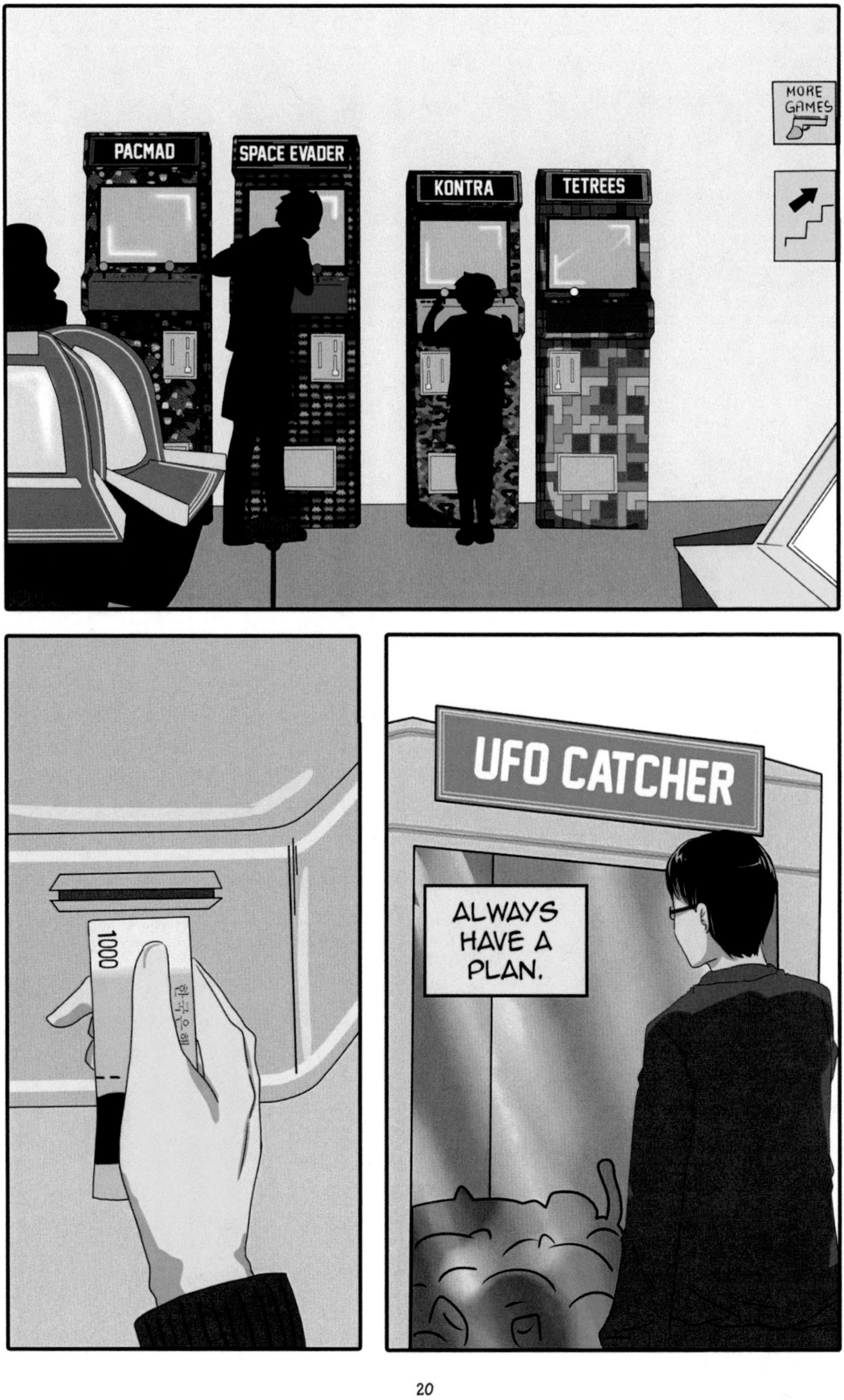

PACMAD
SPACE EVADER
KONTRA
TETREES
MORE GAMES
1000
UFO CATCHER
ALWAYS HAVE A PLAN.

MOVES!
BZZZT!
BZZZT!
MOVES!
BZZZT!
BZZZT!
PRESS!
DOWN!
OPEN!
CLOSES!

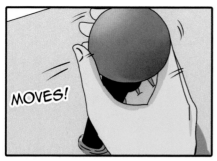

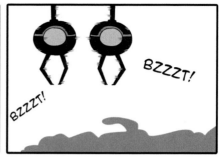

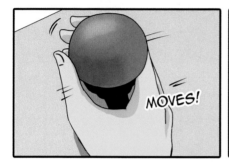

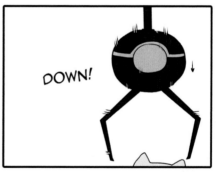

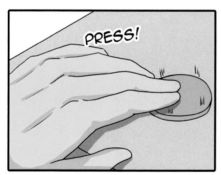

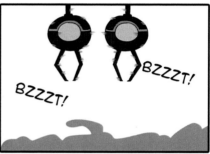

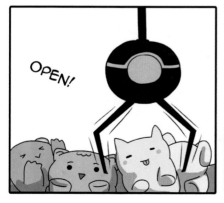

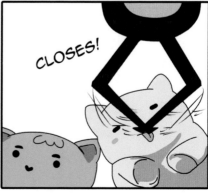

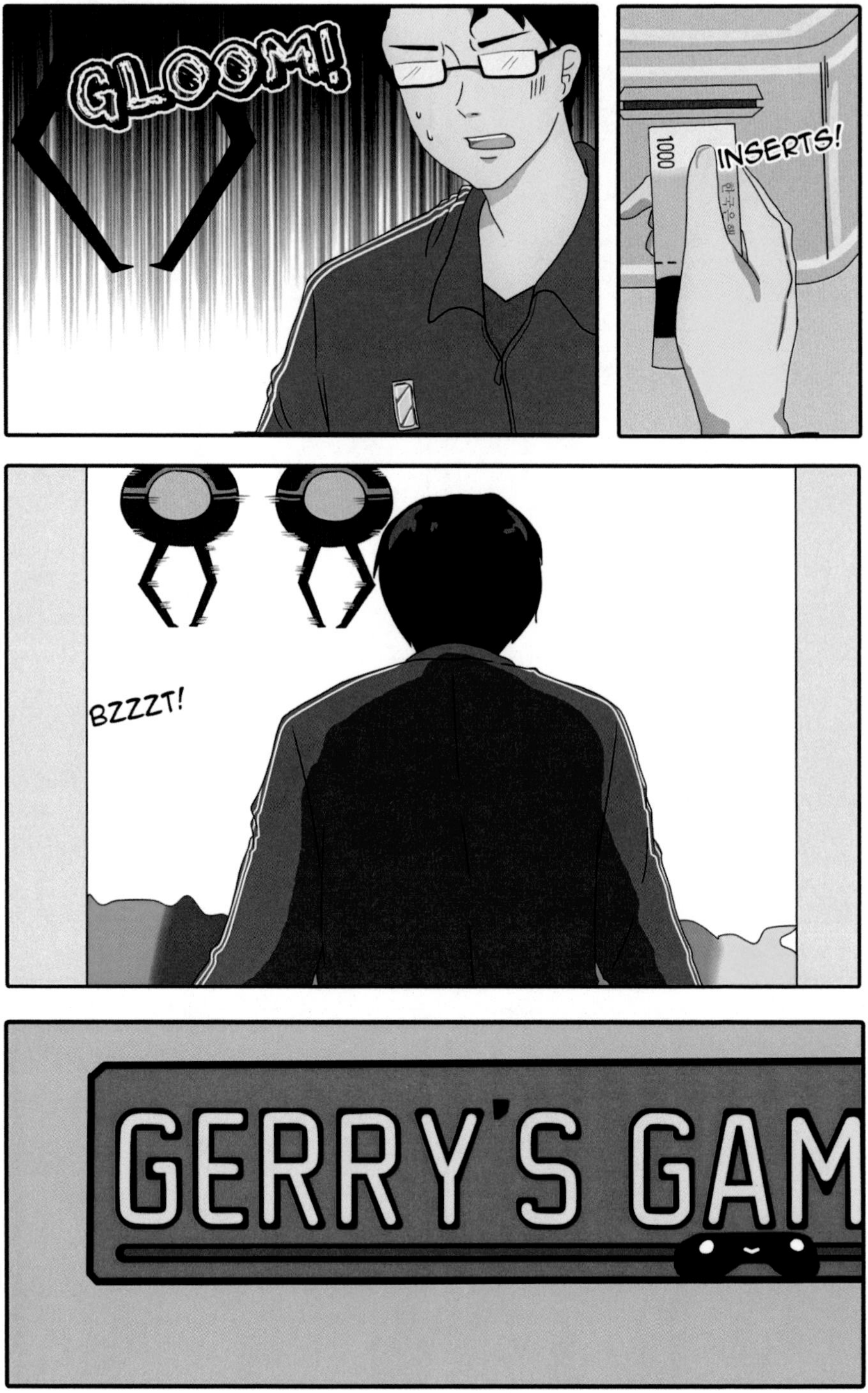
GLOOM!
1000
INSERTS!
BZZZT!
GERRY'S GAM

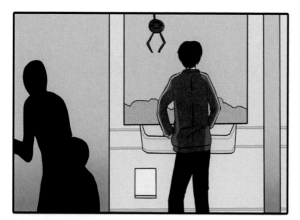

DON'T JUST JUMP IN WITHOUT KNOWING WHAT YOU'RE GOING TO DO.

つづく

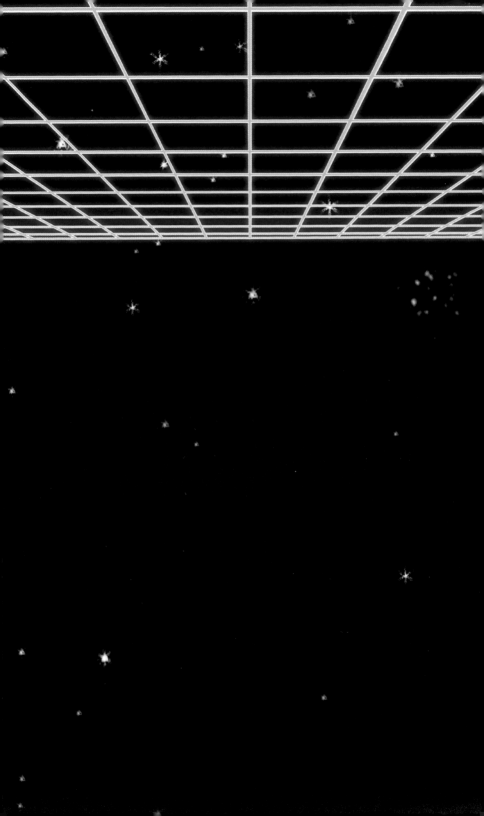

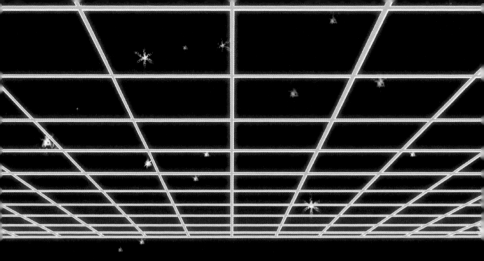

Episode 3:

I Love It When A Plan Comes Together

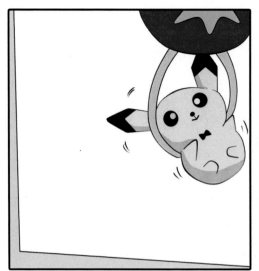

HAVE A
"PLAN B"
(AND A
"PLAN C")
JUST
IN CASE
"PLAN A"
DOESN'T
WORK OUT.

THE HANDLE IS PRETTY WEAK, HUH?

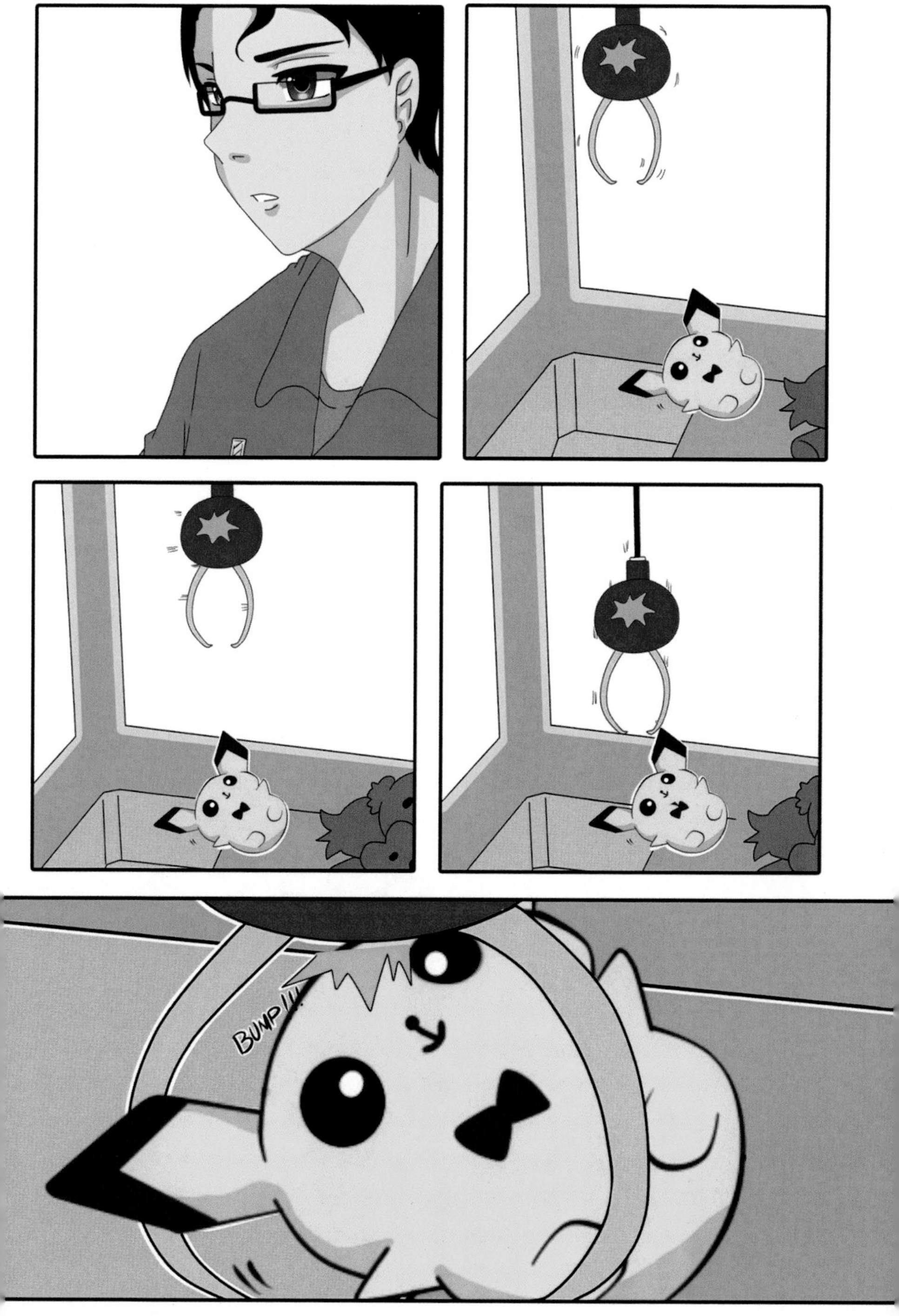
BUMP!!!

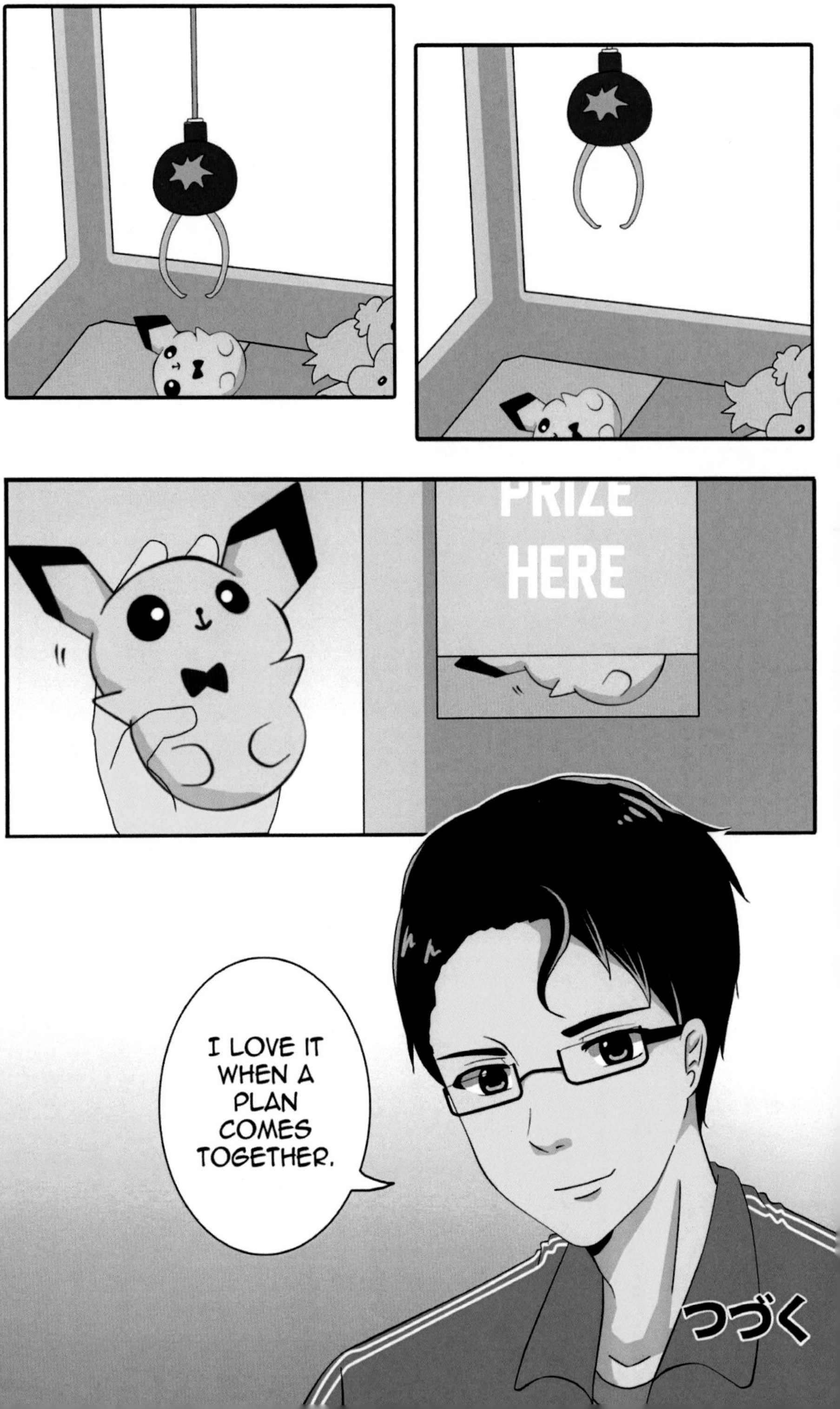
PRIZE
HERE
I LOVE IT WHEN A PLAN COMES TOGETHER.
つづく

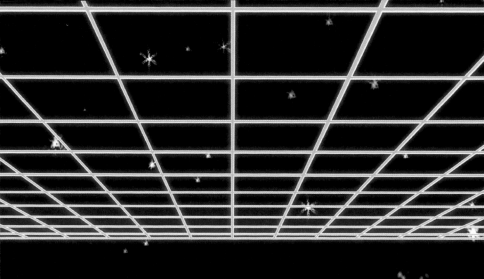

Episode 4:
Stay The Course (AKA Don't "Flip Flop")

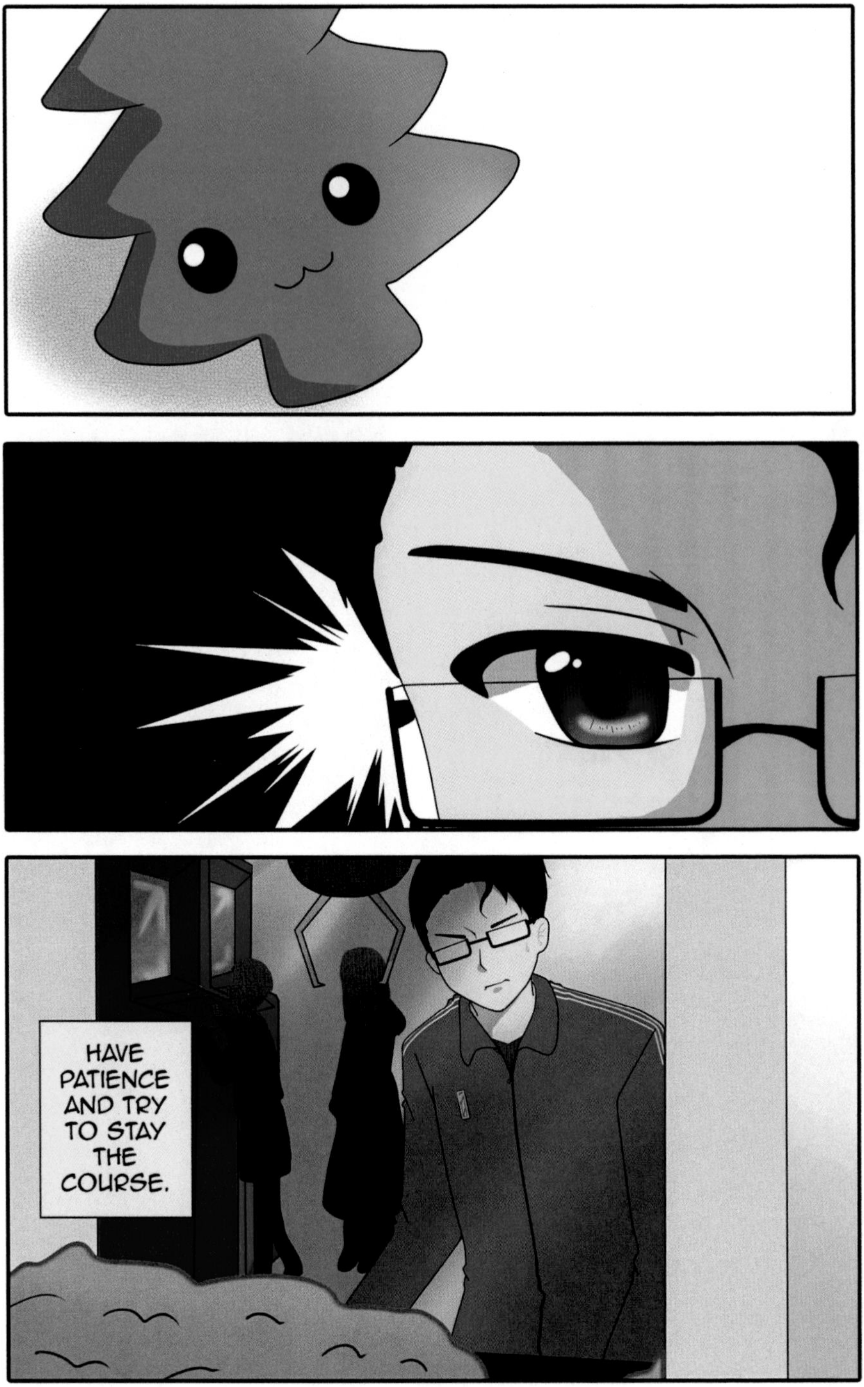
HAVE PATIENCE AND TRY TO STAY THE COURSE.

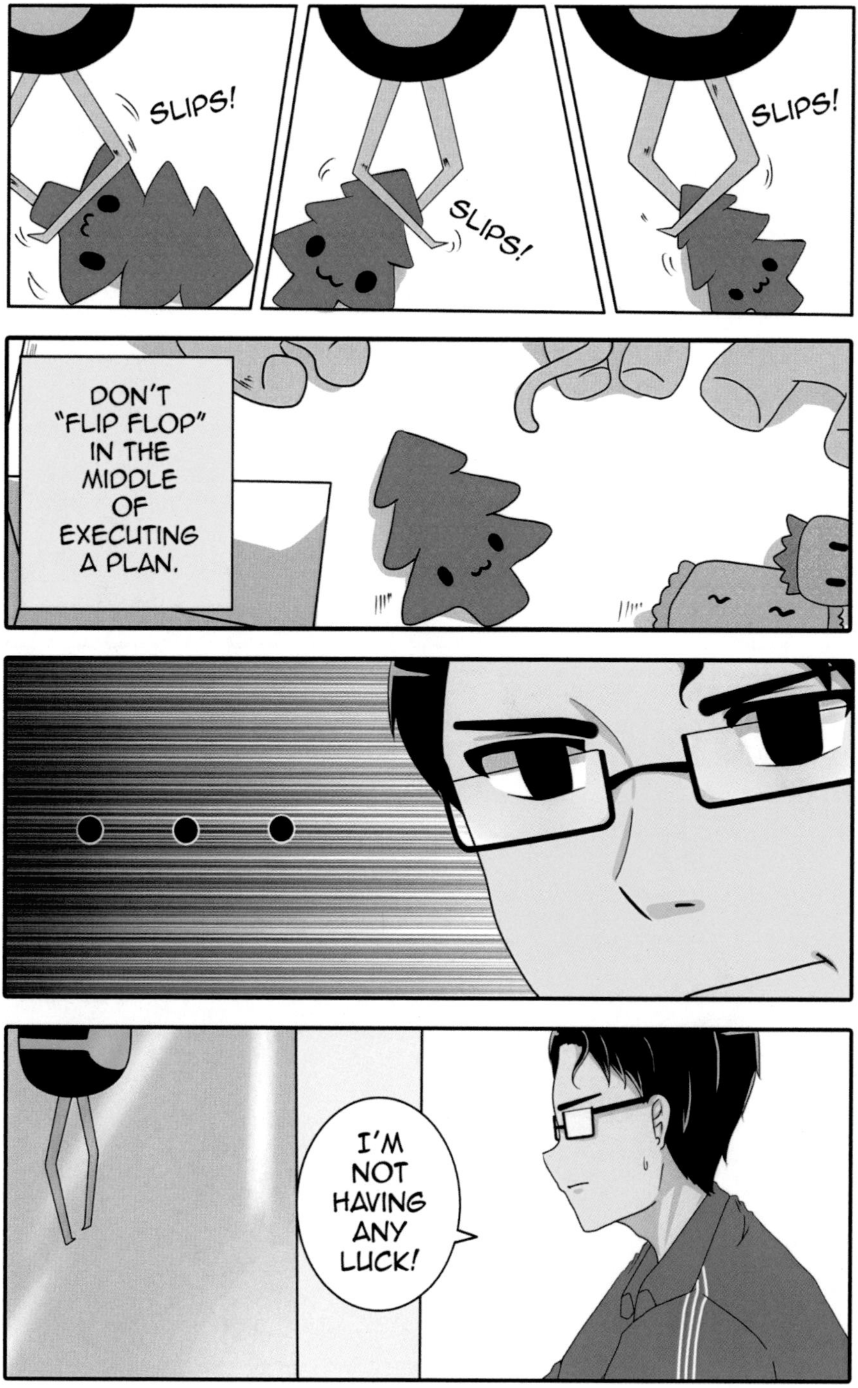
SLIPS!
SLIPS!
SLIPS!
DON'T "FLIP FLOP" IN THE MIDDLE OF EXECUTING A PLAN.
• • •
I'M NOT HAVING ANY LUCK!

I'LL TRY GOING FOR THAT ONE INSTEAD.

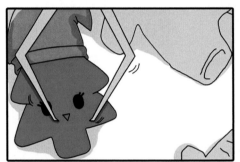

MISSED...

AH, FORGET IT!

32

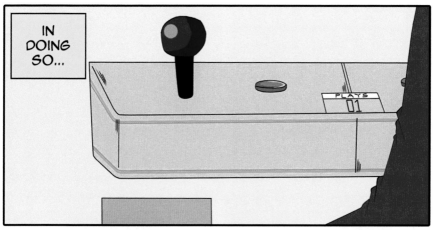

IN DOING SO...

...YOU MAY END UP OPENING THE DOOR TO VICTORY...

Falls...

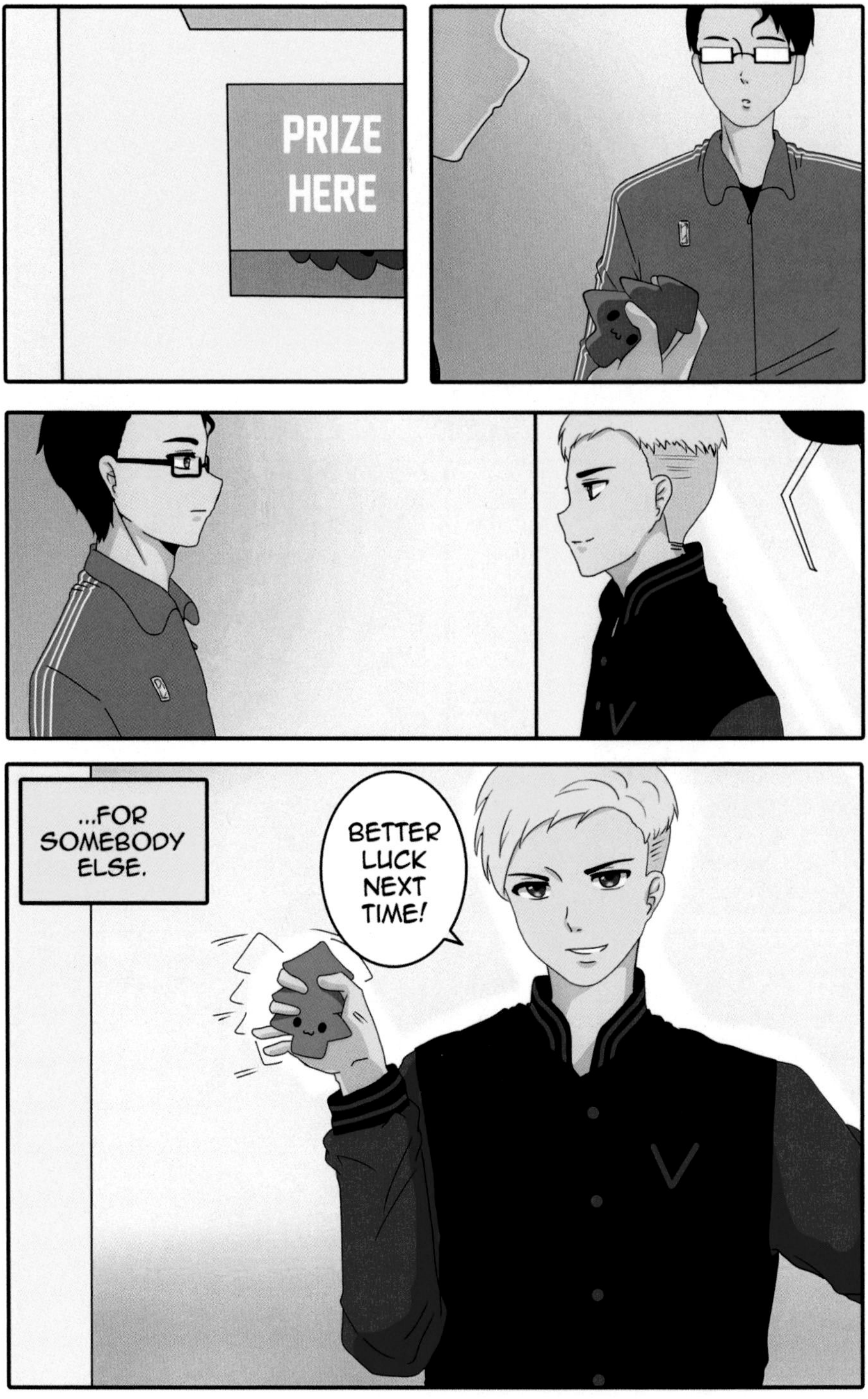
PRIZE HERE
...FOR SOMEBODY ELSE.
BETTER LUCK NEXT TIME!

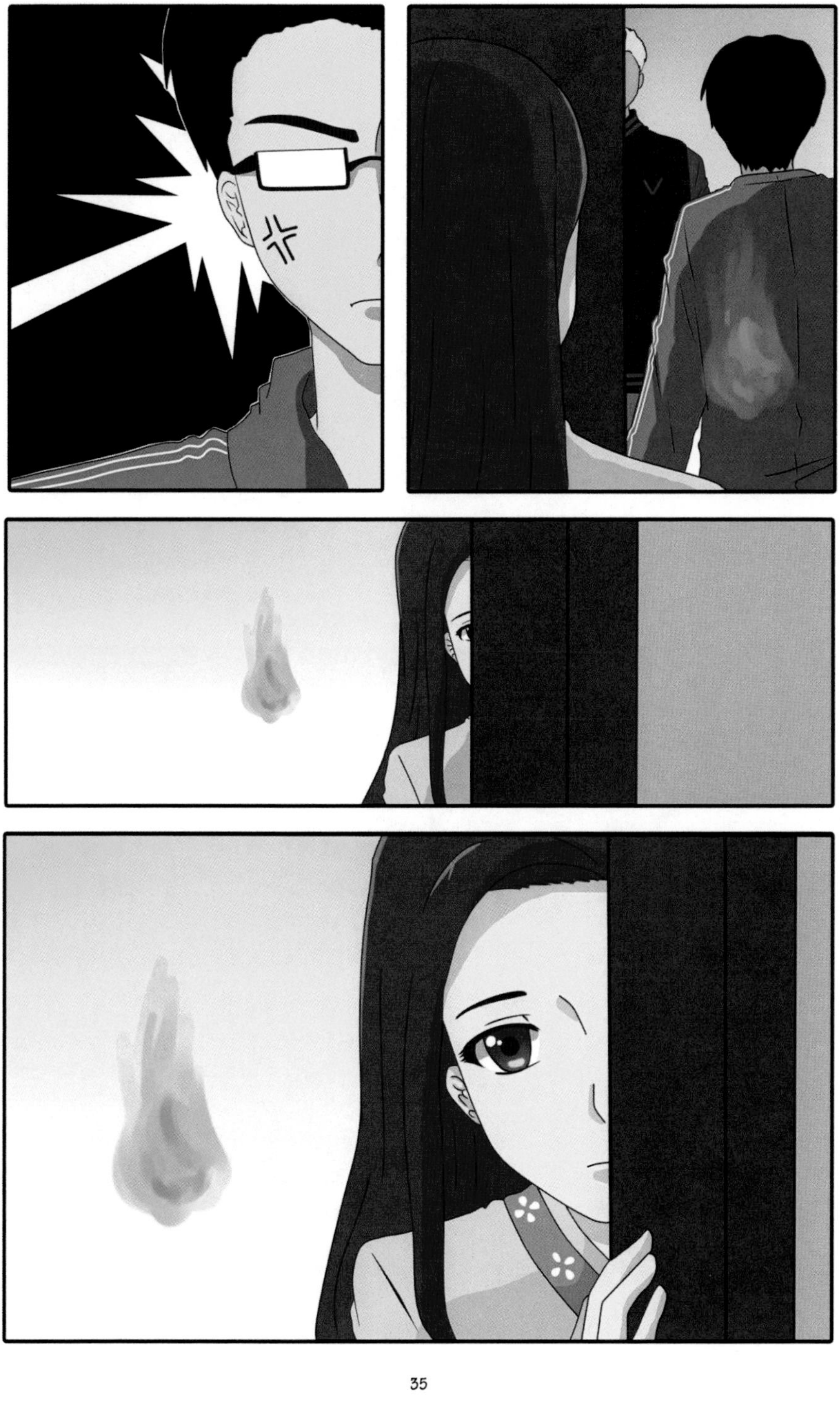

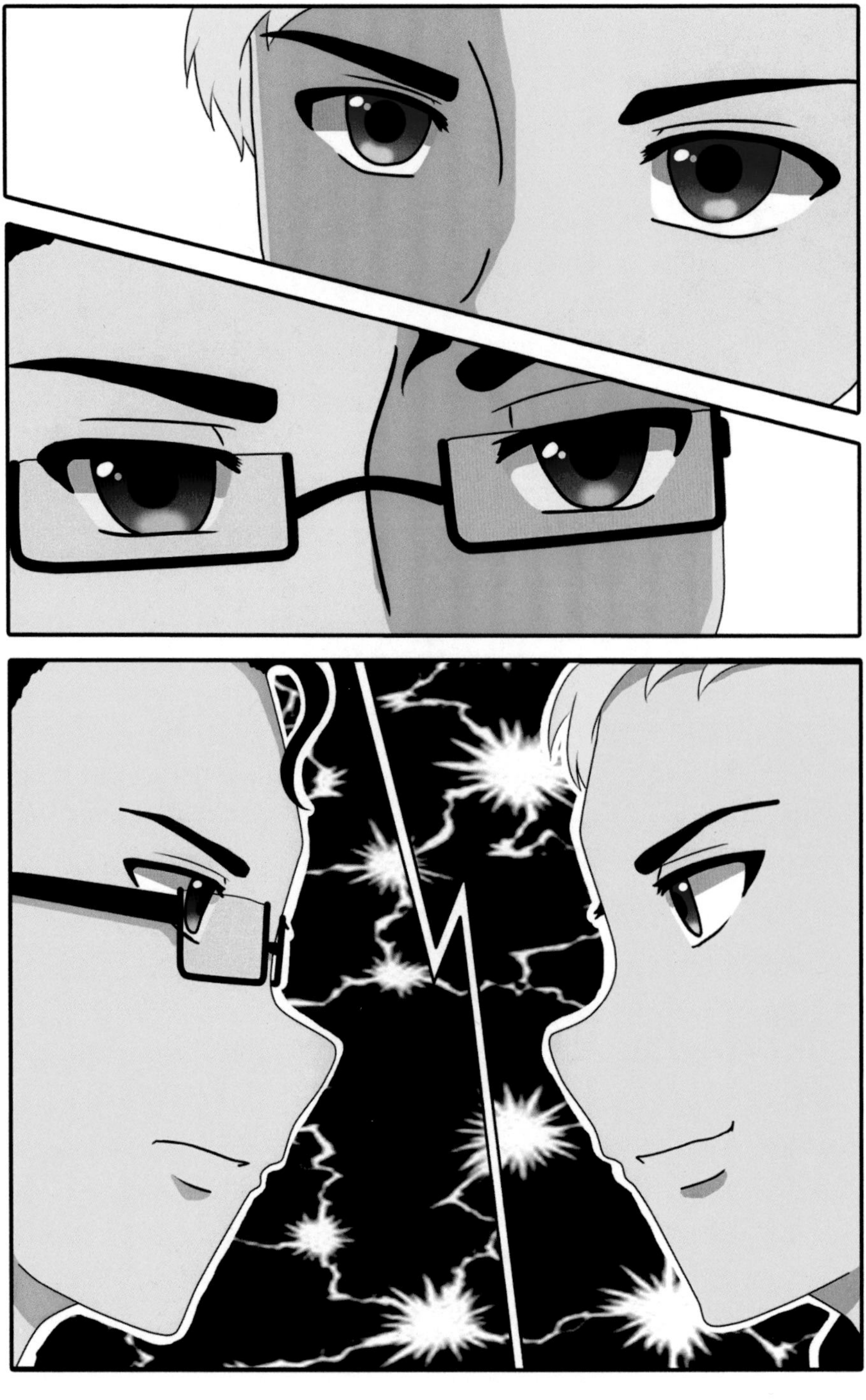

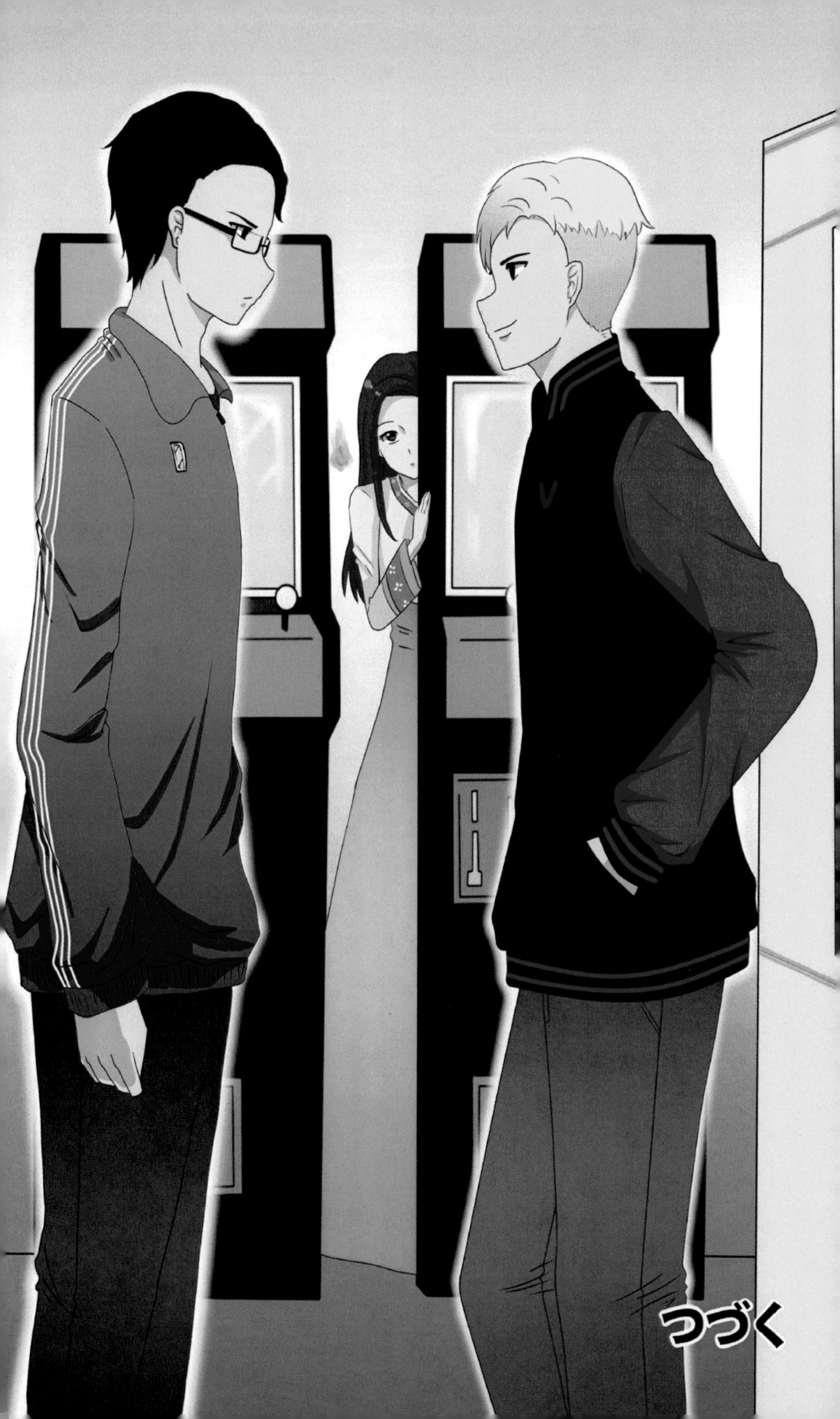
つづく

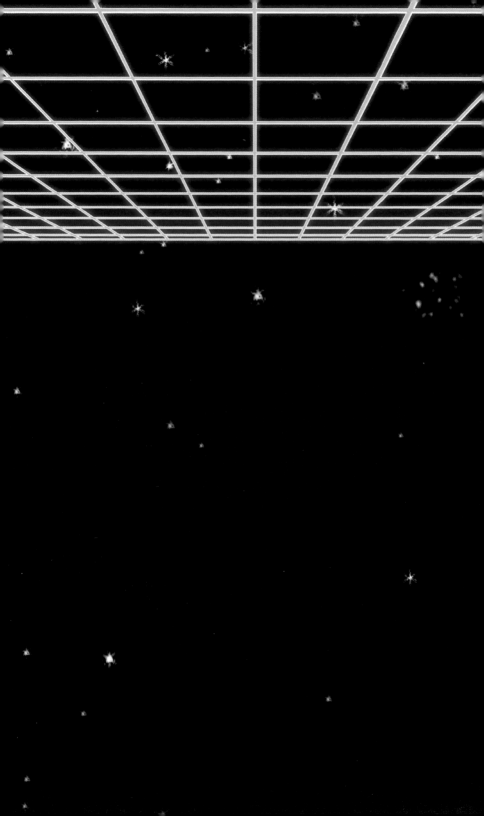

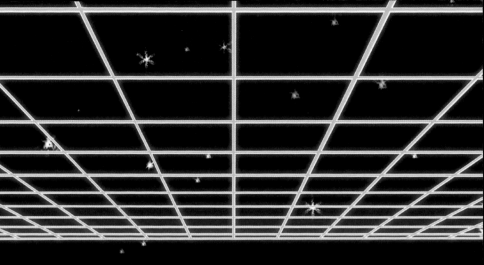

Episode 5:
Don't Tempt Fate

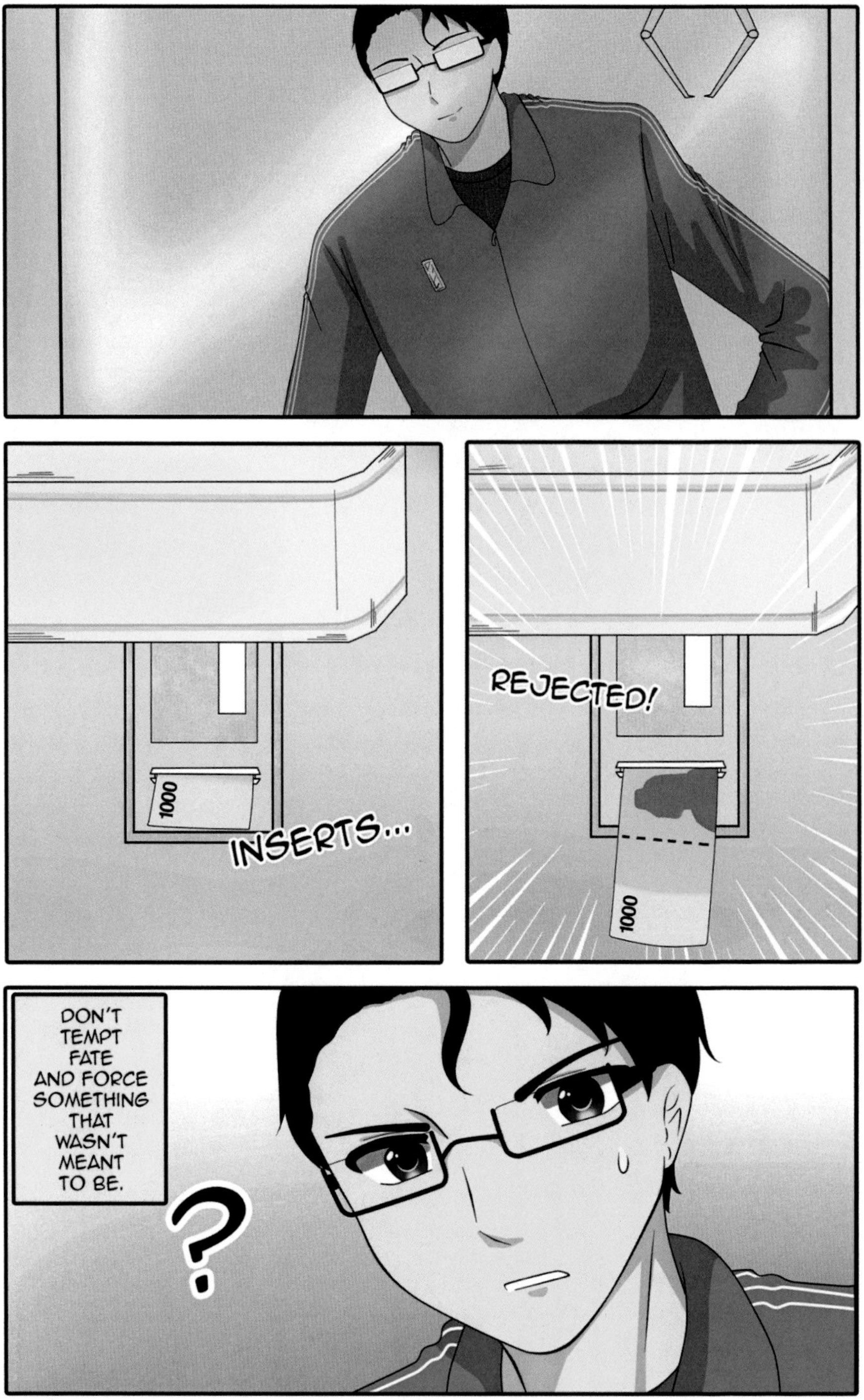
1000
INSERTS...
REJECTED!
1000
DON'T TEMPT FATE AND FORCE SOMETHING THAT WASN'T MEANT TO BE.
?

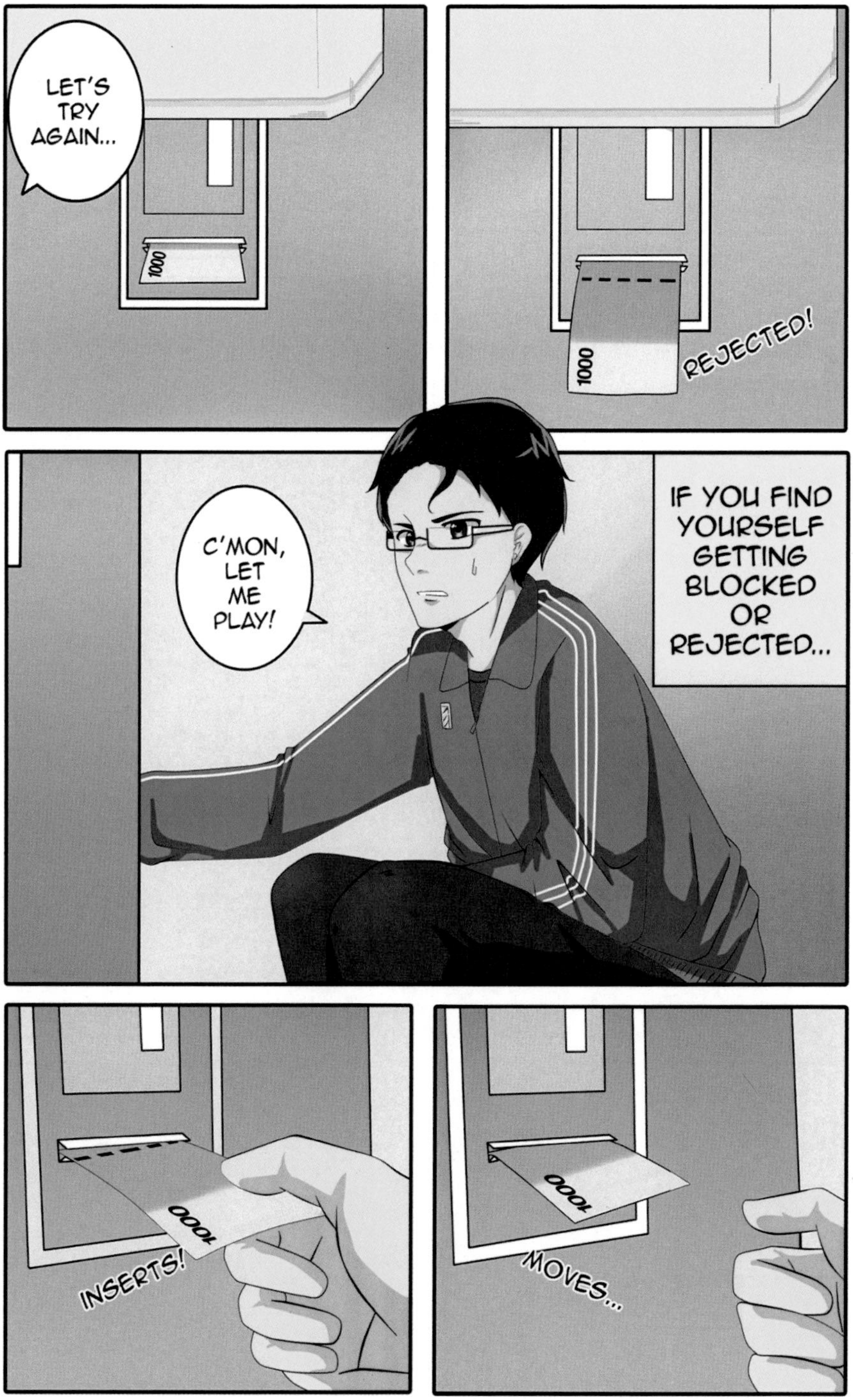
LET'S TRY AGAIN...
1000
1000
REJECTED!
IF YOU FIND YOURSELF GETTING BLOCKED OR REJECTED...
C'MON, LET ME PLAY!
1000
INSERTS!
1000
MOVES...

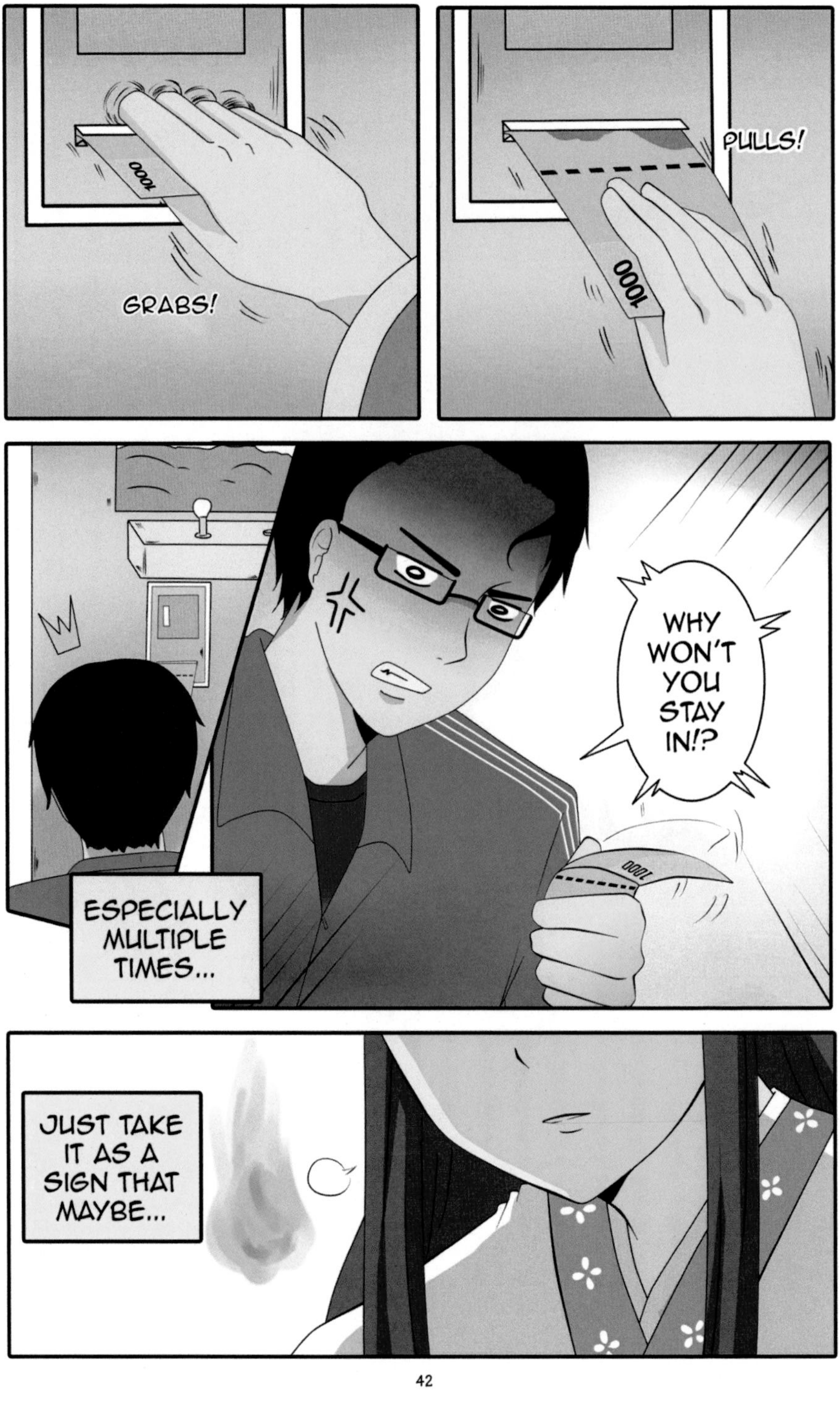
GRABS!
PULLS!
WHY WON'T YOU STAY IN!?
ESPECIALLY MULTIPLE TIMES...
JUST TAKE IT AS A SIGN THAT MAYBE...

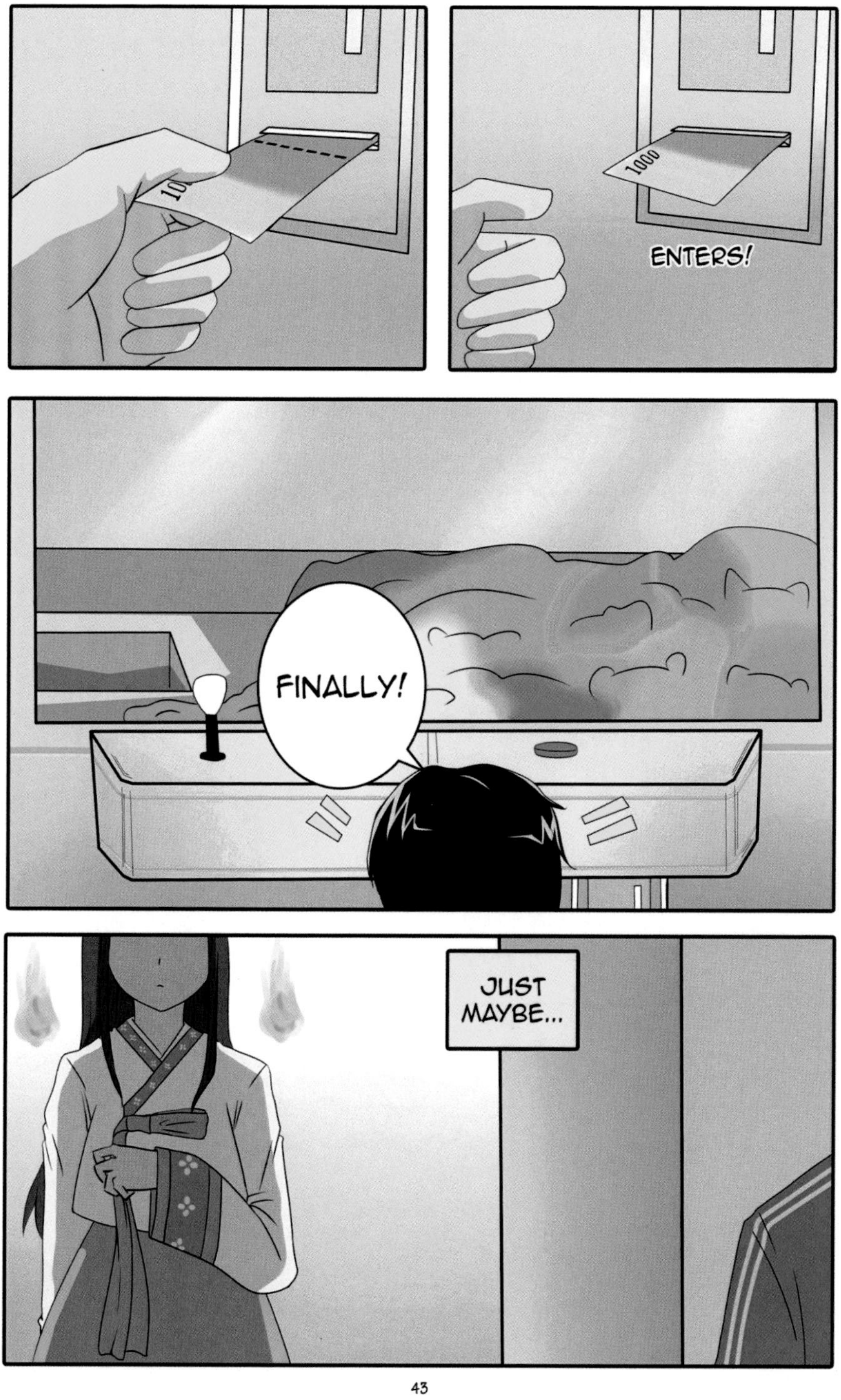
1000
ENTERS!
FINALLY!
JUST MAYBE...

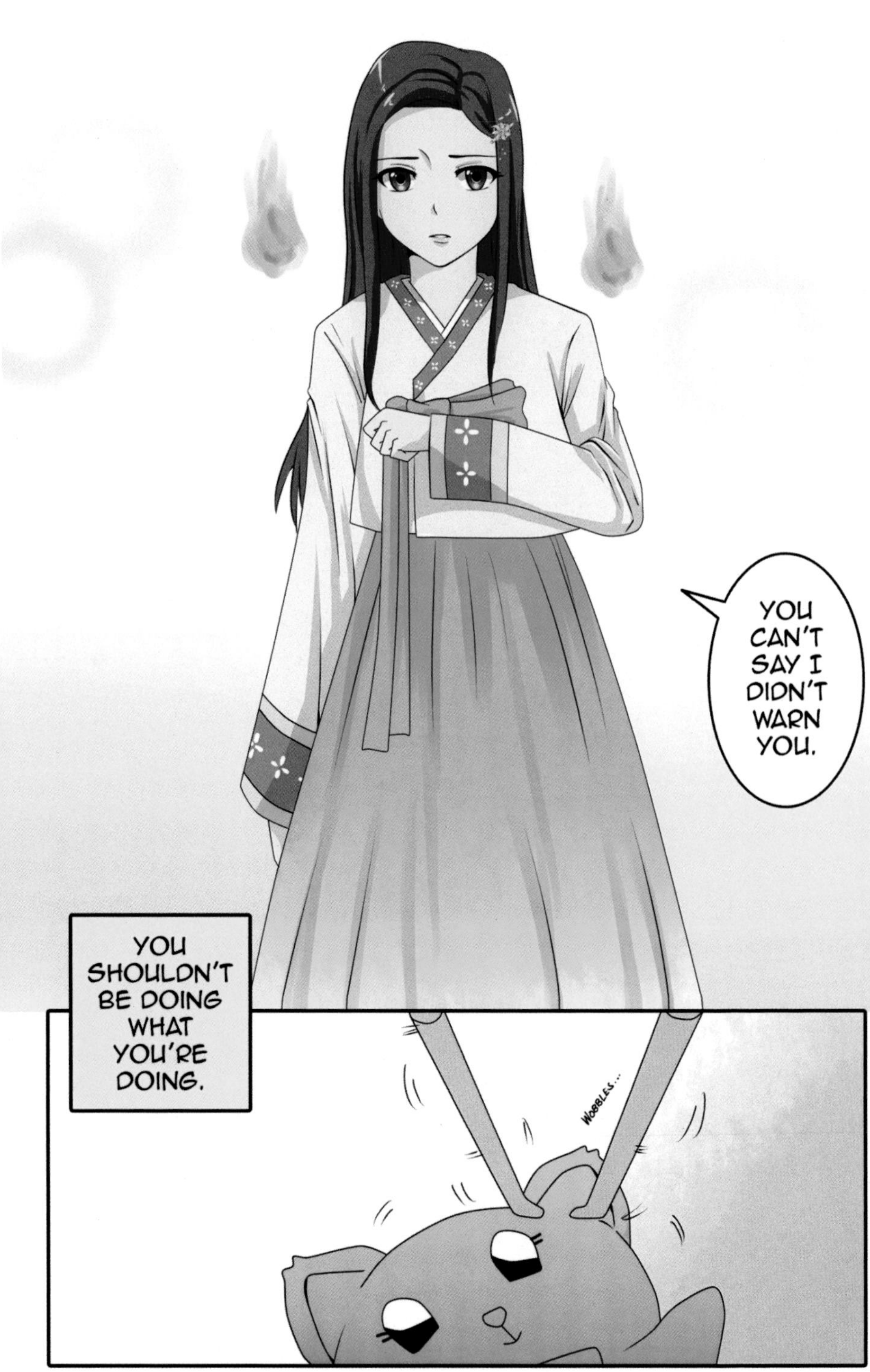
YOU CAN'T SAY I DIDN'T WARN YOU.
YOU SHOULDN'T BE DOING WHAT YOU'RE DOING.
WOBBLES...

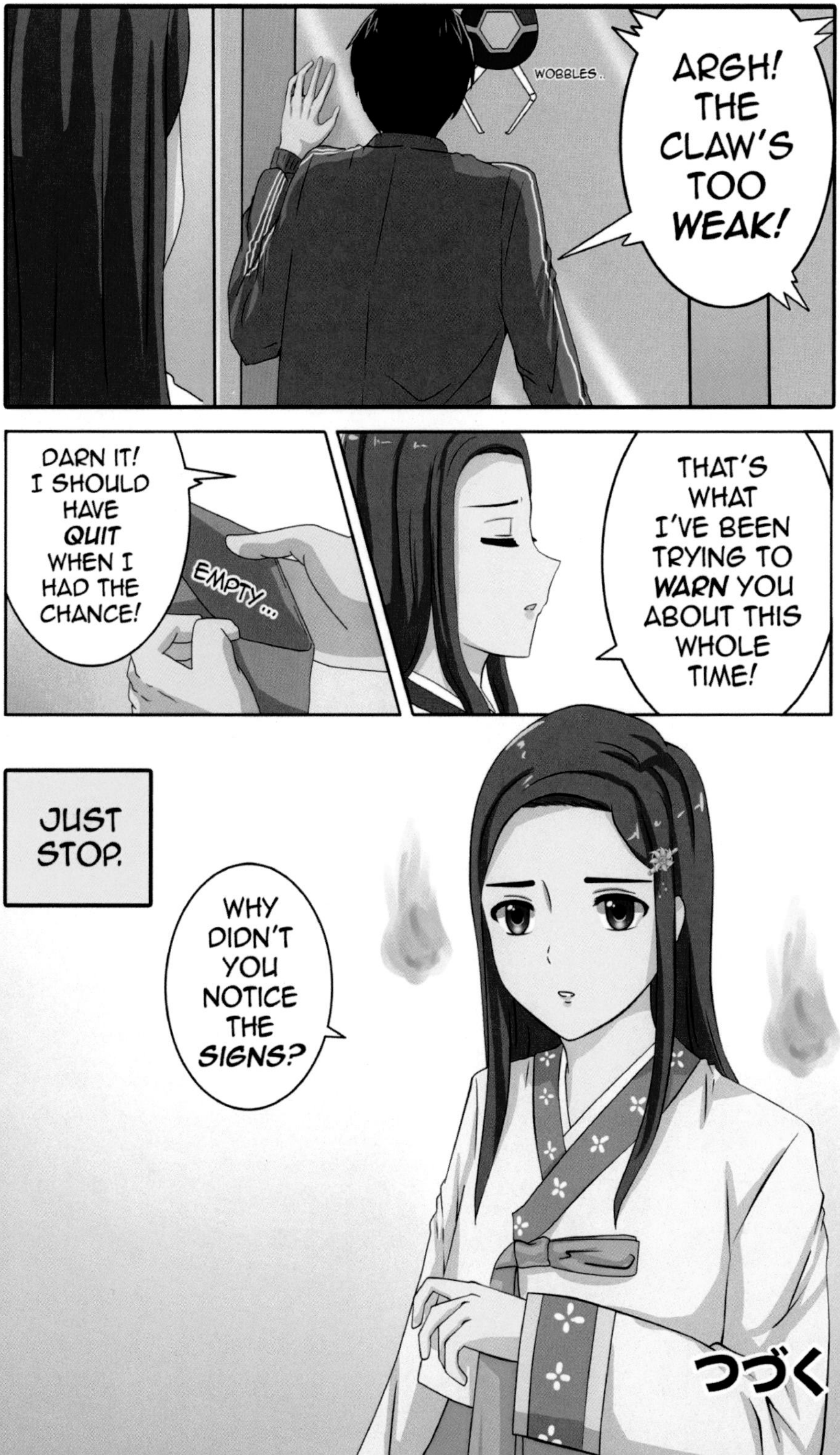
WOBBLES..
ARGH! THE CLAW'S TOO WEAK!
EMPTY...
DARN IT! I SHOULD HAVE QUIT WHEN I HAD THE CHANCE!
THAT'S WHAT I'VE BEEN TRYING TO WARN YOU ABOUT THIS WHOLE TIME!
JUST STOP.
WHY DIDN'T YOU NOTICE THE SIGNS?
つづく

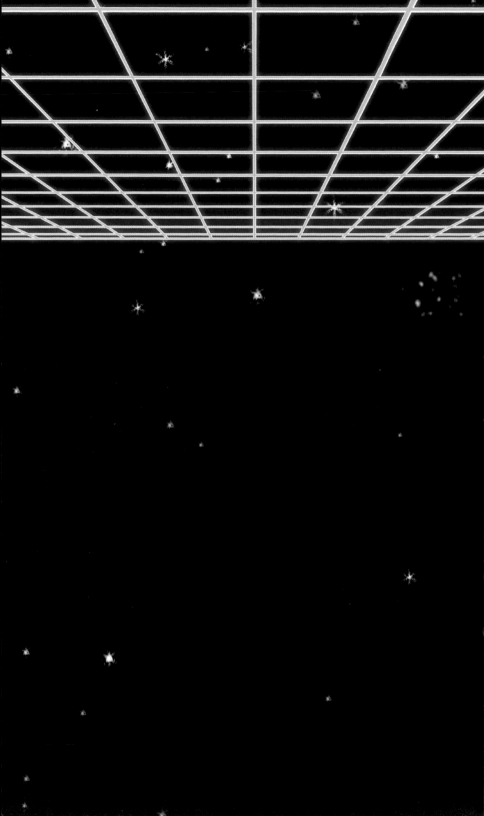

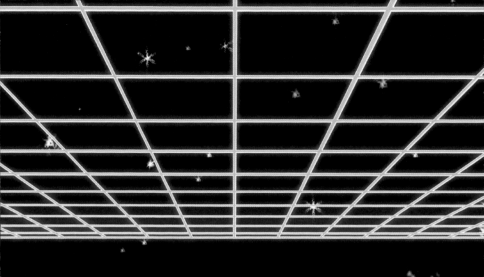

Episode 6:
Get Lucky
(Or Not)

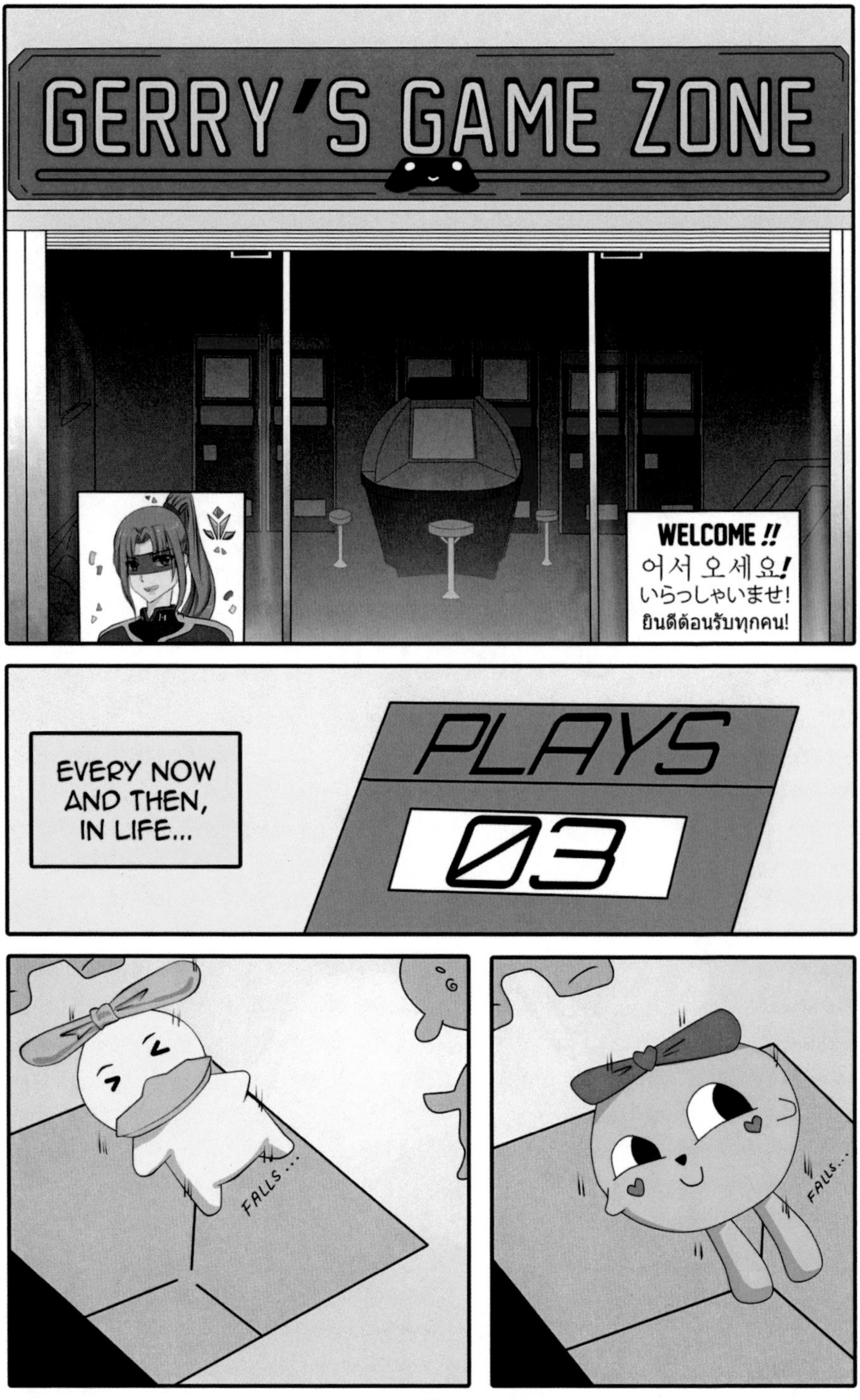
GERRY'S GAME ZONE
WELCOME !!
어서 오세요!
いらっしゃいませ!
ยินดีต้อนรับทุกคน!
EVERY NOW AND THEN, IN LIFE...
PLAYS
03
FALLS...
FALLS...

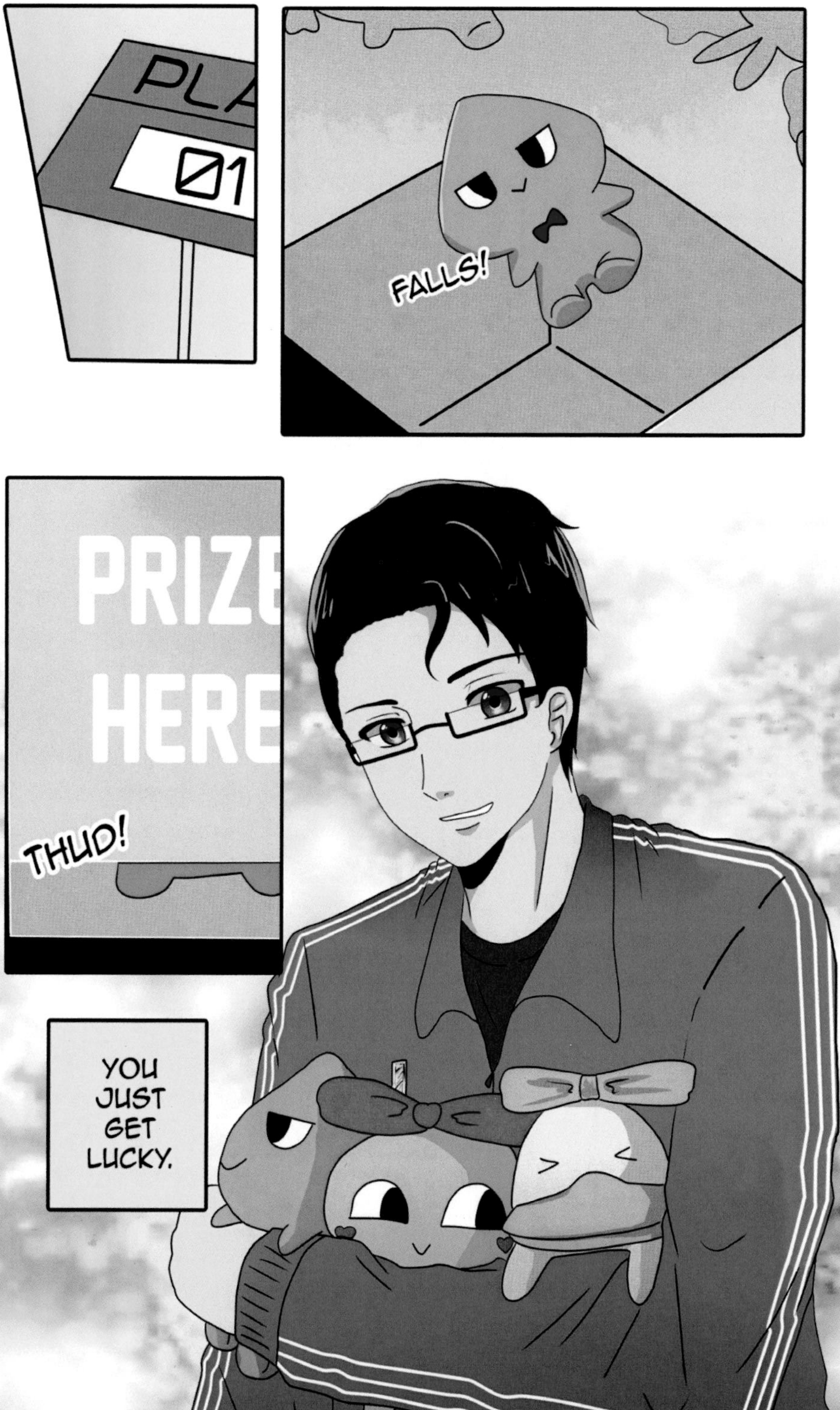
PLA
01
FALLS!
PRIZE
HERE
THUD!
YOU JUST GET LUCKY.

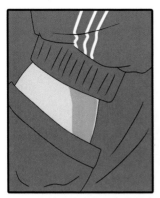

CLICK!

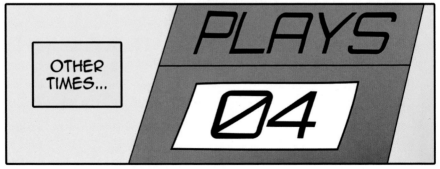

OTHER TIMES...

PLAYS

04

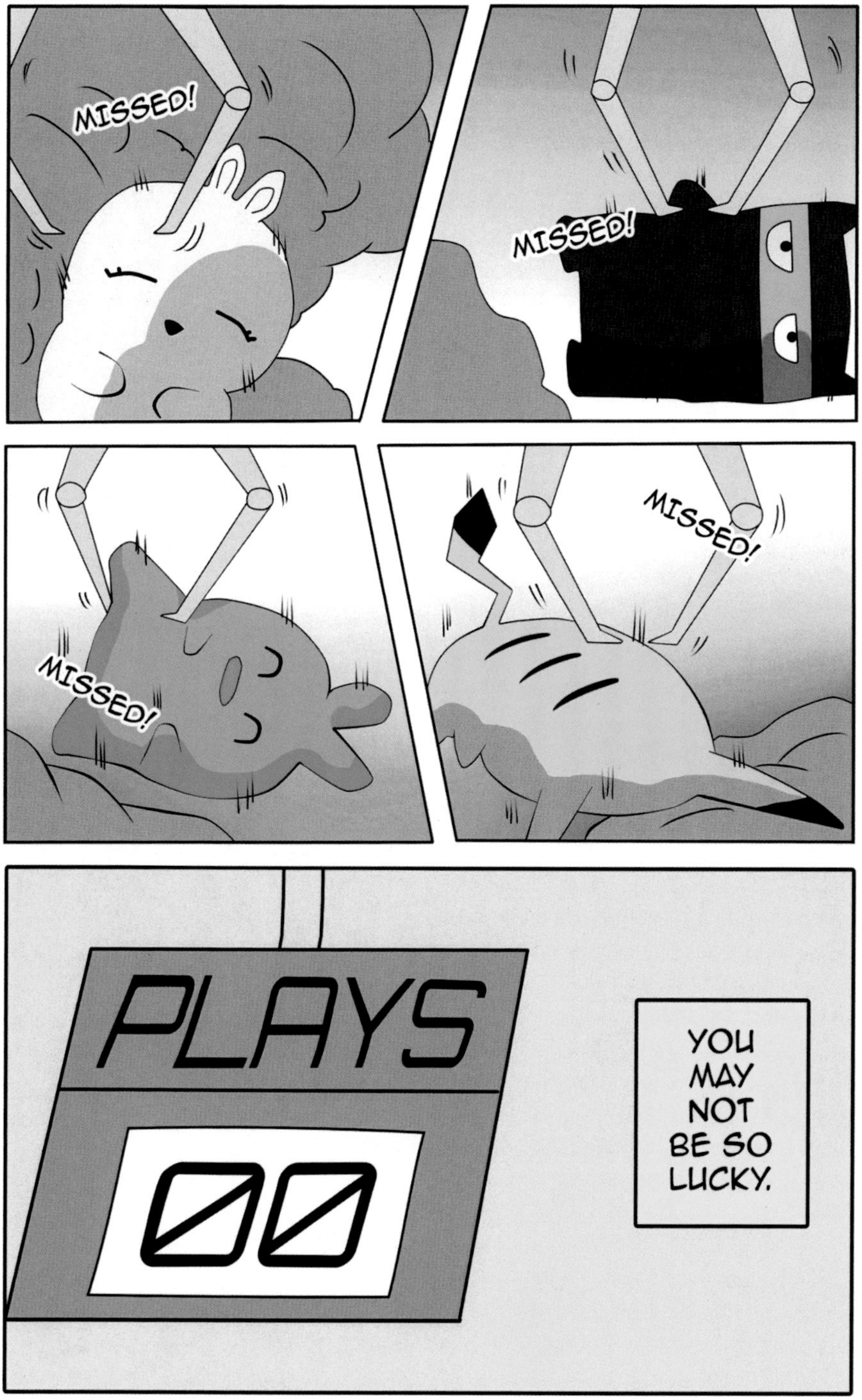
MISSED!
MISSED!
MISSED!
MISSED!
PLAYS
00
YOU MAY NOT BE SO LUCKY.

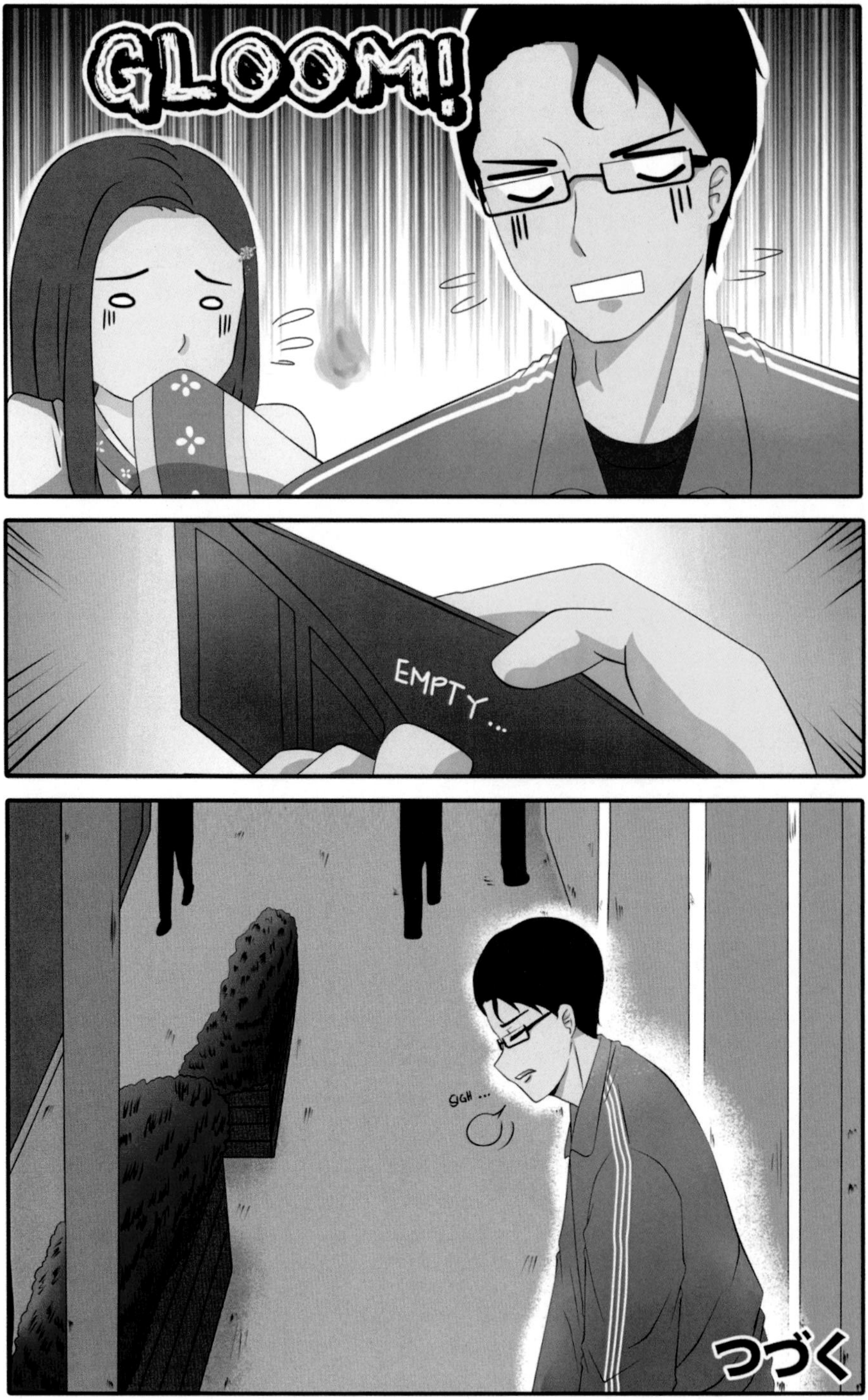
GLOOM!
EMPTY...
SIGH...
つづく

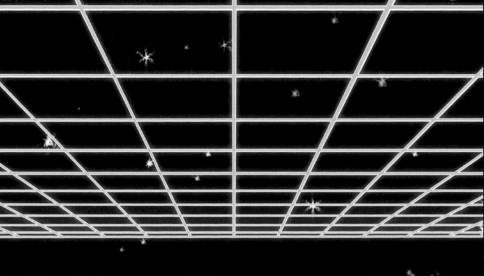

Episode 7:
One Shot
(Or Not)

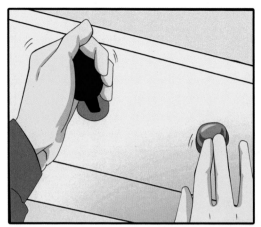

SLIPS....

DON'T GIVE UP!

DON'T ALWAYS EXPECT TO WIN IN ONE SHOT.

SLIPS...

YOU CAN DO IT!

SLIPS ...
화이팅!
FALLS ...
頑張って！
FALLS ...
สู้ต่อไปนะคะ!
MISSED ...
加油!

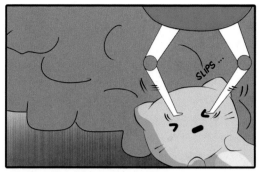

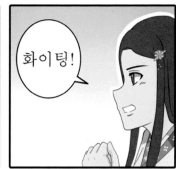

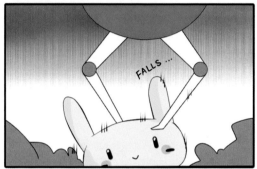

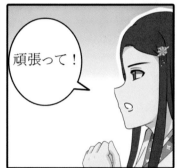

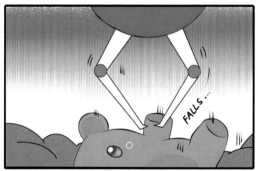

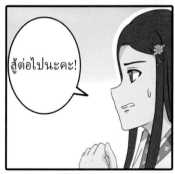

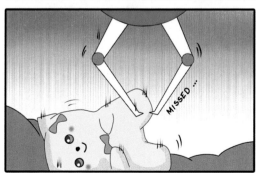

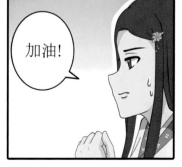

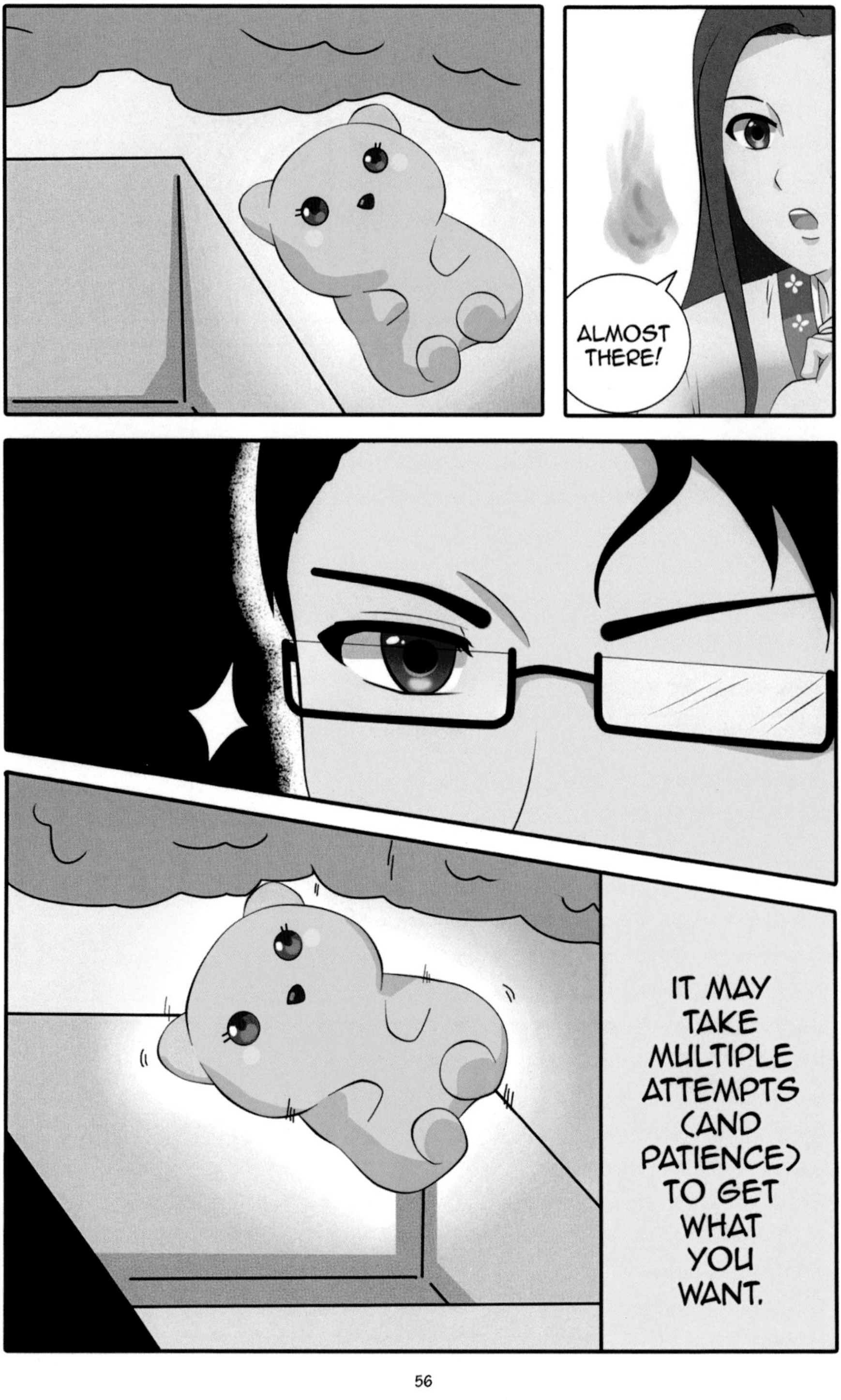
ALMOST THERE!
IT MAY TAKE MULTIPLE ATTEMPTS (AND PATIENCE) TO GET WHAT YOU WANT.

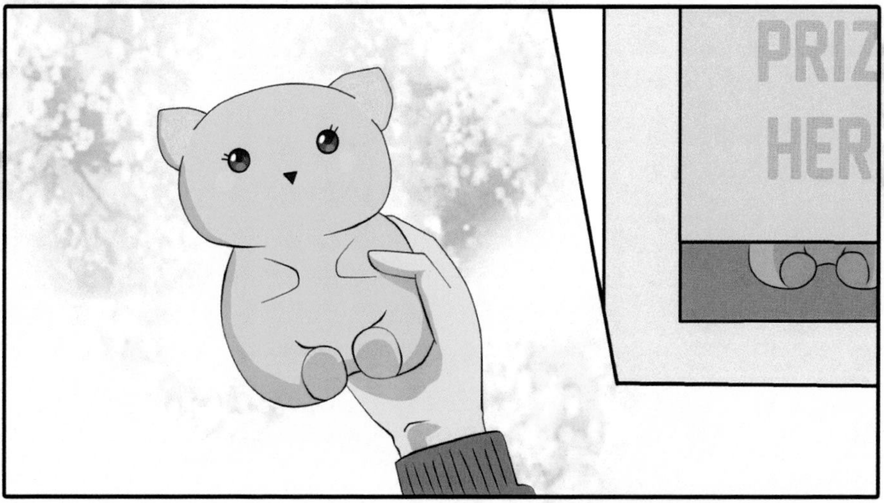
PRIZ
HER

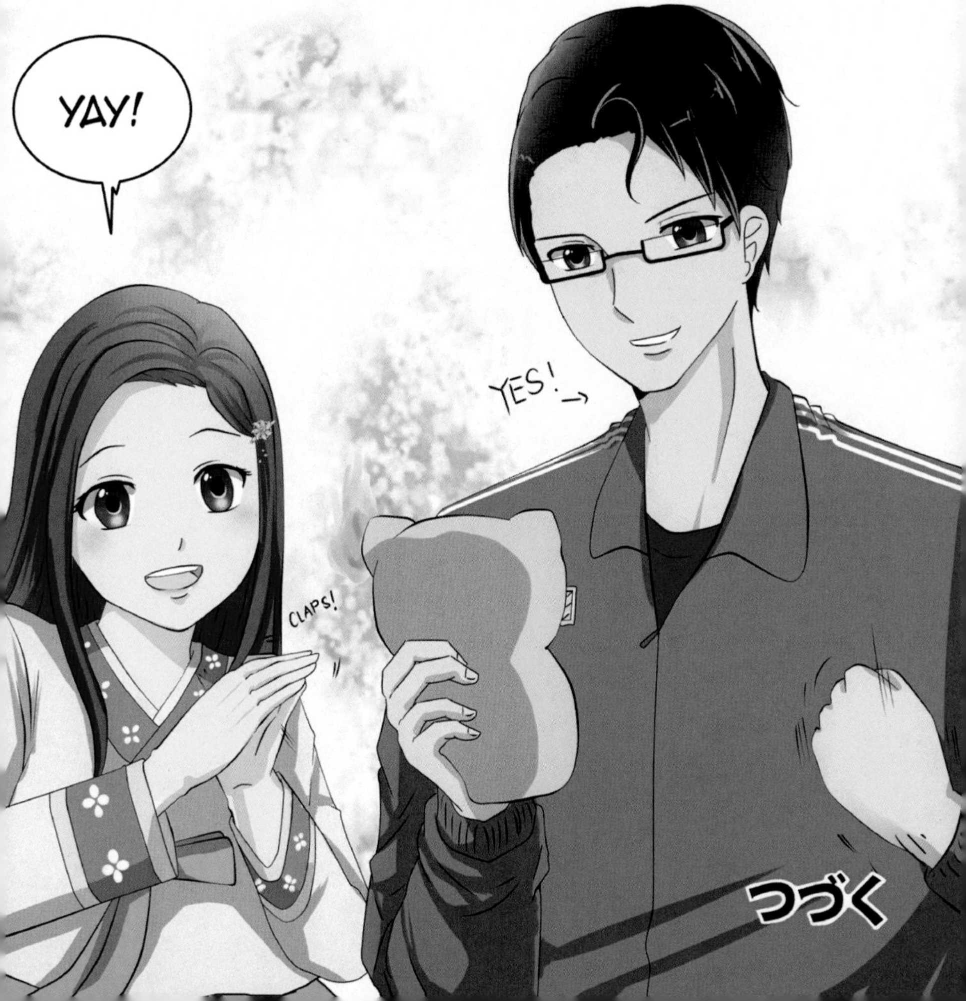
YAY!
YES!
CLAPS!
つづく

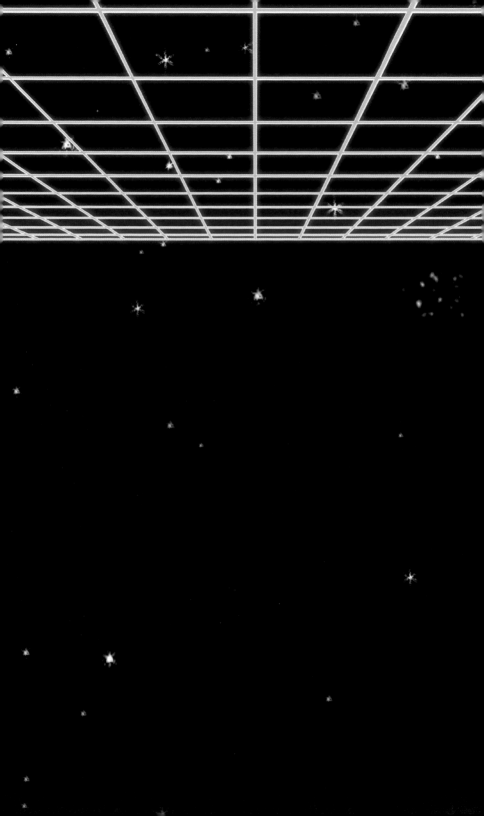

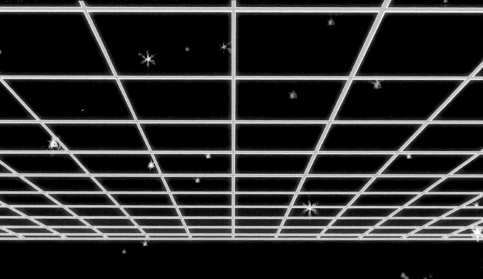

Episode 8:
A Blessing in Disguise

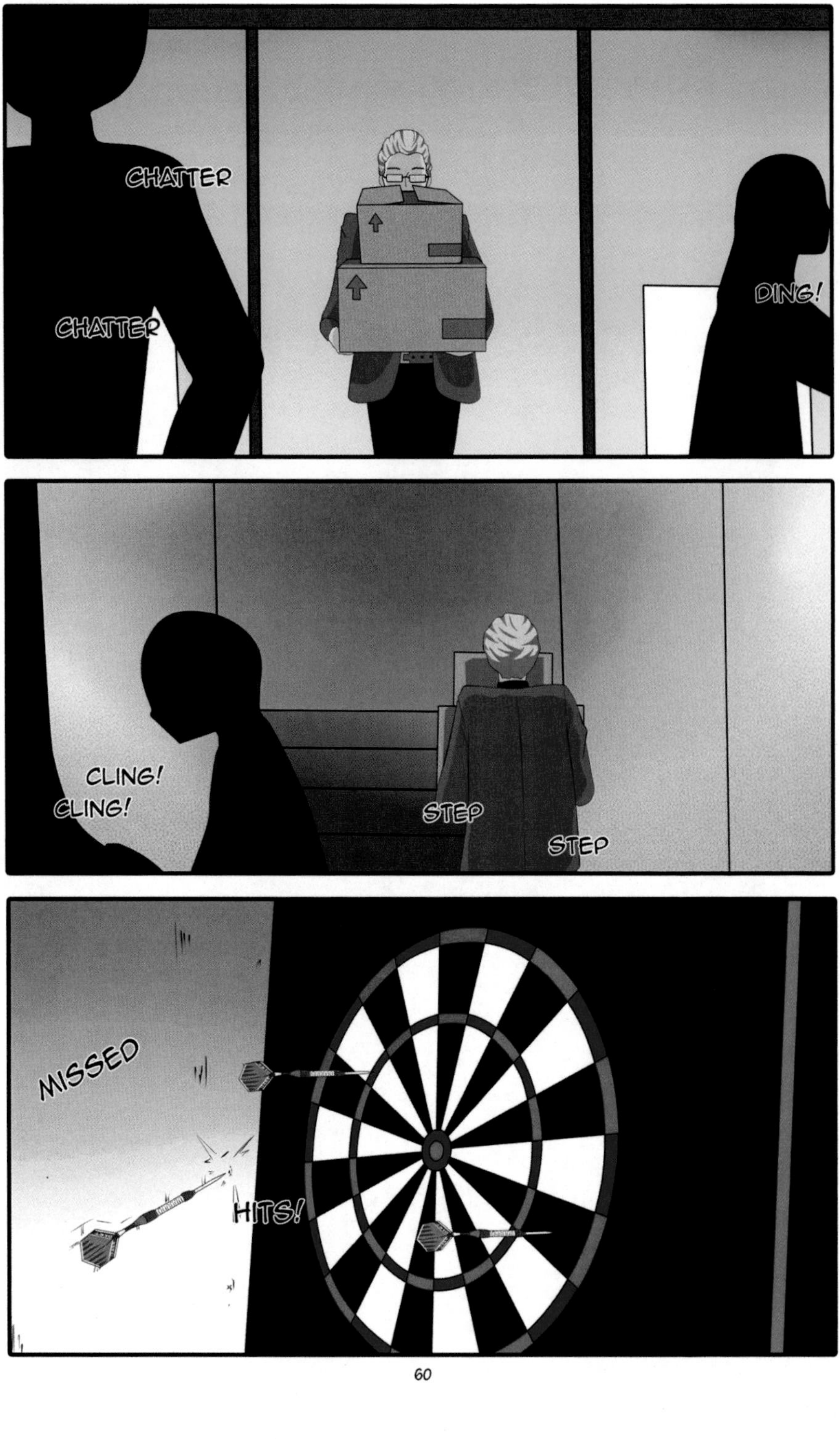
CHATTER
CHATTER
DING!
CLING!
CLING!
STEP
STEP
MISSED
HITS!

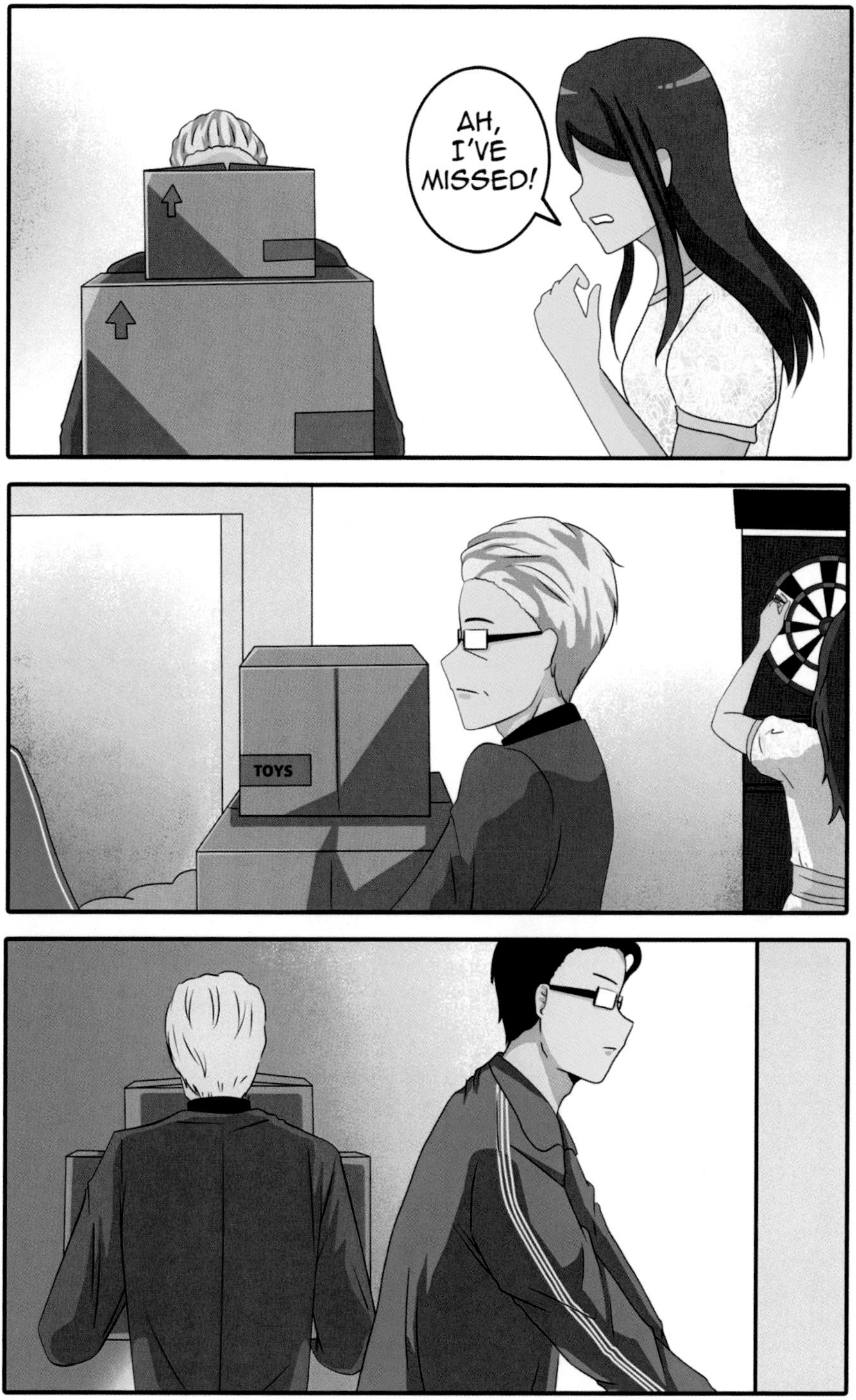
AH, I'VE MISSED!
TOYS

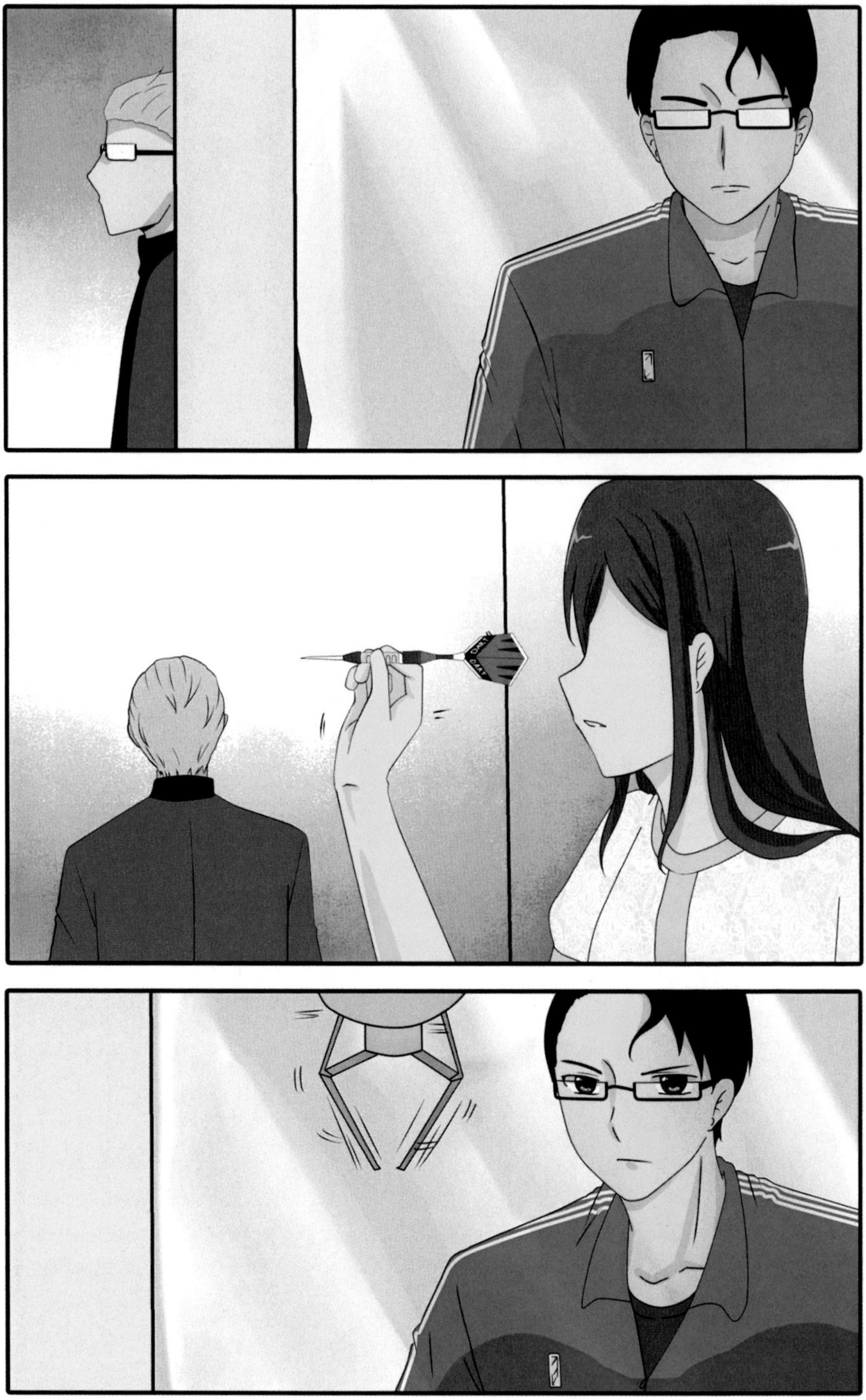

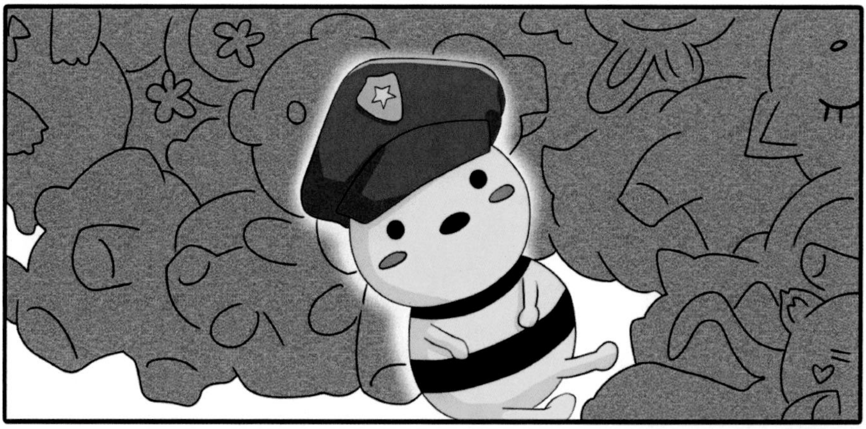

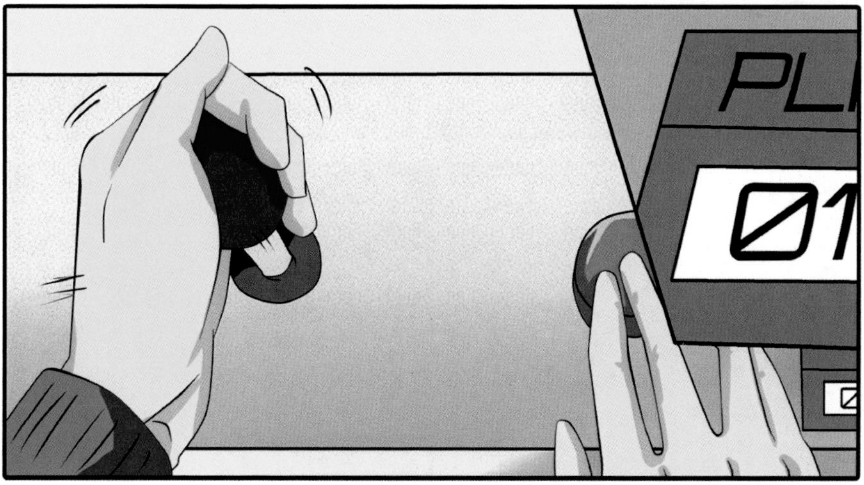

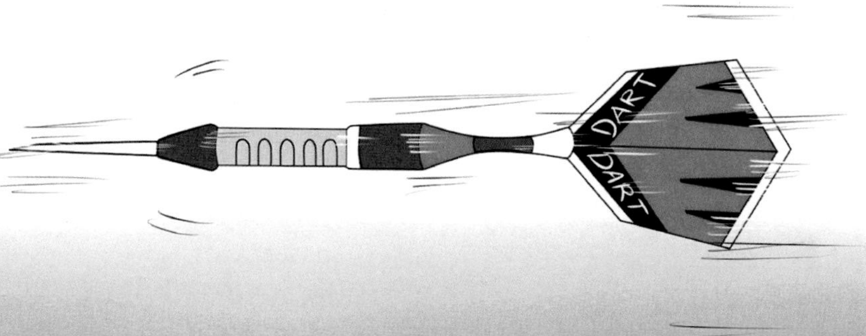
DART
DART

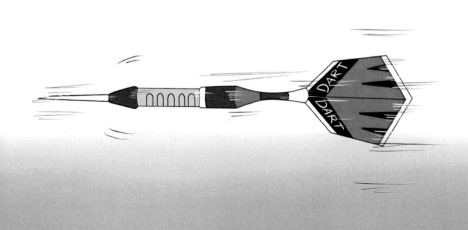

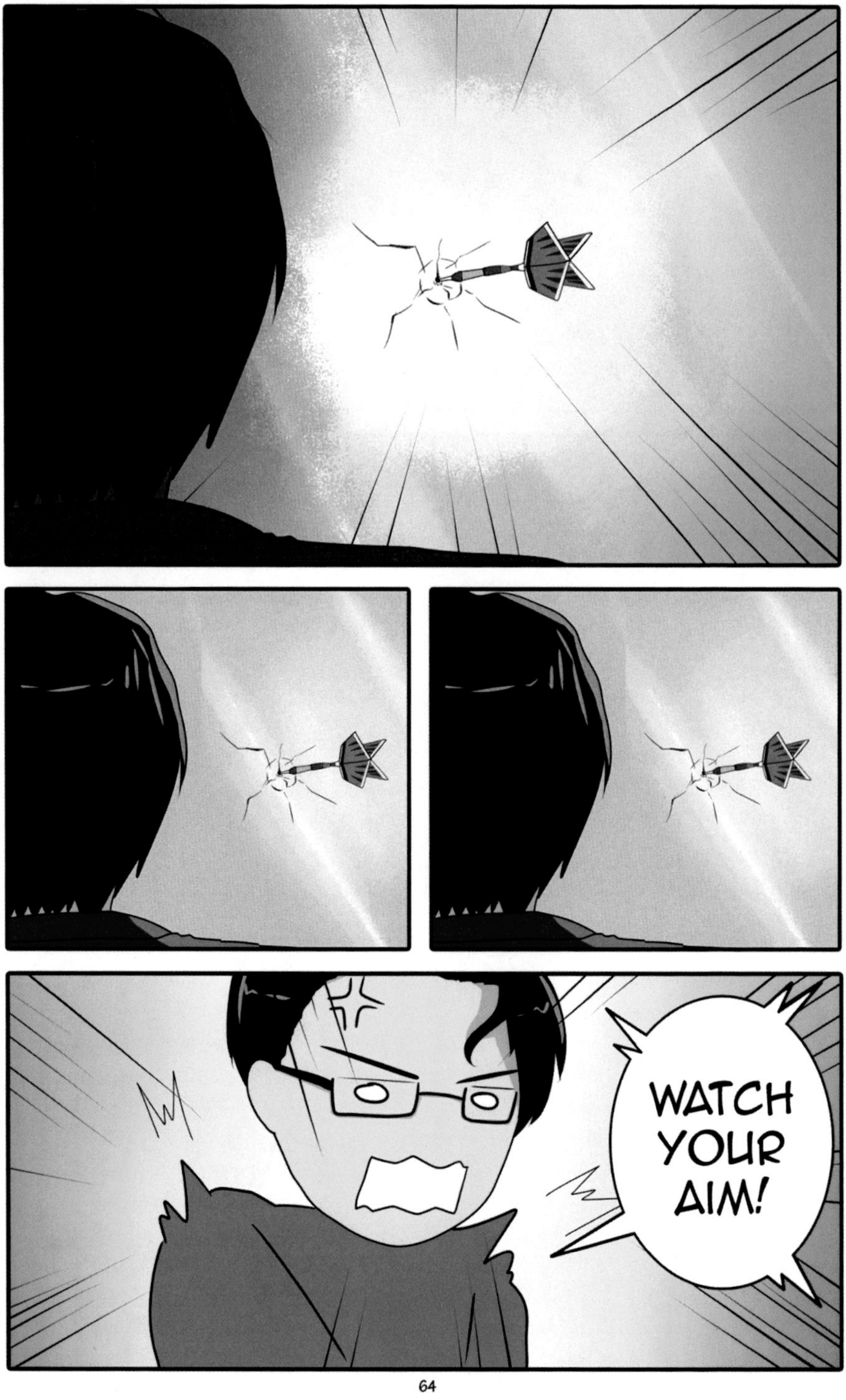
WATCH YOUR AIM!

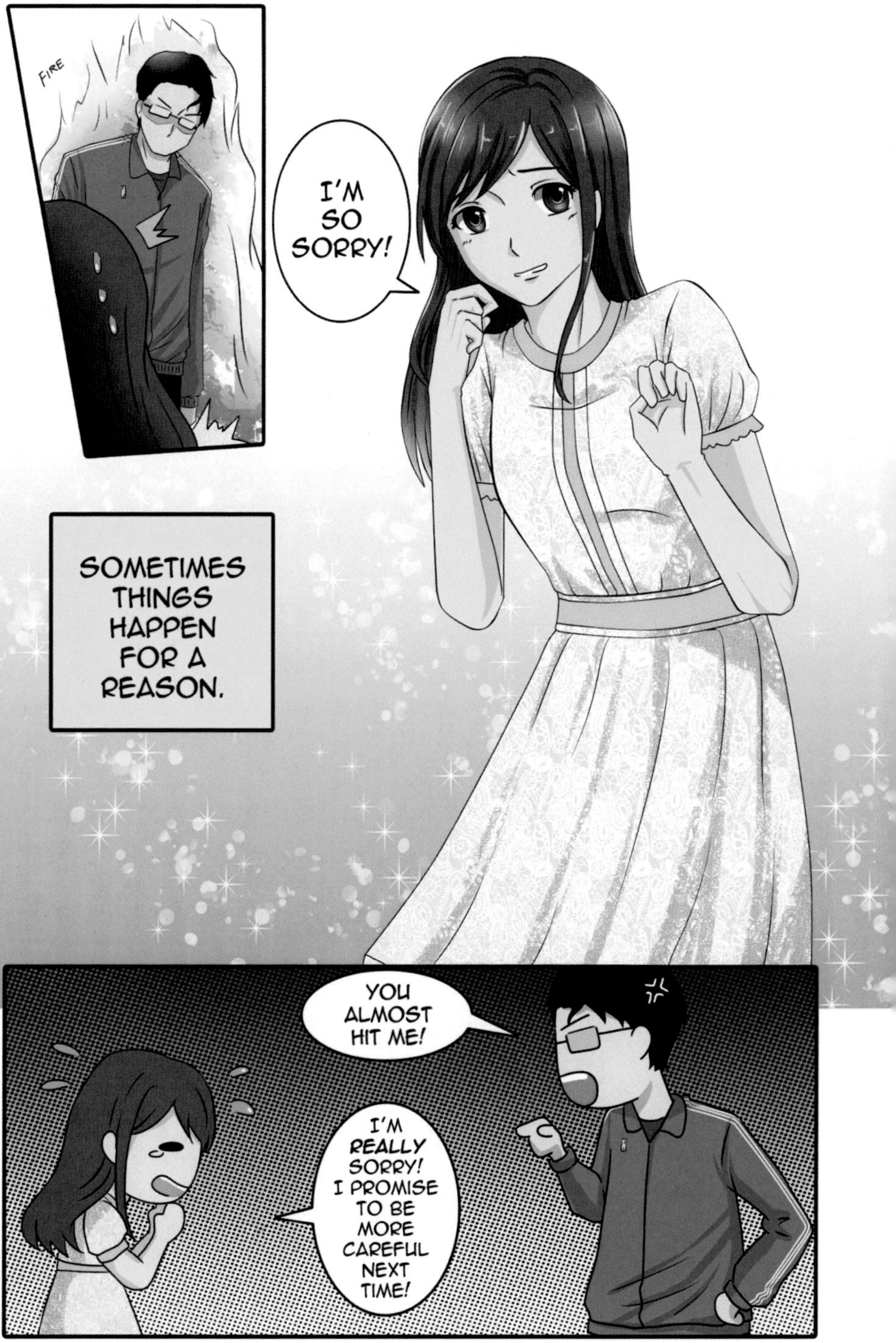
FIRE
I'M SO SORRY!
SOMETIMES THINGS HAPPEN FOR A REASON.
YOU ALMOST HIT ME!
I'M REALLY SORRY! I PROMISE TO BE MORE CAREFUL NEXT TIME!

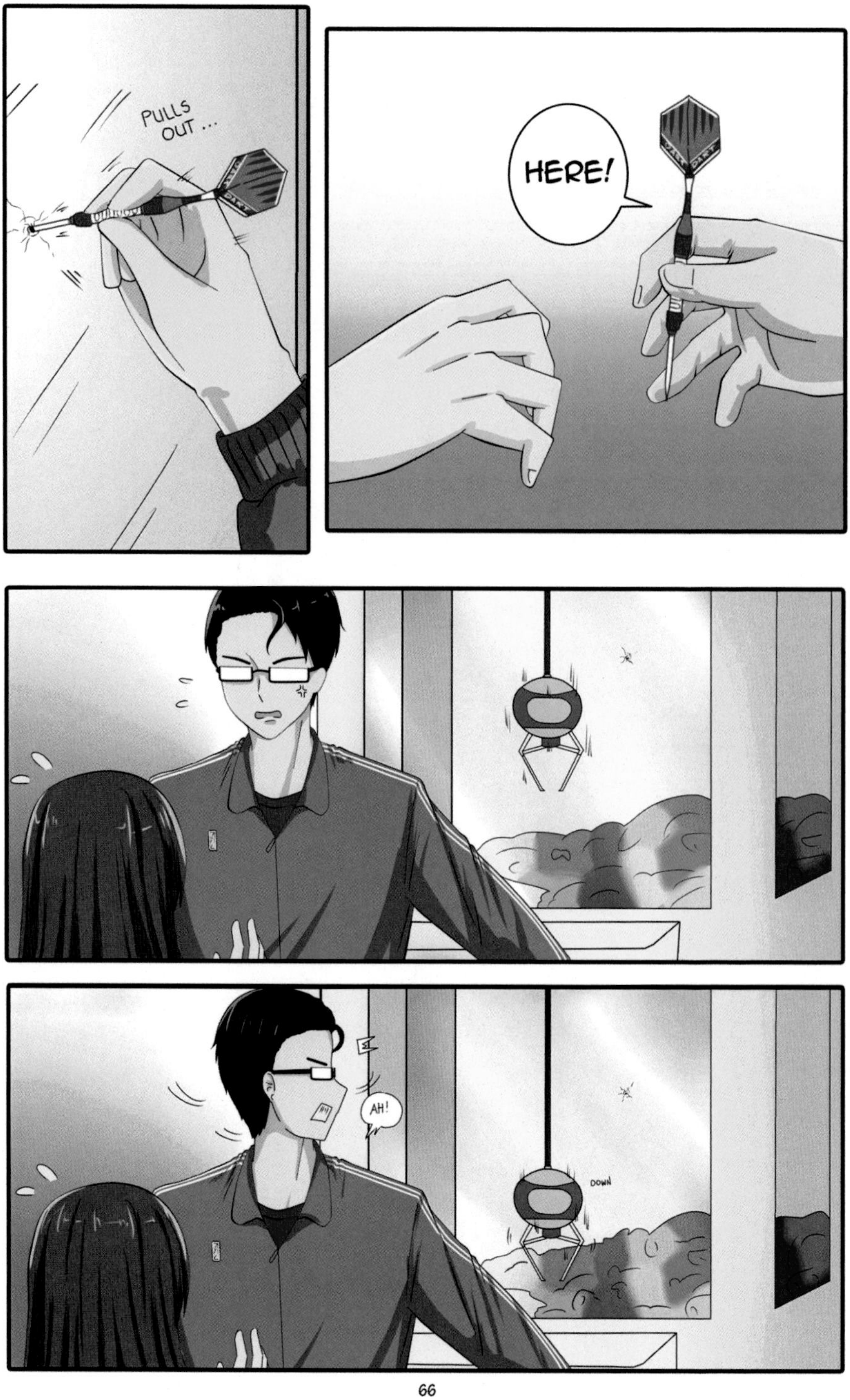
PULLS OUT ...
HERE!
AH!
DOWN

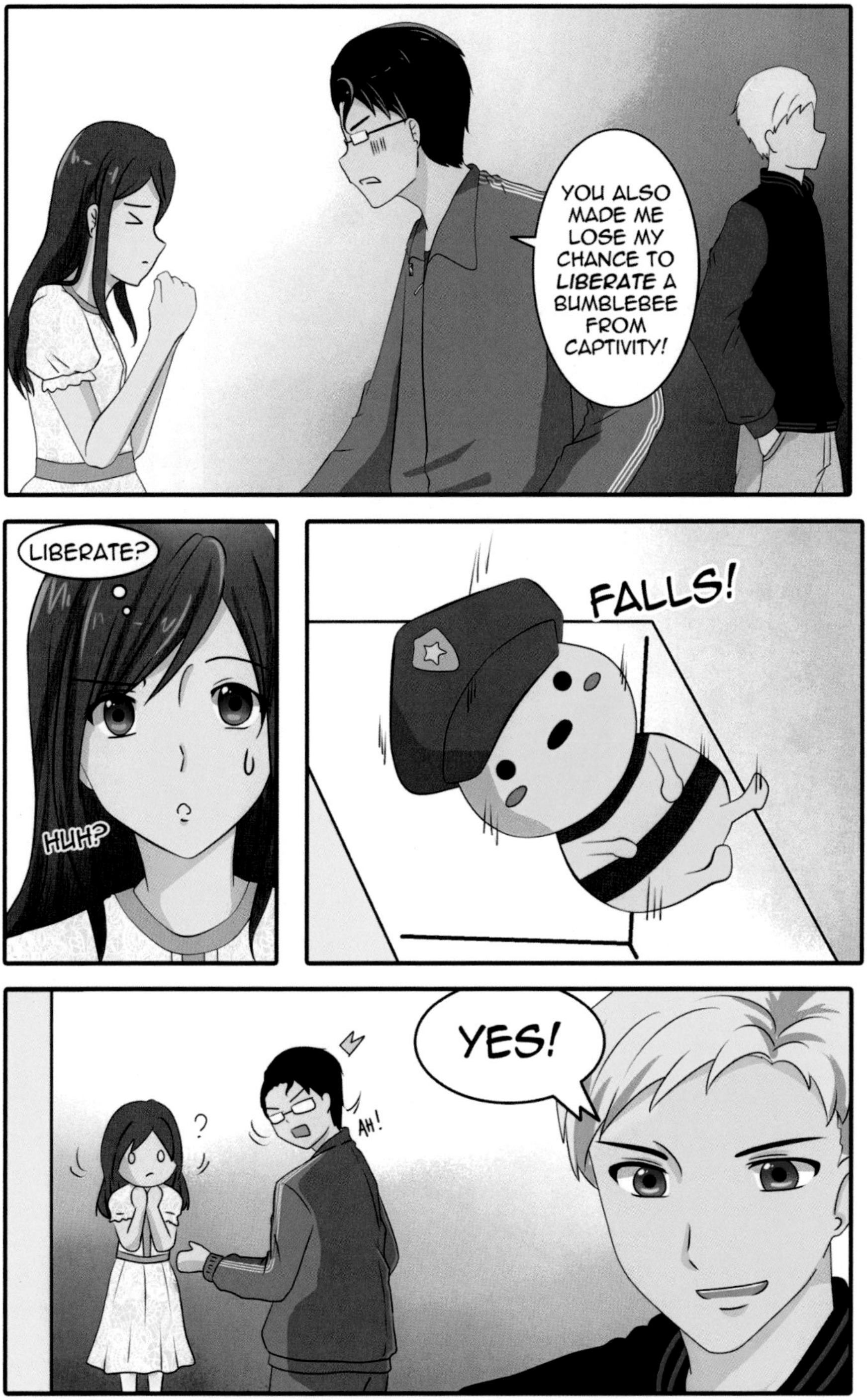
YOU ALSO MADE ME LOSE MY CHANCE TO LIBERATE A BUMBLEBEE FROM CAPTIVITY!
LIBERATE?
HUH?
FALLS!
YES!
AH!
?

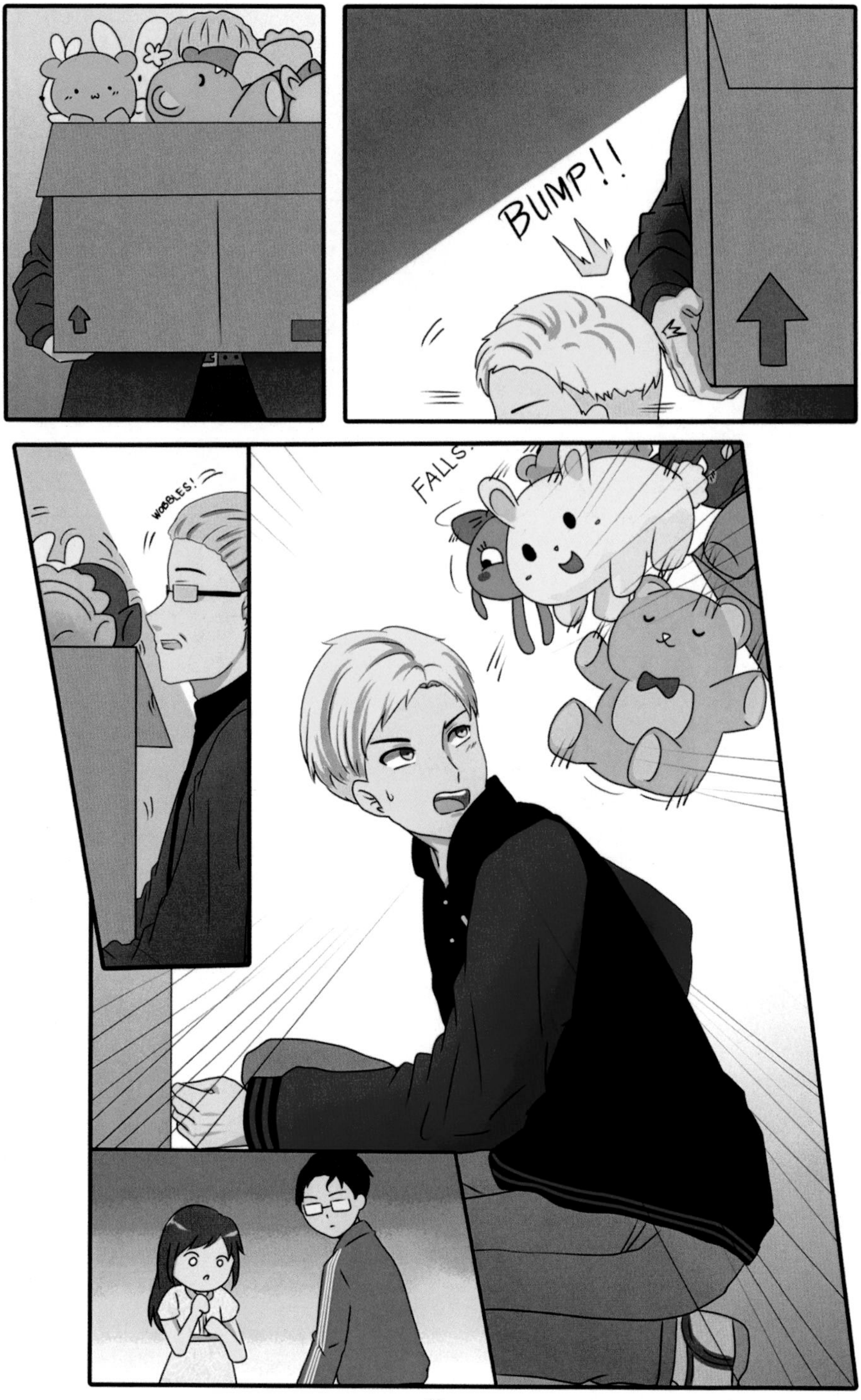
BUMP!!
WOBBLES!
FALLS!

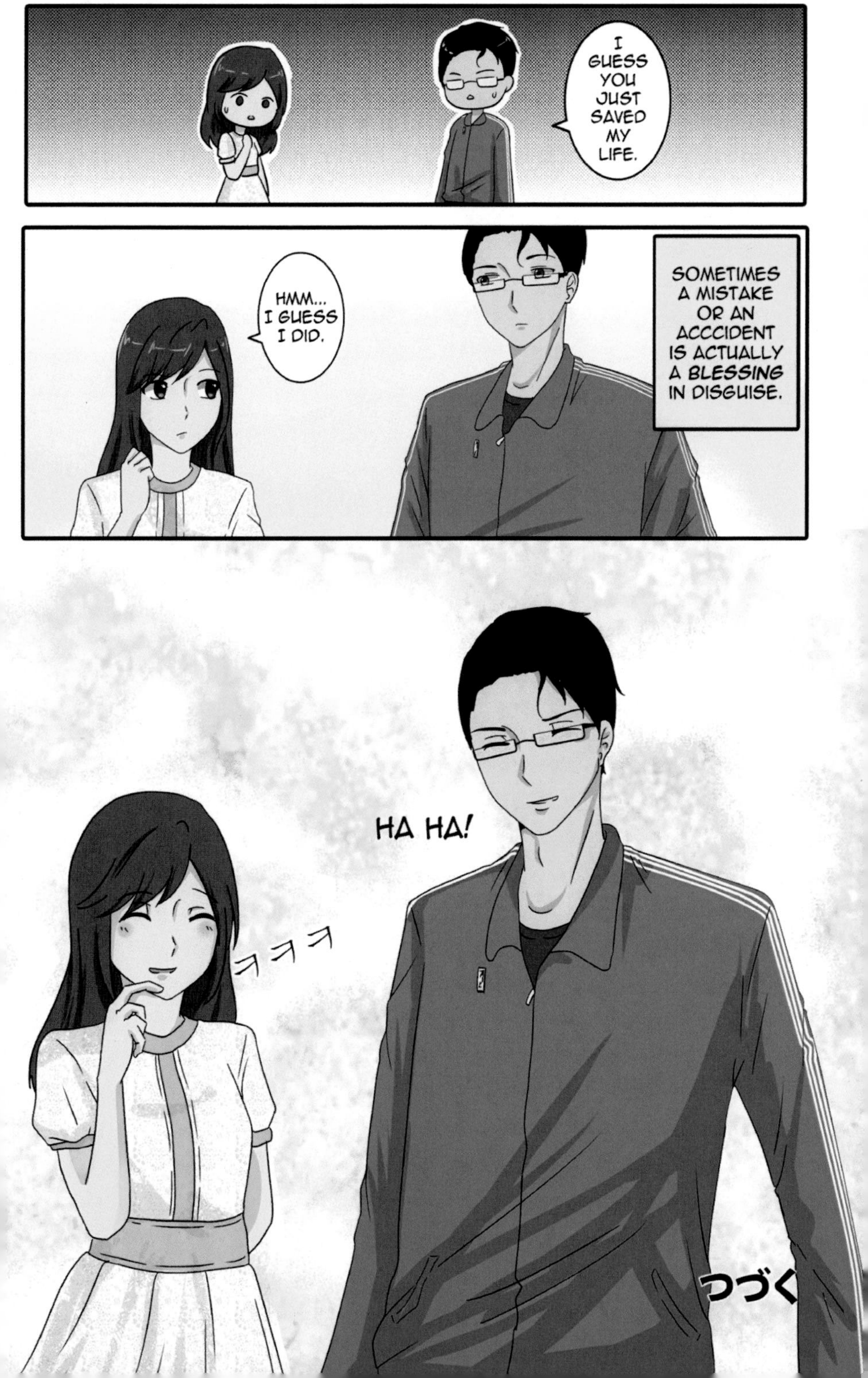
I GUESS YOU JUST SAVED MY LIFE.
HMM... I GUESS I DID.
SOMETIMES A MISTAKE OR AN ACCCIDENT IS ACTUALLY A BLESSING IN DISGUISE.
HA HA!
ヲヲヲ
つづく

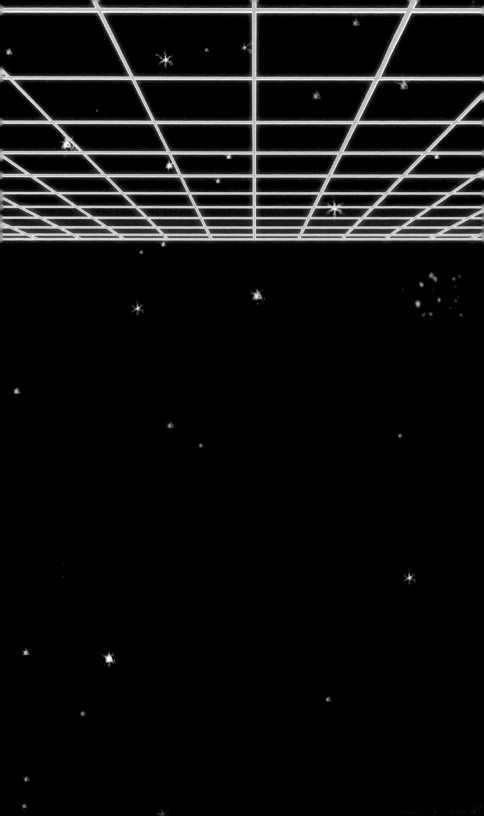

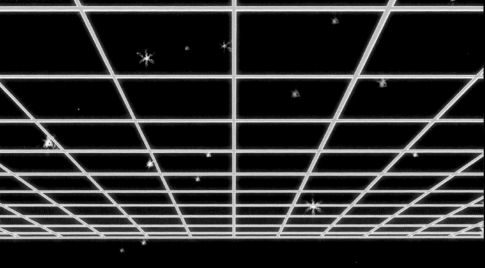

Episode 9:
A Good Samaritan

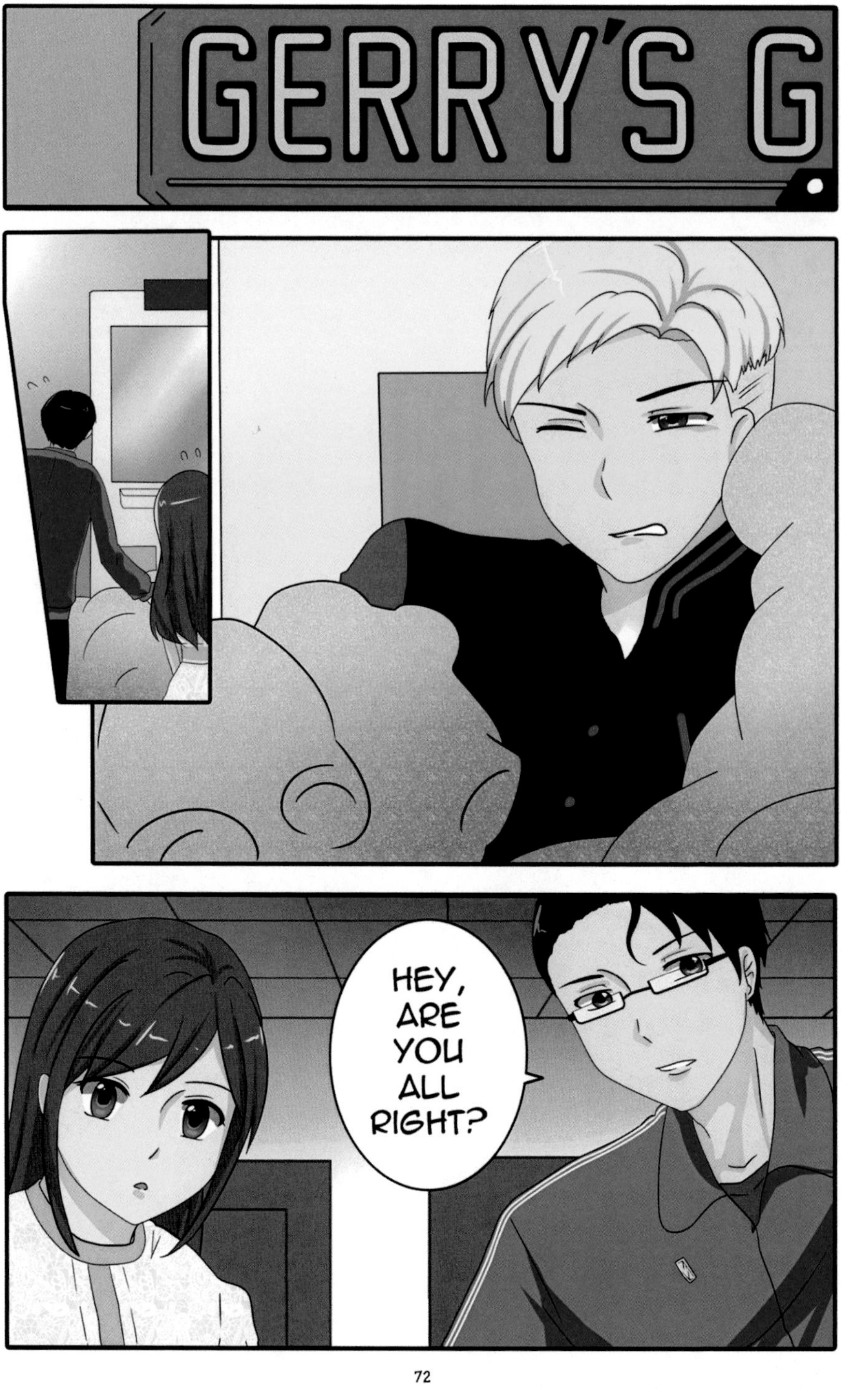
GERRY'S G
HEY, ARE YOU ALL RIGHT?

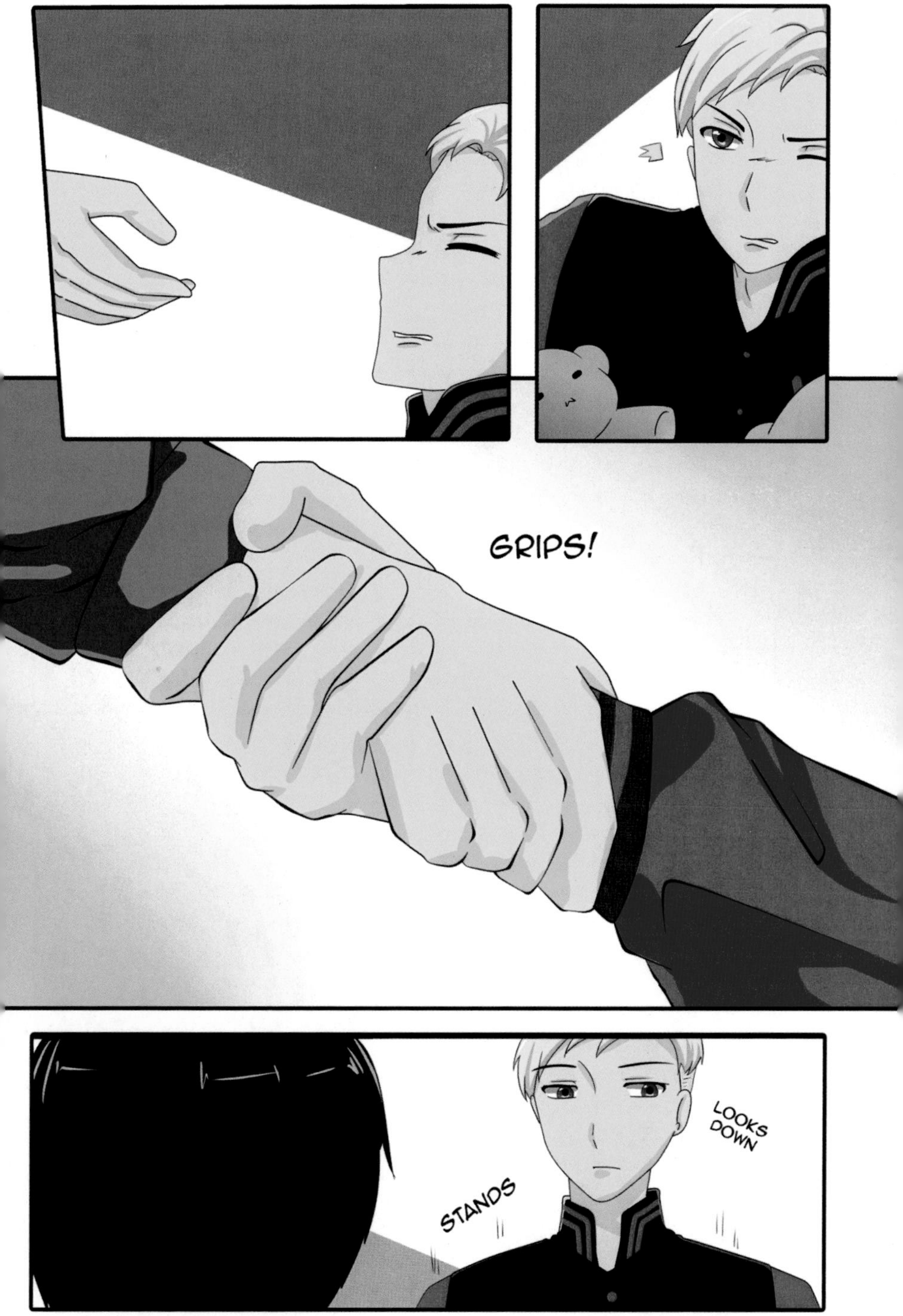
GRIPS!
LOOKS DOWN
STANDS

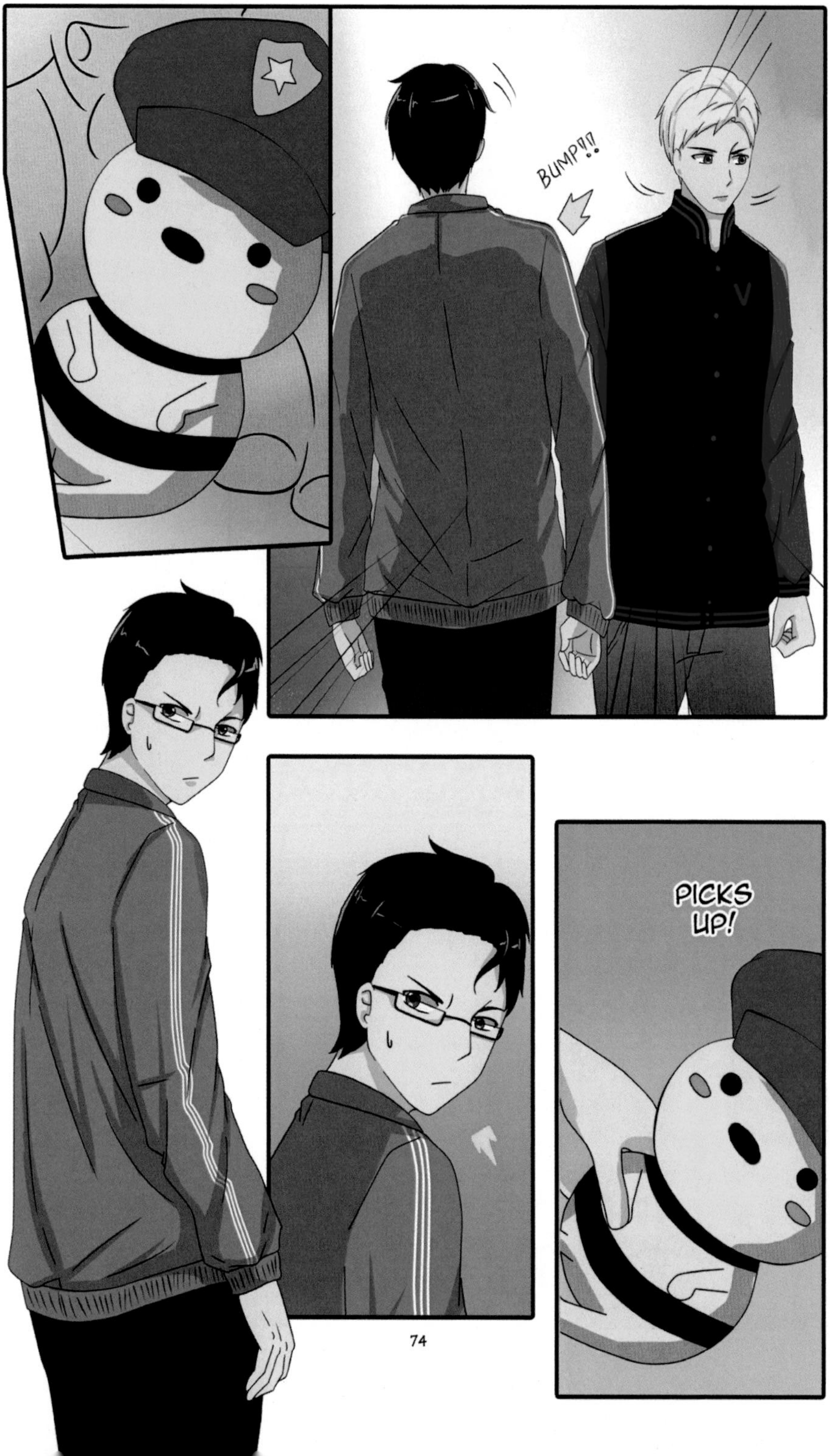
BUMP?!?
PICKS UP!

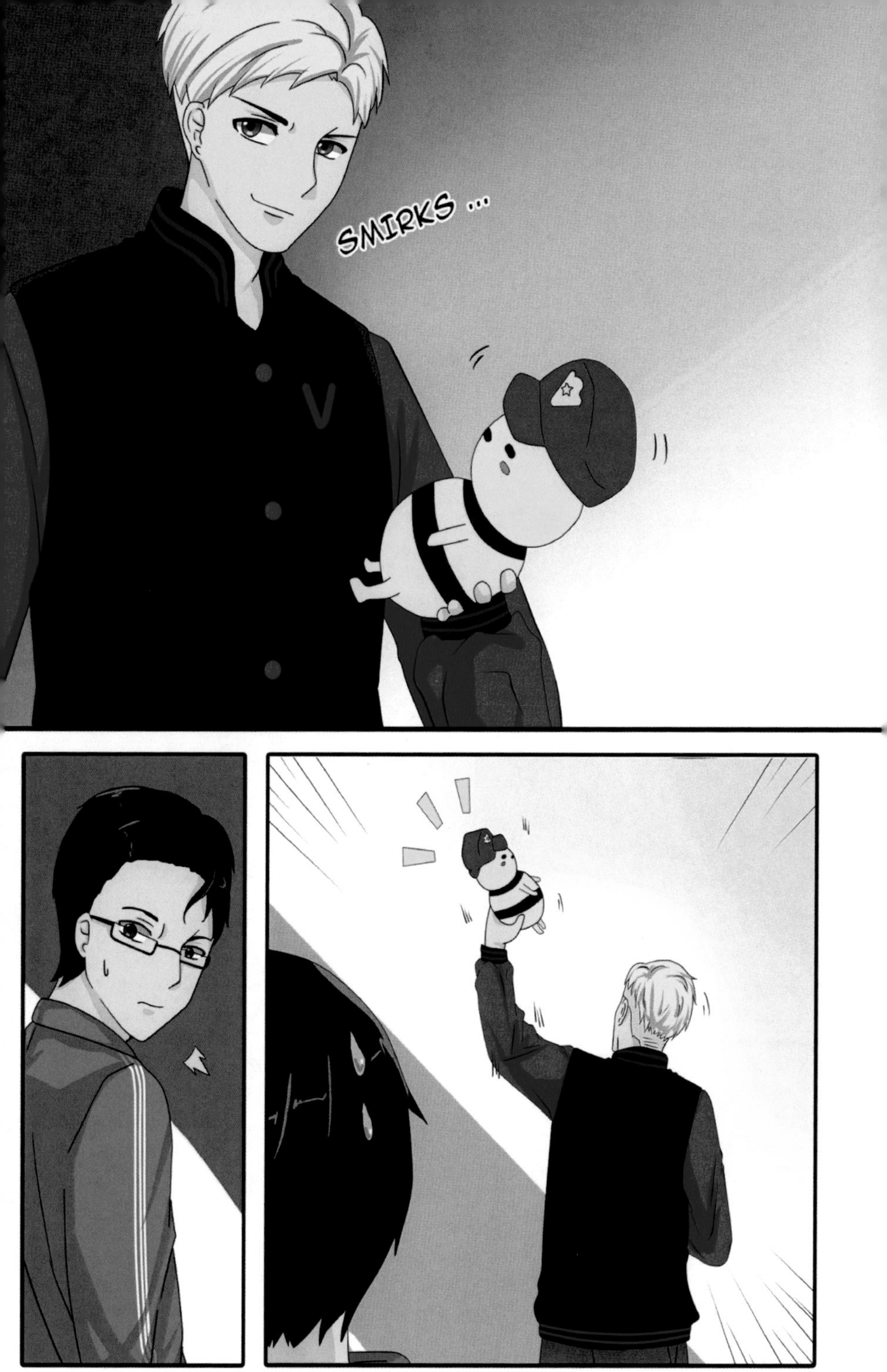
SMIRKS ...

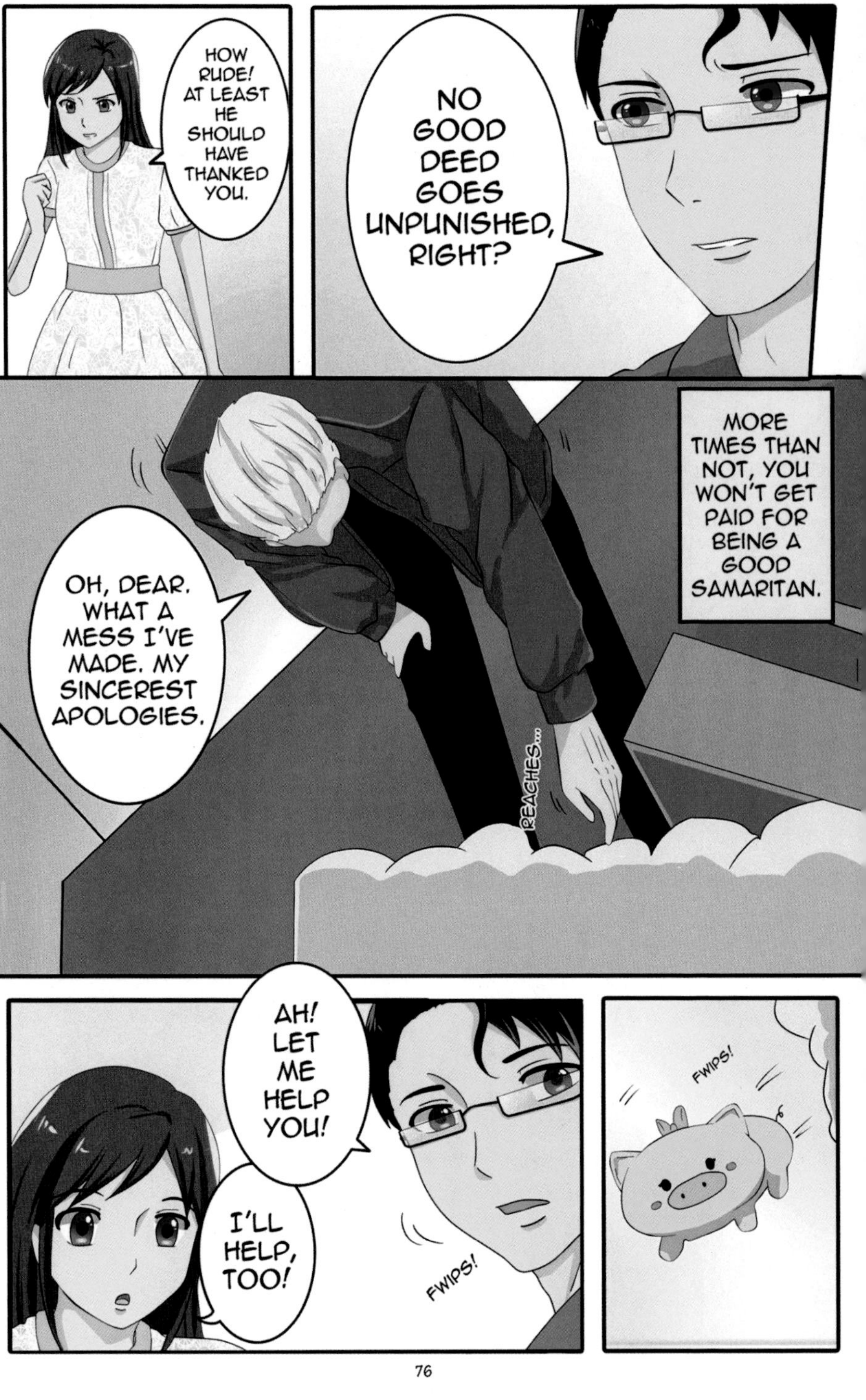
HOW RUDE! AT LEAST HE SHOULD HAVE THANKED YOU.
NO GOOD DEED GOES UNPUNISHED, RIGHT?
MORE TIMES THAN NOT, YOU WON'T GET PAID FOR BEING A GOOD SAMARITAN.
OH, DEAR. WHAT A MESS I'VE MADE. MY SINCEREST APOLOGIES.
REACHES...
AH! LET ME HELP YOU!
I'LL HELP, TOO!
FWIPS!
FWIPS!

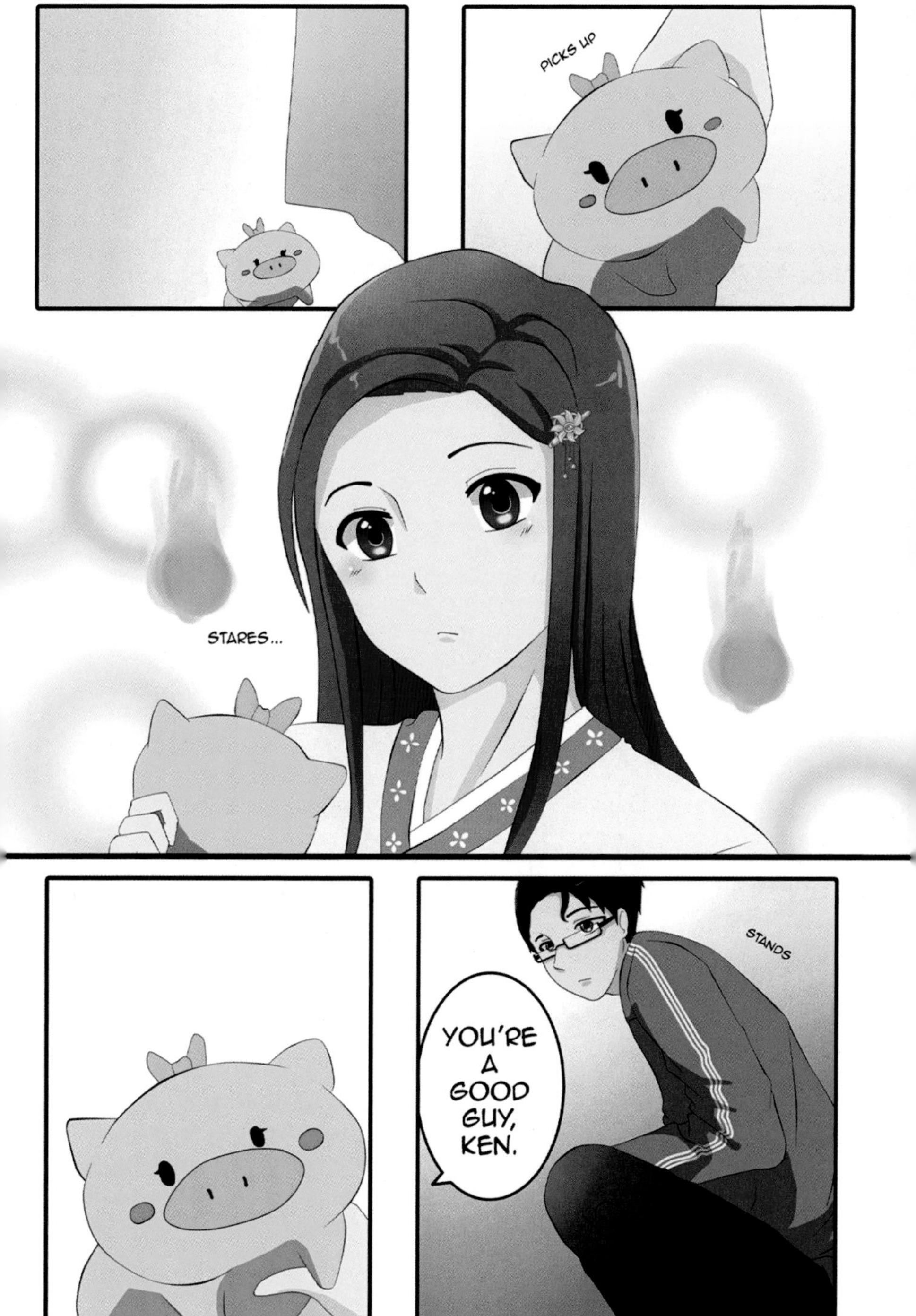
PICKS UP
STARES...
YOU'RE A GOOD GUY, KEN.
STANDS

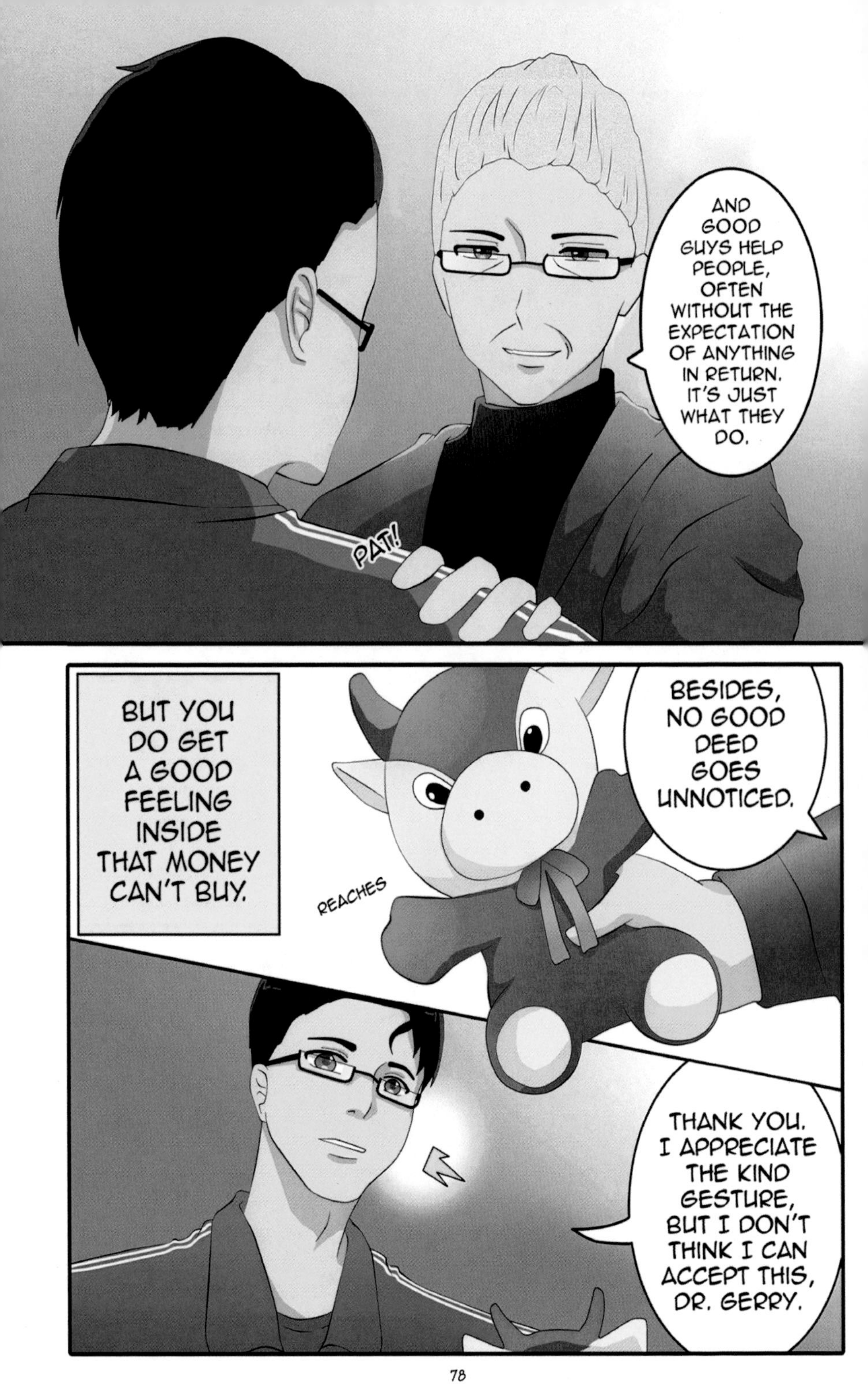
AND GOOD GUYS HELP PEOPLE, OFTEN WITHOUT THE EXPECTATION OF ANYTHING IN RETURN. IT'S JUST WHAT THEY DO.
PAT!
BUT YOU DO GET A GOOD FEELING INSIDE THAT MONEY CAN'T BUY.
BESIDES, NO GOOD DEED GOES UNNOTICED.
REACHES
THANK YOU. I APPRECIATE THE KIND GESTURE, BUT I DON'T THINK I CAN ACCEPT THIS, DR. GERRY.

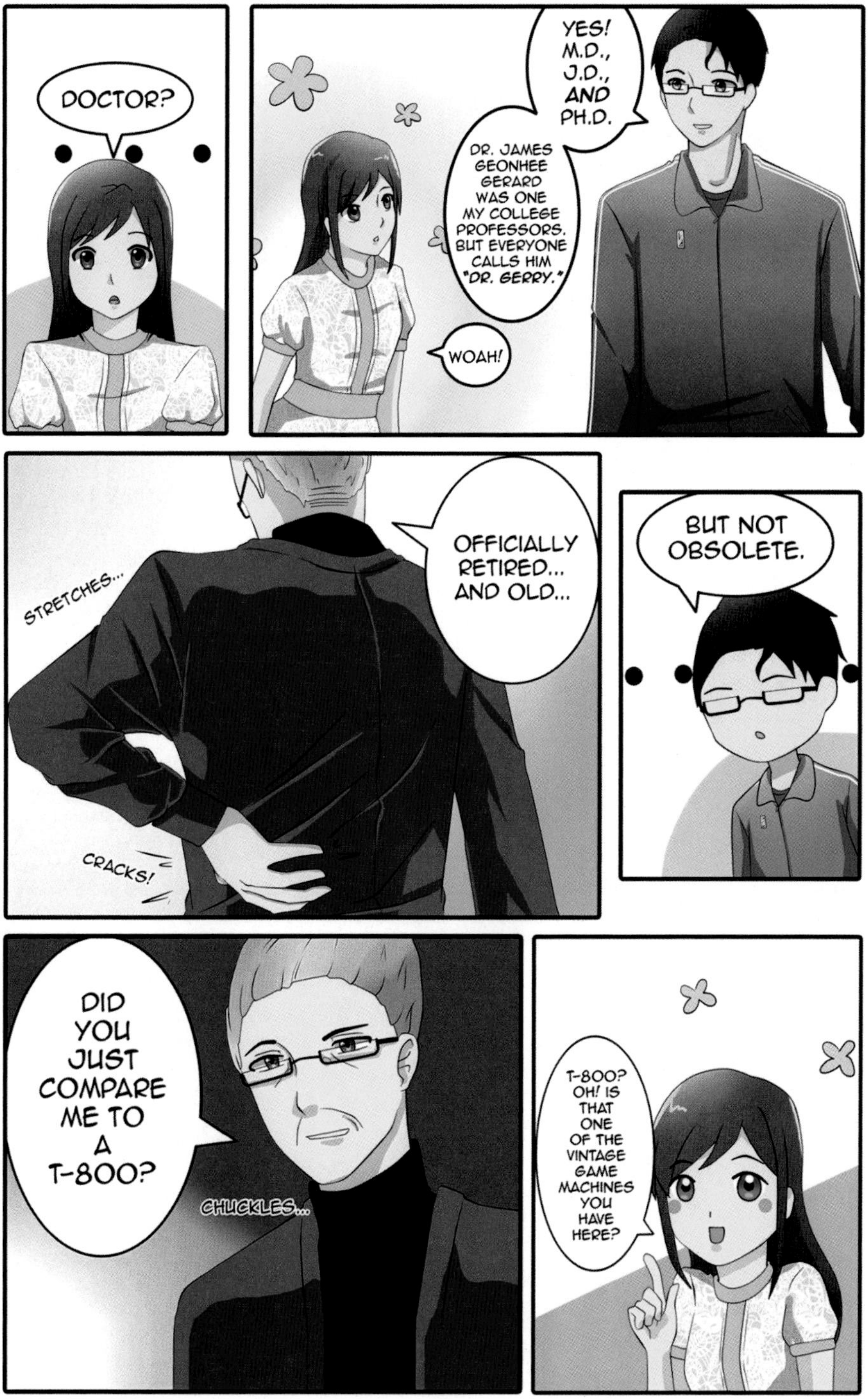
DOCTOR?
YES! M.D., J.D., AND PH.D.
DR. JAMES GEONHEE GERARD WAS ONE MY COLLEGE PROFESSORS. BUT EVERYONE CALLS HIM "DR. GERRY."
WOAH!
OFFICIALLY RETIRED... AND OLD...
STRETCHES...
CRACKS!
BUT NOT OBSOLETE.
DID YOU JUST COMPARE ME TO A T-800?
CHUCKLES...
T-800? OH! IS THAT ONE OF THE VINTAGE GAME MACHINES YOU HAVE HERE?

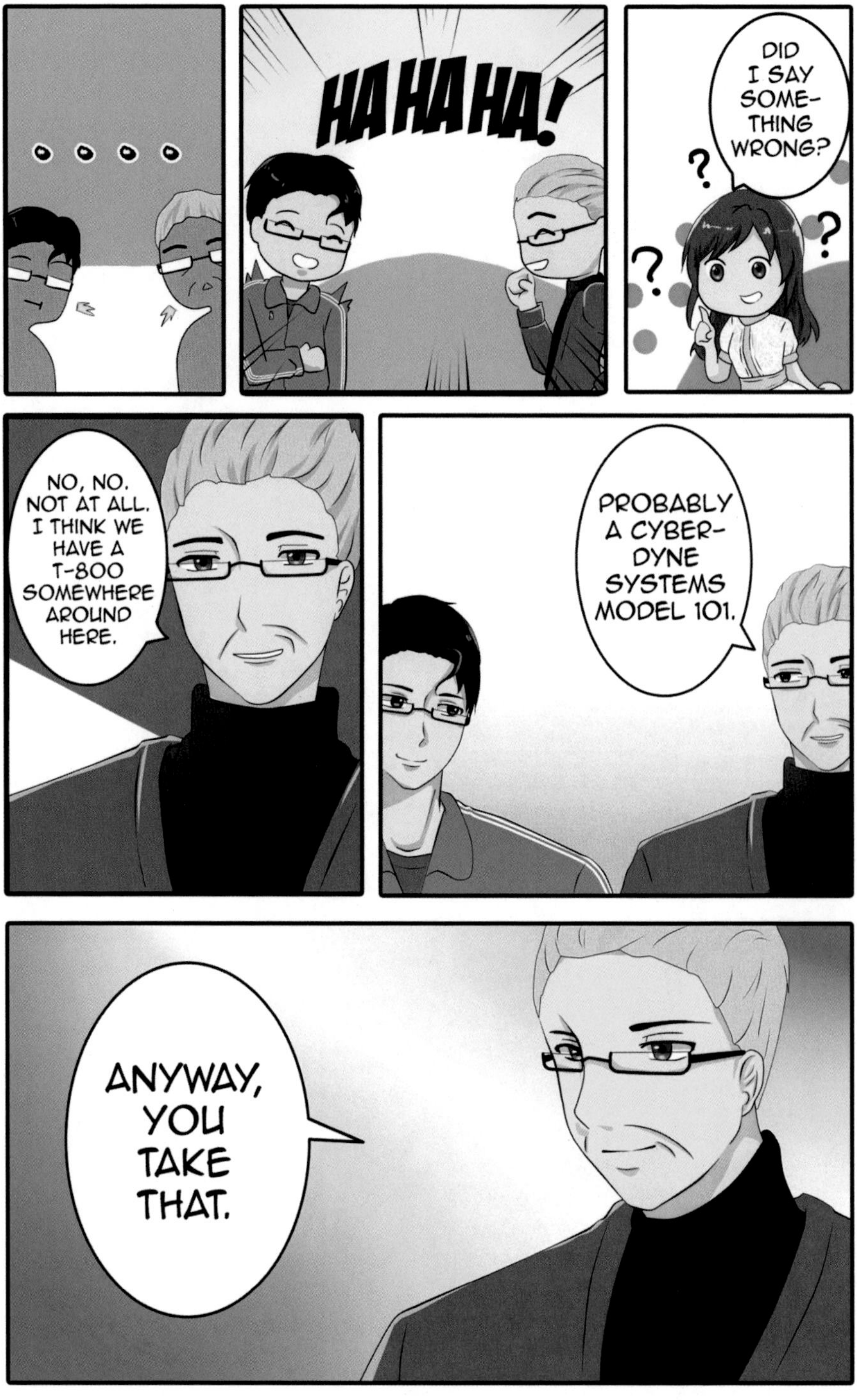

HA HA HA!
DID I SAY SOME-THING WRONG?
? ? ?
NO, NO. NOT AT ALL. I THINK WE HAVE A T-800 SOMEWHERE AROUND HERE.
PROBABLY A CYBER-DYNE SYSTEMS MODEL 101.
ANYWAY, YOU TAKE THAT.

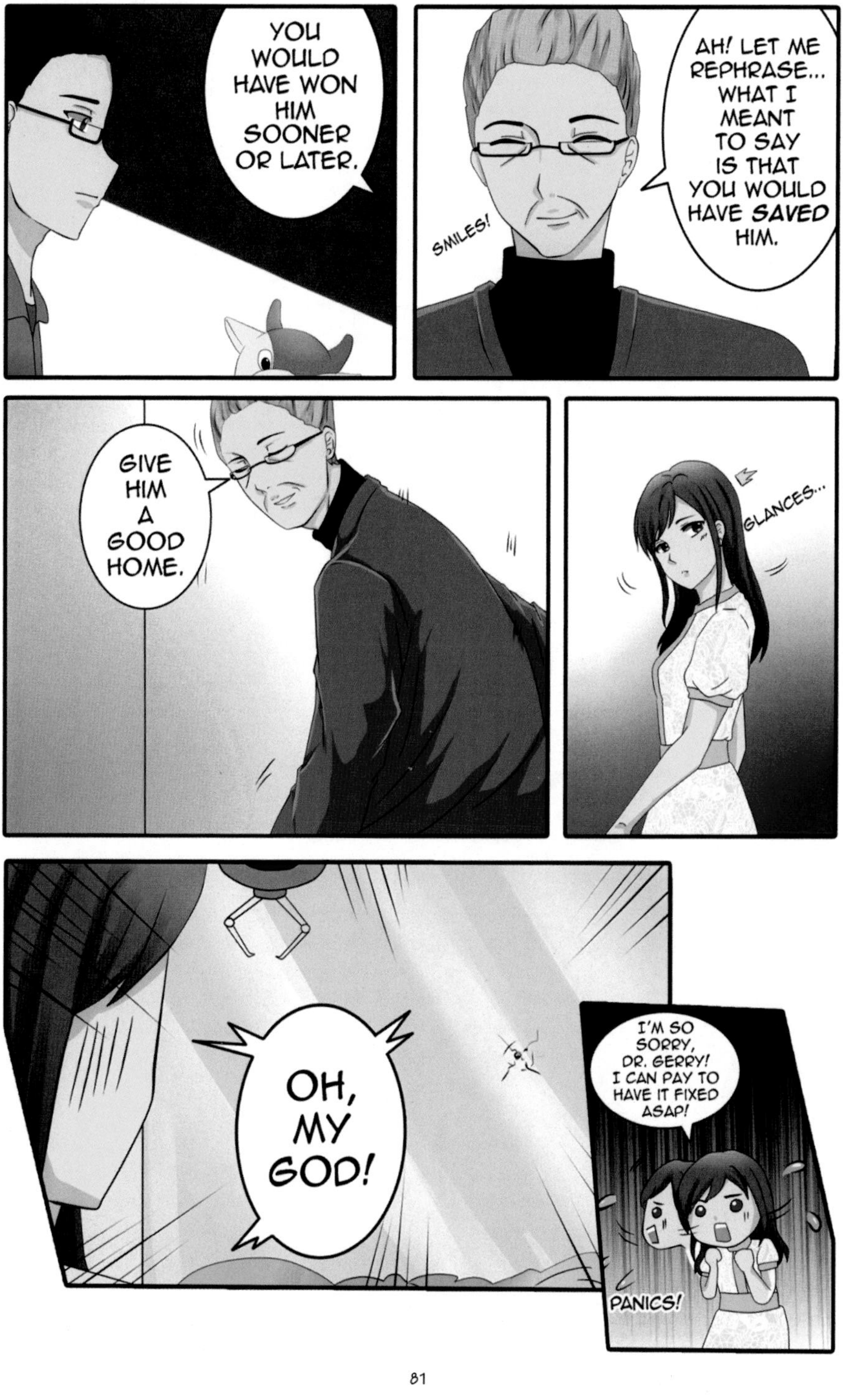
YOU WOULD HAVE WON HIM SOONER OR LATER.
AH! LET ME REPHRASE... WHAT I MEANT TO SAY IS THAT YOU WOULD HAVE SAVED HIM.
SMILES!
GIVE HIM A GOOD HOME.
GLANCES...
OH, MY GOD!
I'M SO SORRY, DR. GERRY! I CAN PAY TO HAVE IT FIXED ASAP!
PANICS!

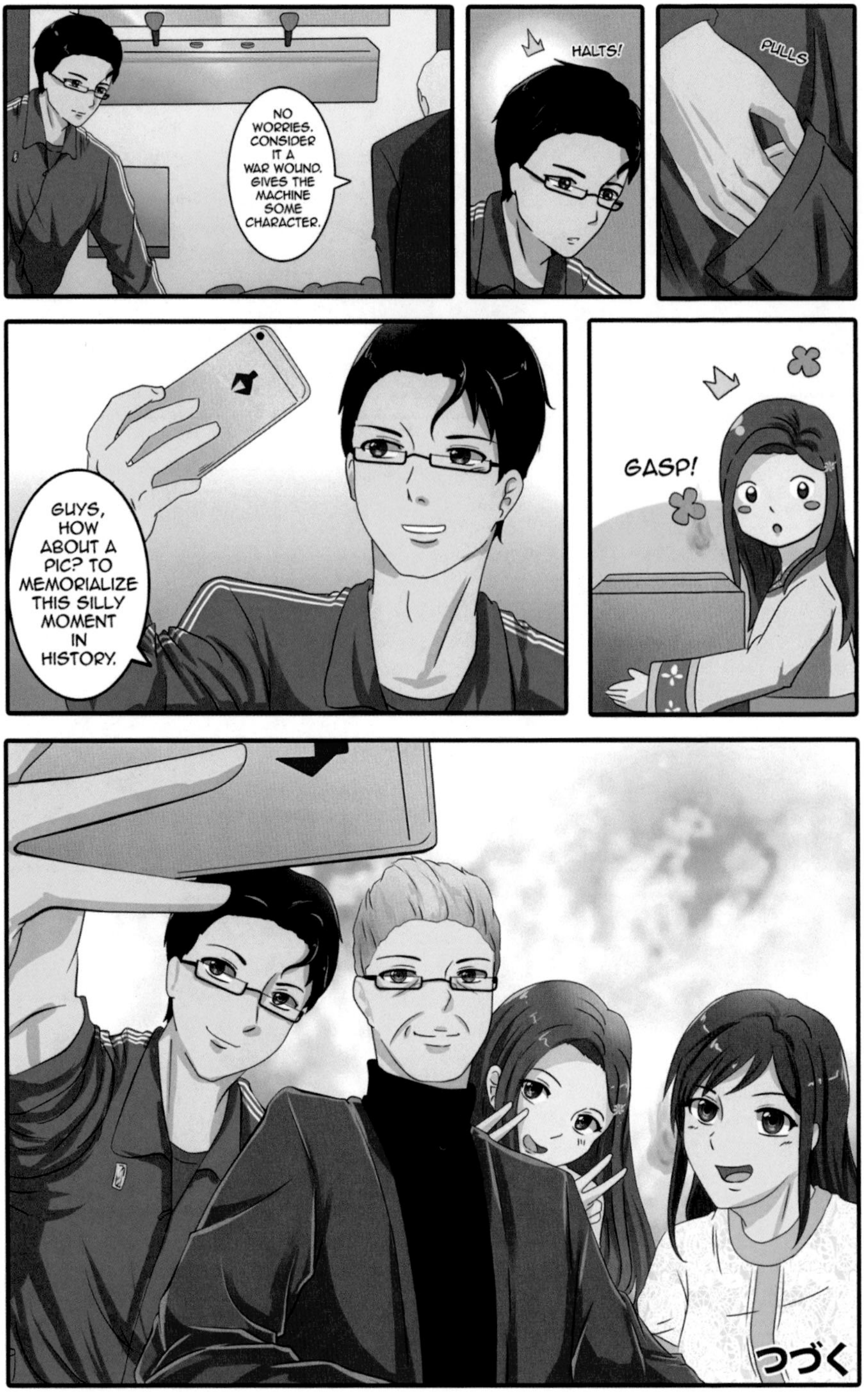
NO WORRIES. CONSIDER IT A WAR WOUND. GIVES THE MACHINE SOME CHARACTER.
HALTS!
PULLS
GUYS, HOW ABOUT A PIC? TO MEMORIALIZE THIS SILLY MOMENT IN HISTORY.
GASP!
つづく

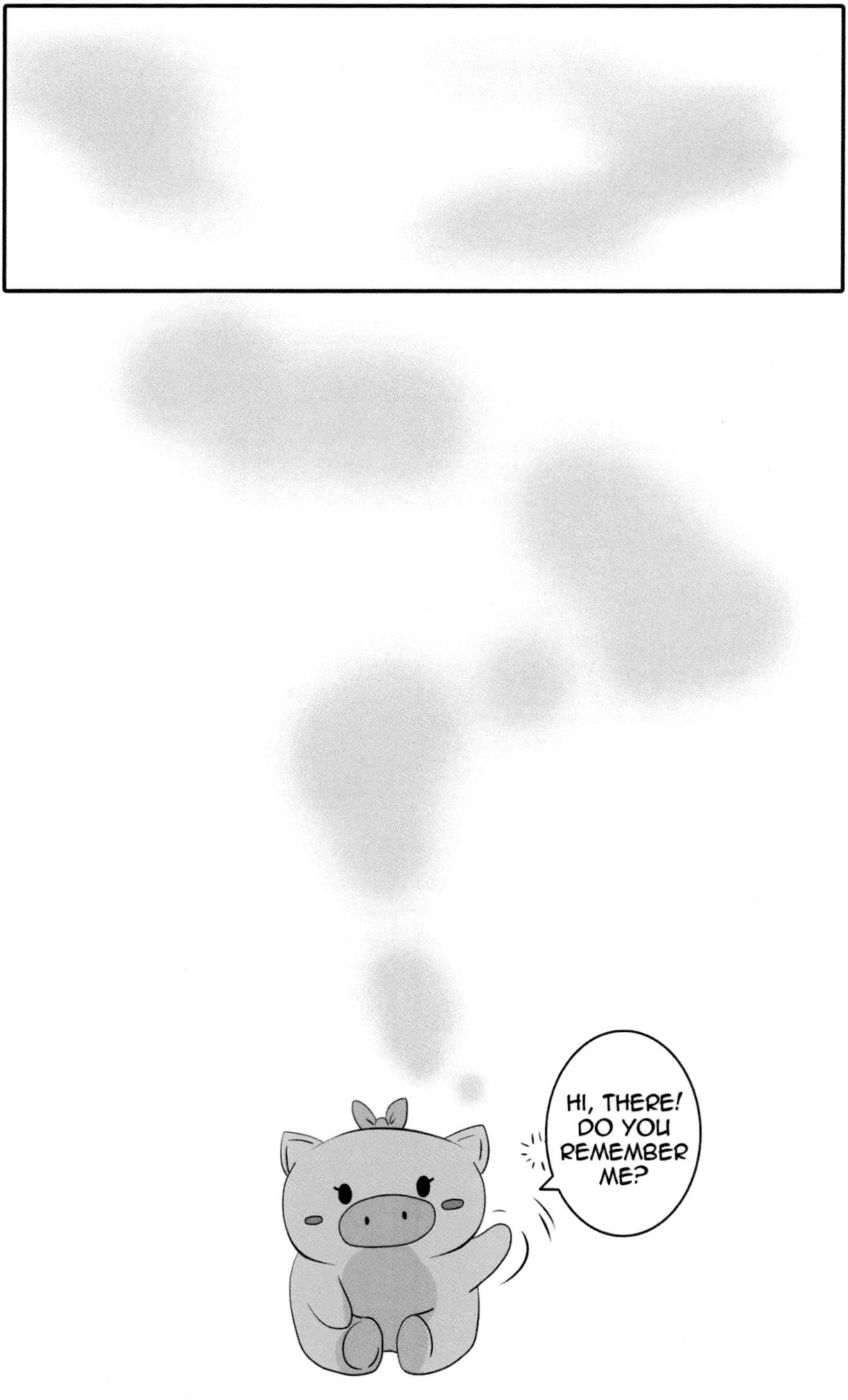
HI, THERE! DO YOU REMEMBER ME?

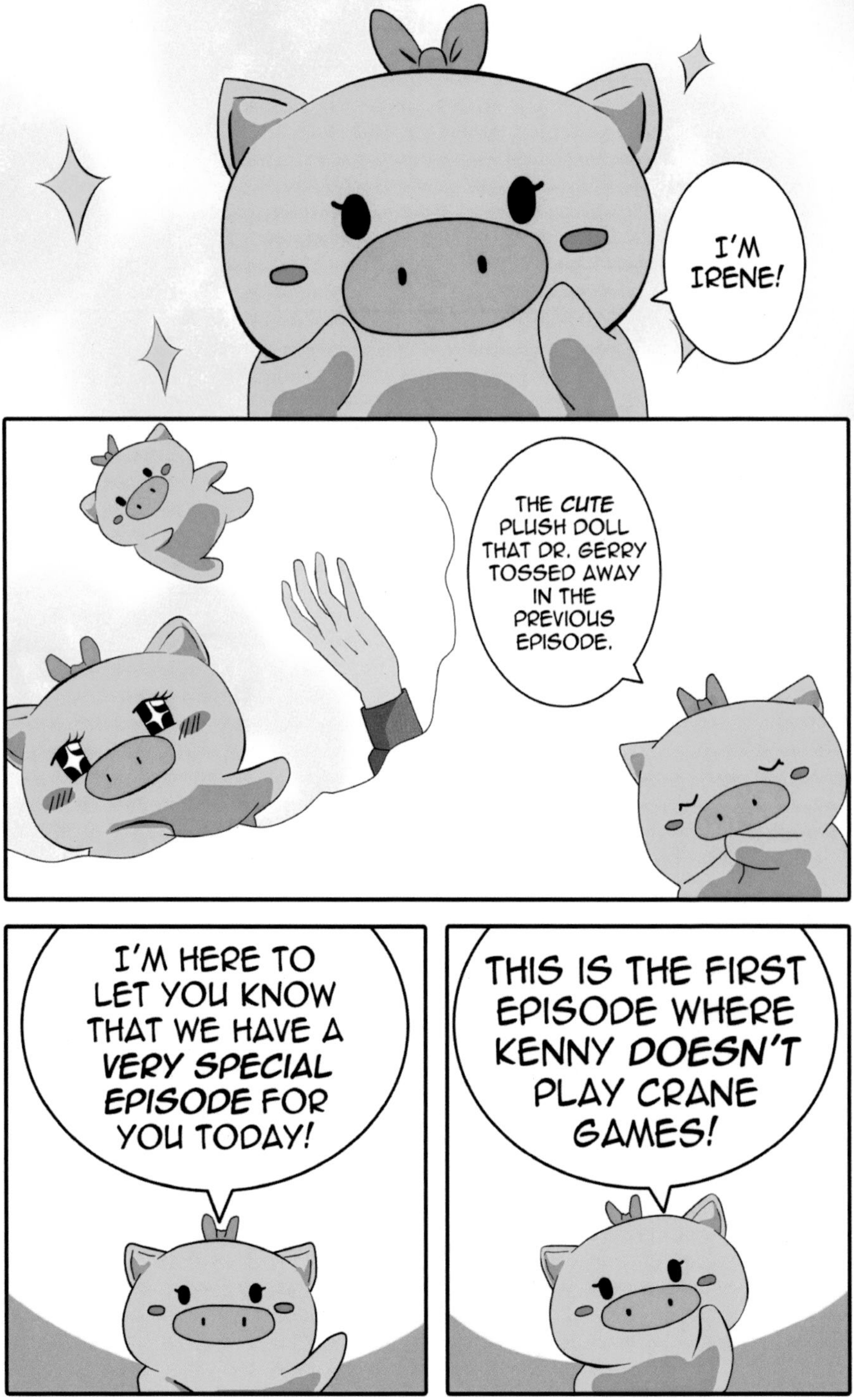
I'M IRENE!
THE CUTE PLUSH DOLL THAT DR. GERRY TOSSED AWAY IN THE PREVIOUS EPISODE.
I'M HERE TO LET YOU KNOW THAT WE HAVE A VERY SPECIAL EPISODE FOR YOU TODAY!
THIS IS THE FIRST EPISODE WHERE KENNY DOESN'T PLAY CRANE GAMES!

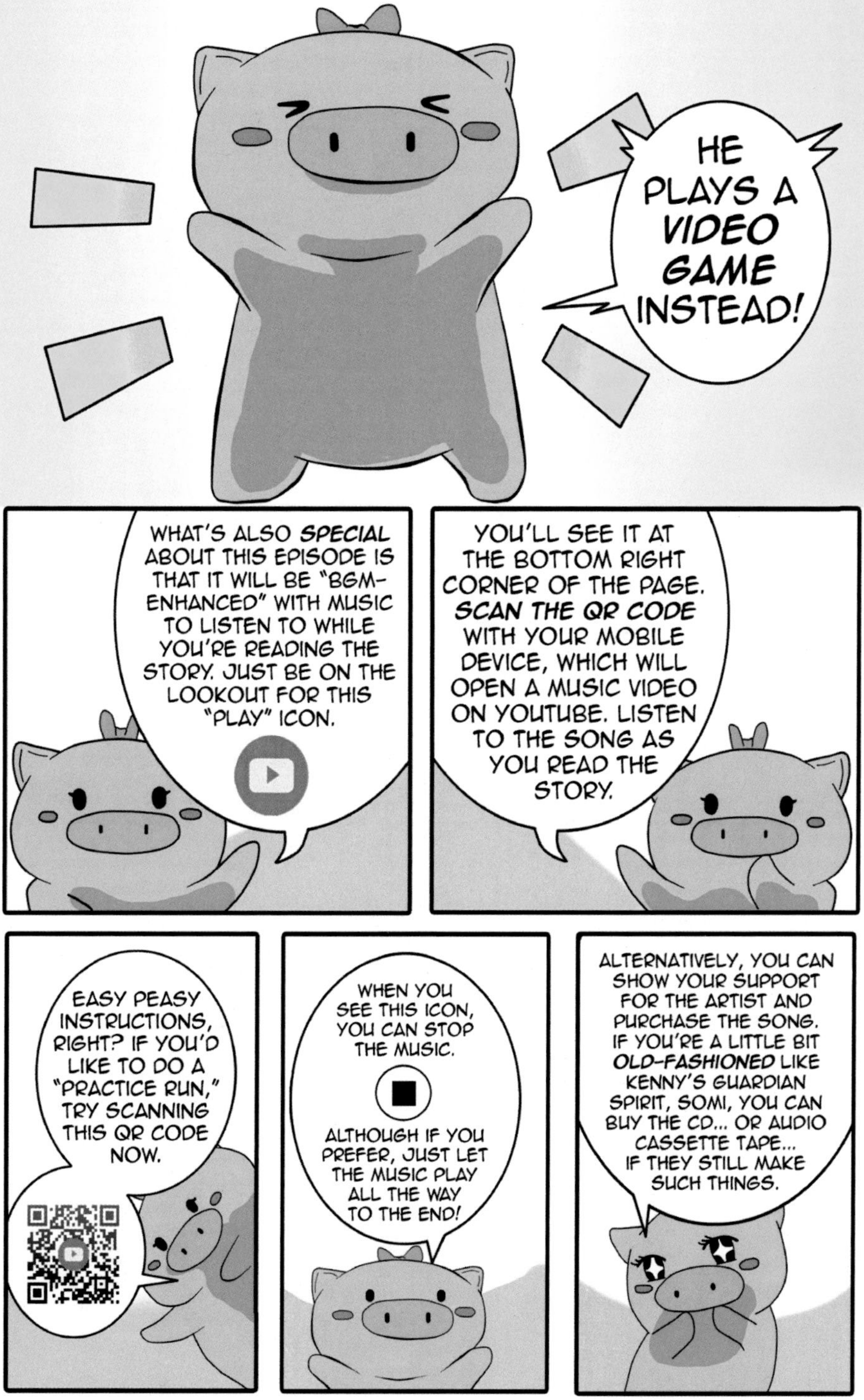
HE PLAYS A VIDEO GAME INSTEAD!
WHAT'S ALSO SPECIAL ABOUT THIS EPISODE IS THAT IT WILL BE "BGM-ENHANCED" WITH MUSIC TO LISTEN TO WHILE YOU'RE READING THE STORY. JUST BE ON THE LOOKOUT FOR THIS "PLAY" ICON.
YOU'LL SEE IT AT THE BOTTOM RIGHT CORNER OF THE PAGE. SCAN THE QR CODE WITH YOUR MOBILE DEVICE, WHICH WILL OPEN A MUSIC VIDEO ON YOUTUBE. LISTEN TO THE SONG AS YOU READ THE STORY.
EASY PEASY INSTRUCTIONS, RIGHT? IF YOU'D LIKE TO DO A "PRACTICE RUN," TRY SCANNING THIS QR CODE NOW.
WHEN YOU SEE THIS ICON, YOU CAN STOP THE MUSIC.
ALTHOUGH IF YOU PREFER, JUST LET THE MUSIC PLAY ALL THE WAY TO THE END!
ALTERNATIVELY, YOU CAN SHOW YOUR SUPPORT FOR THE ARTIST AND PURCHASE THE SONG. IF YOU'RE A LITTLE BIT OLD-FASHIONED LIKE KENNY'S GUARDIAN SPIRIT, SOMI, YOU CAN BUY THE CD... OR AUDIO CASSETTE TAPE... IF THEY STILL MAKE SUCH THINGS.

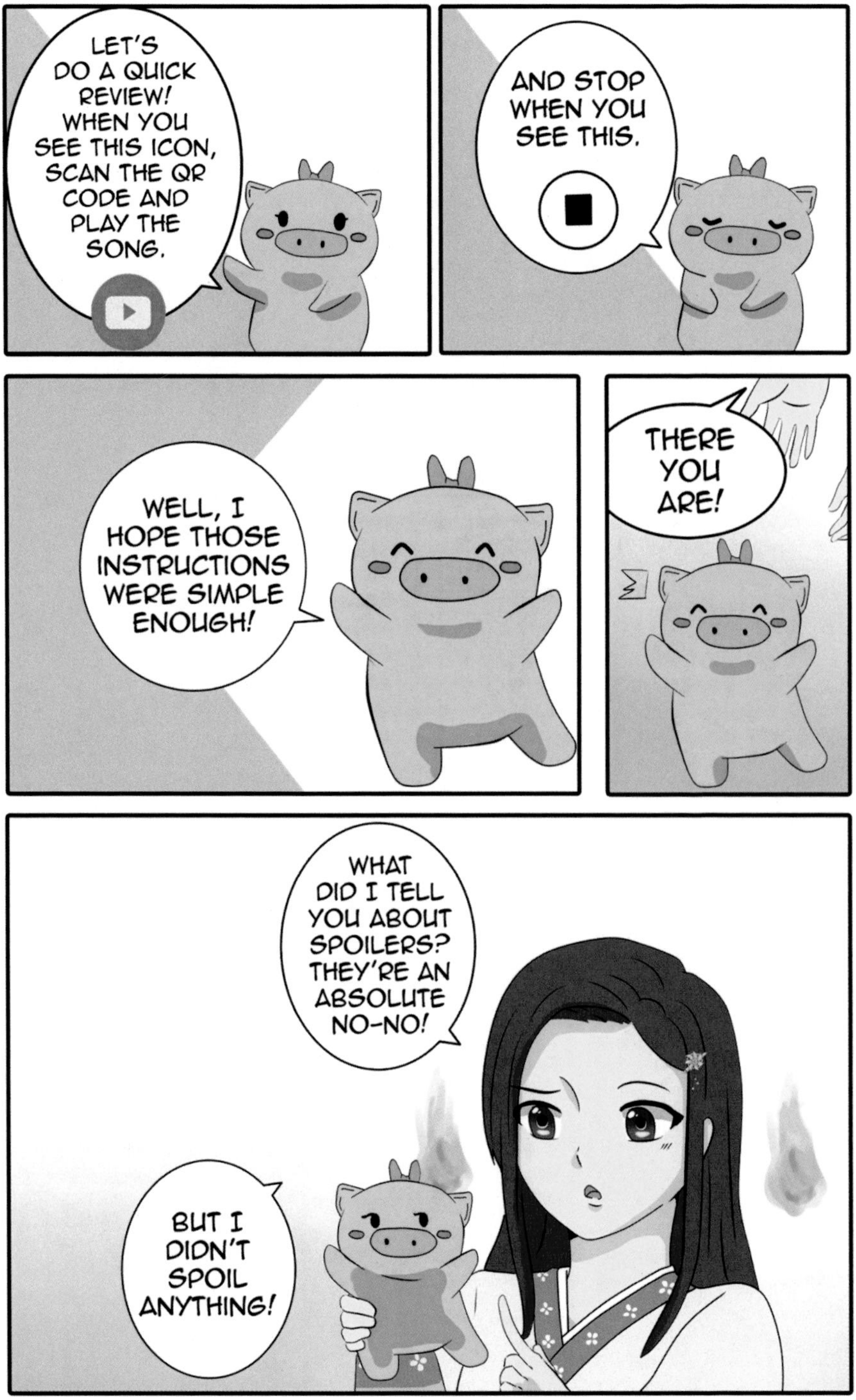
LET'S DO A QUICK REVIEW! WHEN YOU SEE THIS ICON, SCAN THE QR CODE AND PLAY THE SONG.
AND STOP WHEN YOU SEE THIS.
WELL, I HOPE THOSE INSTRUCTIONS WERE SIMPLE ENOUGH!
THERE YOU ARE!
WHAT DID I TELL YOU ABOUT SPOILERS? THEY'RE AN ABSOLUTE NO-NO!
BUT I DIDN'T SPOIL ANYTHING!

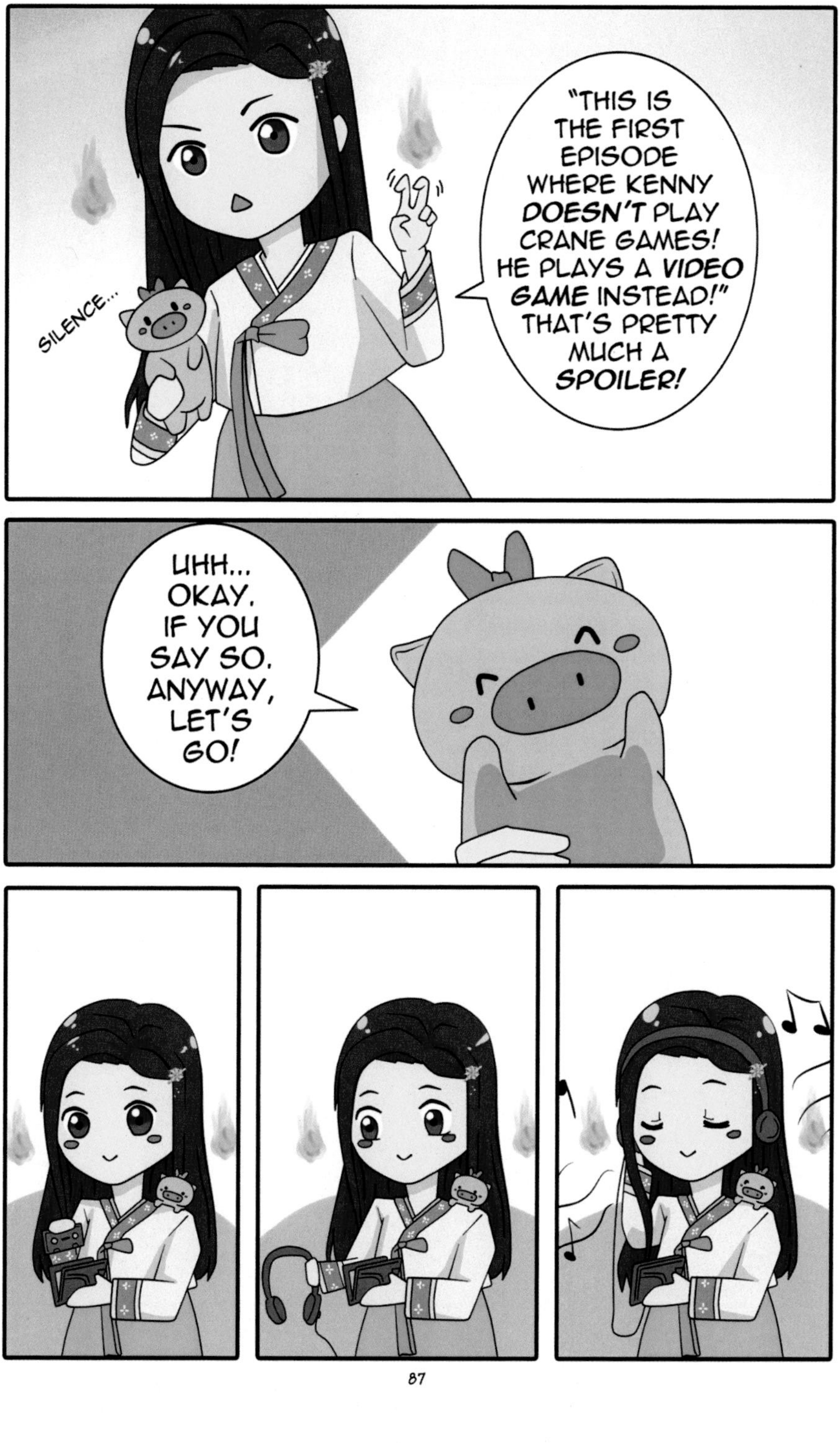

SILENCE...
"THIS IS THE FIRST EPISODE WHERE KENNY DOESN'T PLAY CRANE GAMES! HE PLAYS A VIDEO GAME INSTEAD!" THAT'S PRETTY MUCH A SPOILER!
UHH... OKAY. IF YOU SAY SO. ANYWAY, LET'S GO!

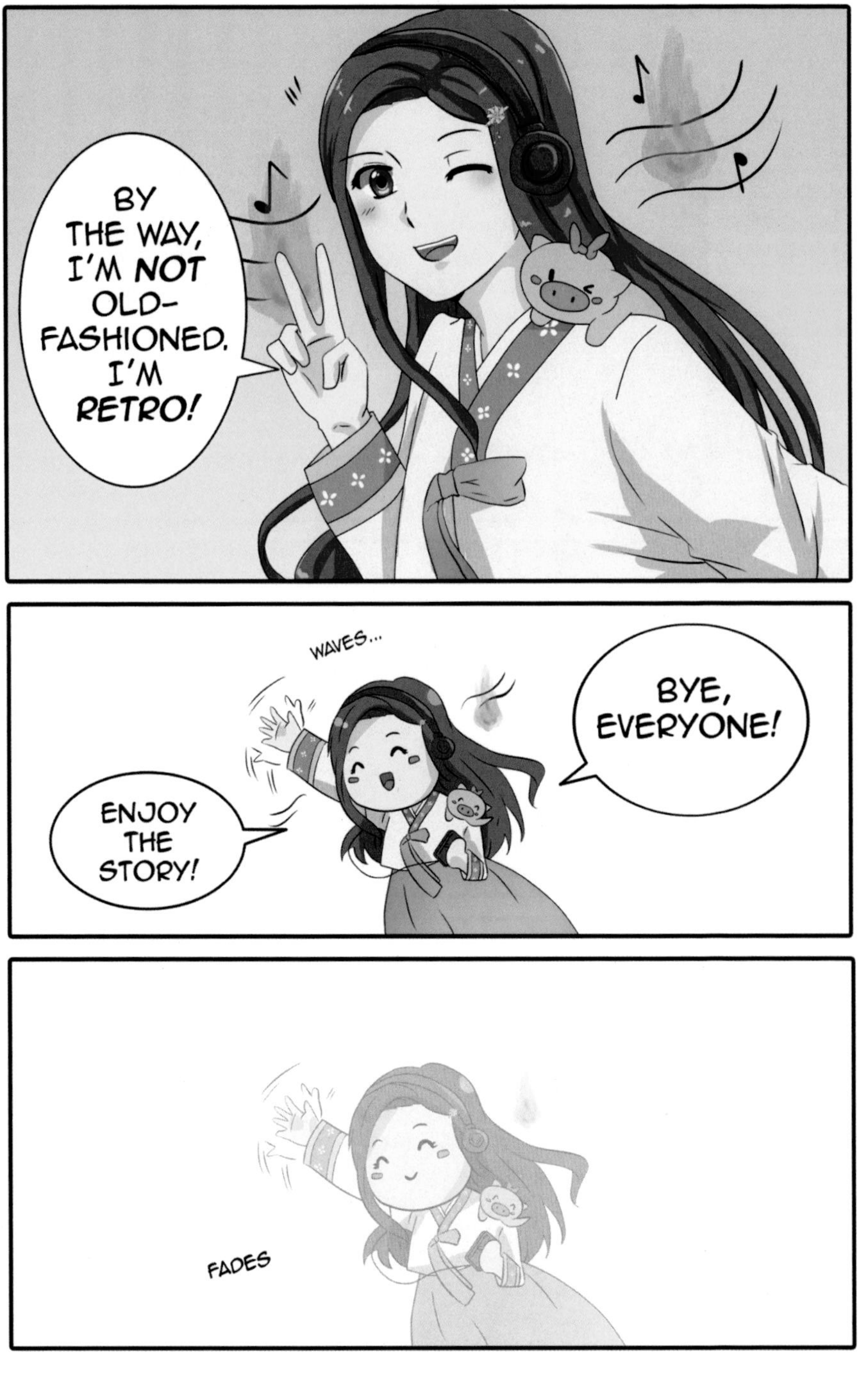
BY THE WAY, I'M NOT OLD-FASHIONED. I'M RETRO!
WAVES...
BYE, EVERYONE!
ENJOY THE STORY!
FADES

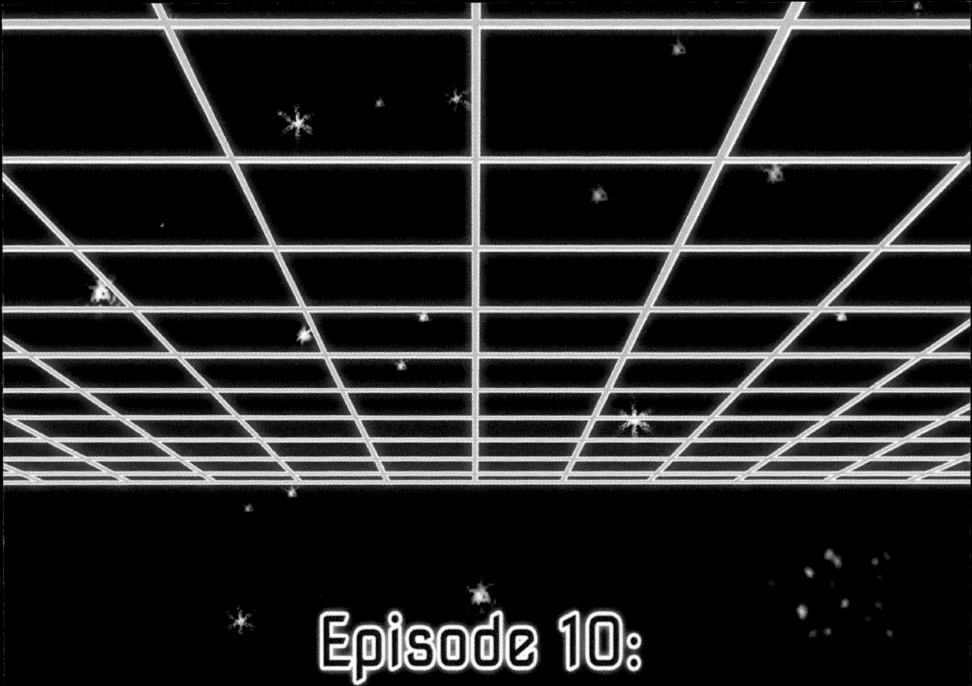

Episode 10:

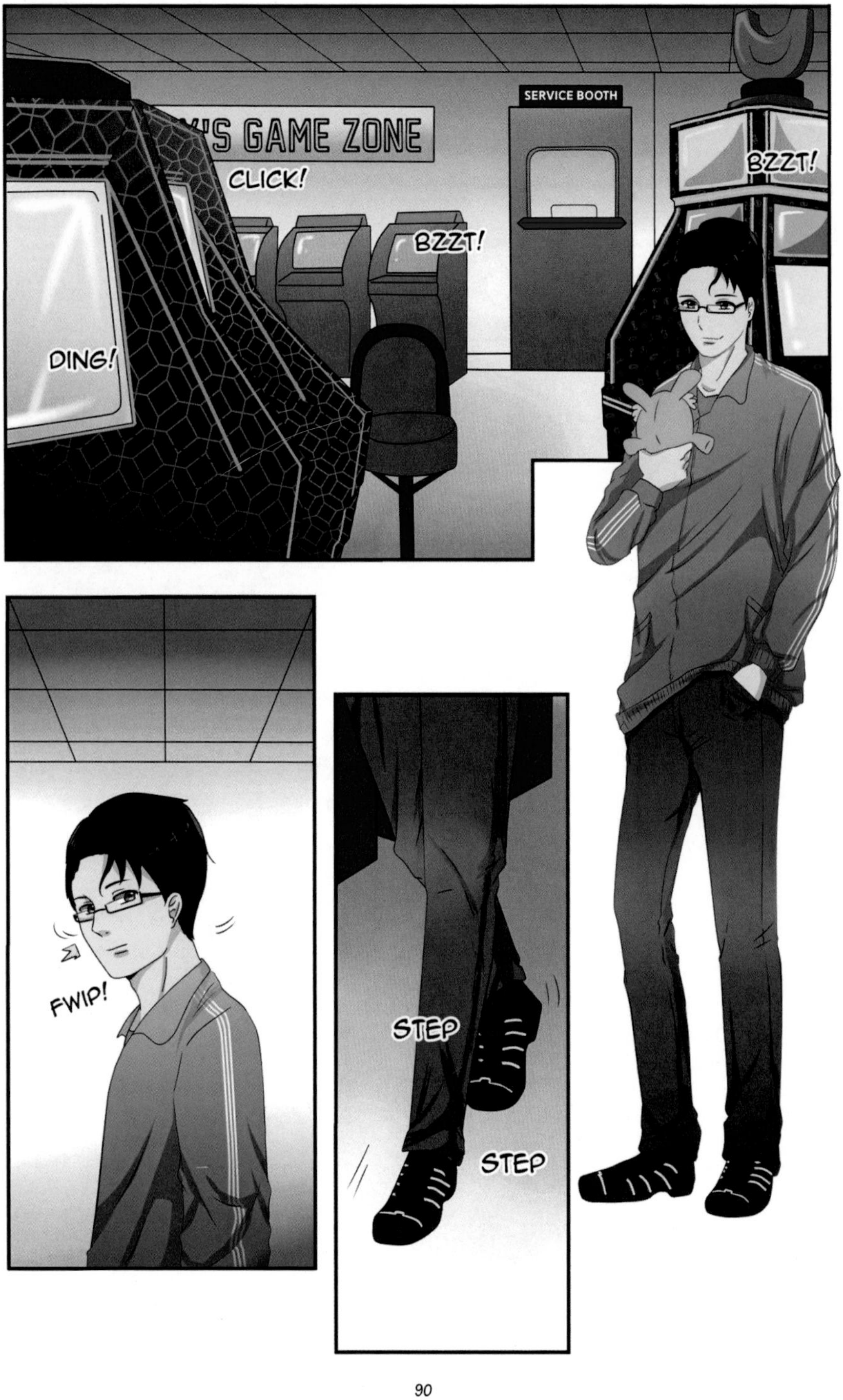

SERVICE BOOTH
'S GAME ZONE
CLICK!
BZZT!
BZZT!
DING!
FWIP!
STEP
STEP

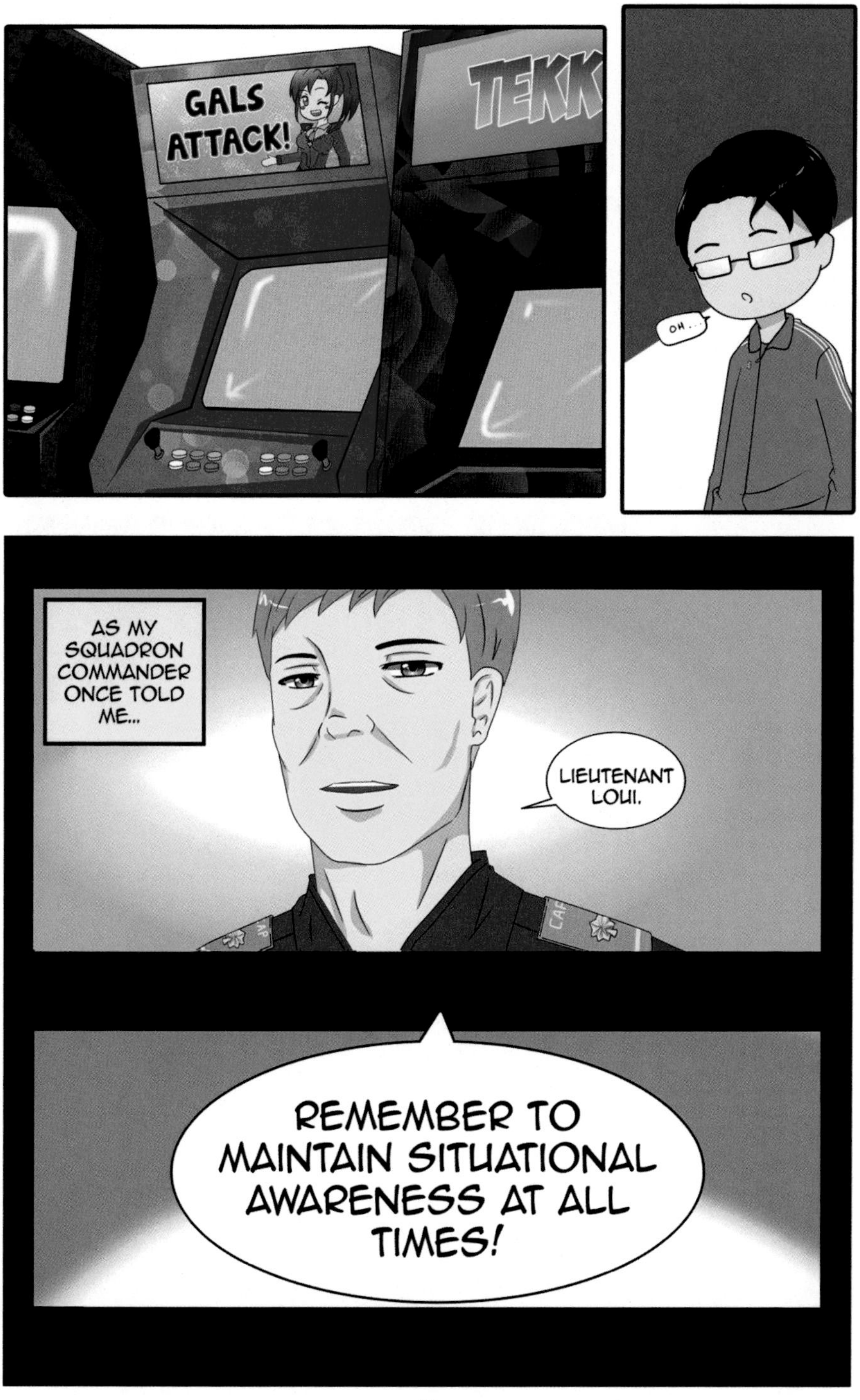
GALS ATTACK!
TEKK
OH...
AS MY SQUADRON COMMANDER ONCE TOLD ME...
LIEUTENANT LOUI.
REMEMBER TO MAINTAIN SITUATIONAL AWARENESS AT ALL TIMES!

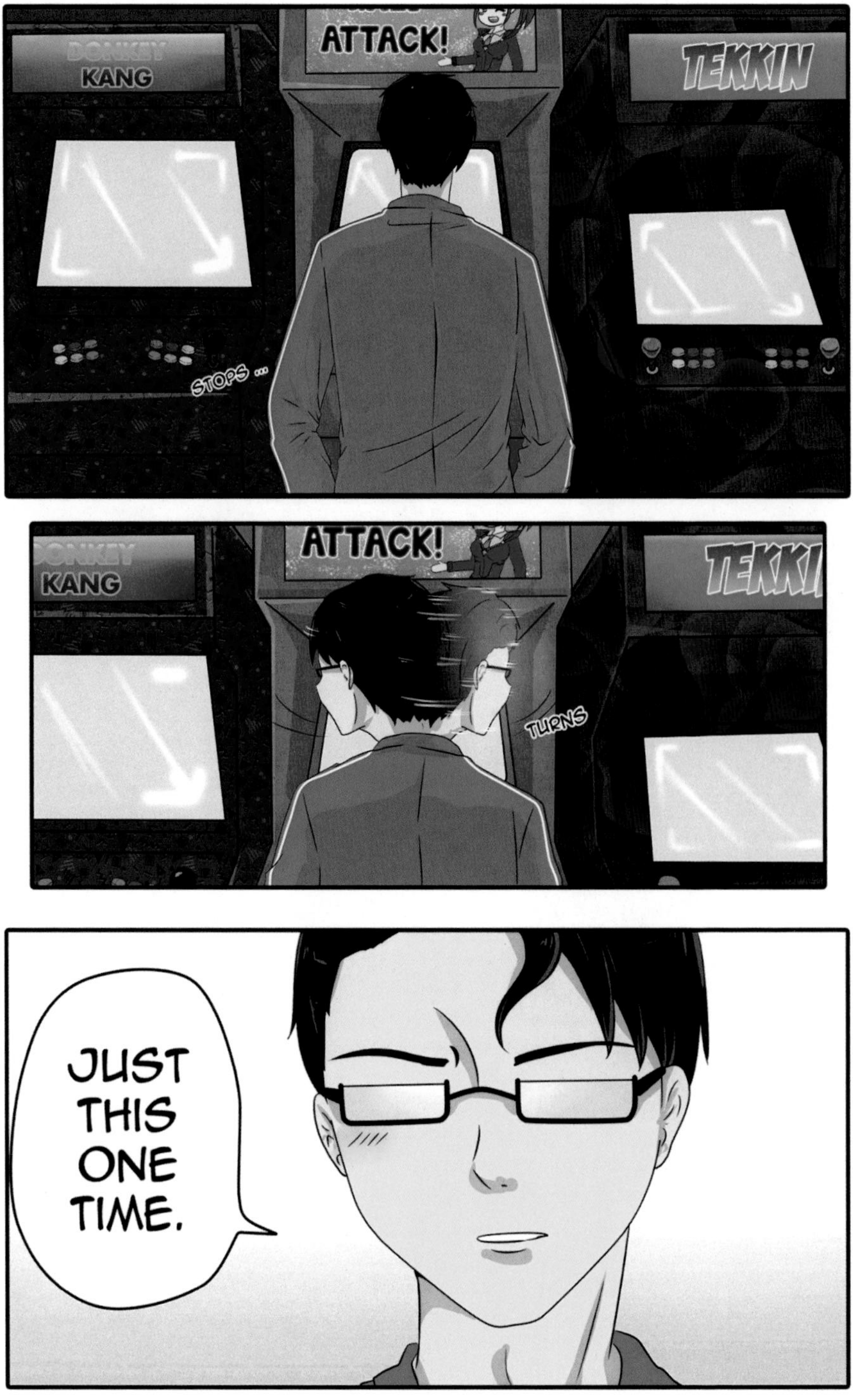
ATTACK!
DONKEY KANG
TEKKIN
STOPS ...
ATTACK!
DONKEY KANG
TEKKIN
TURNS
JUST THIS ONE TIME.

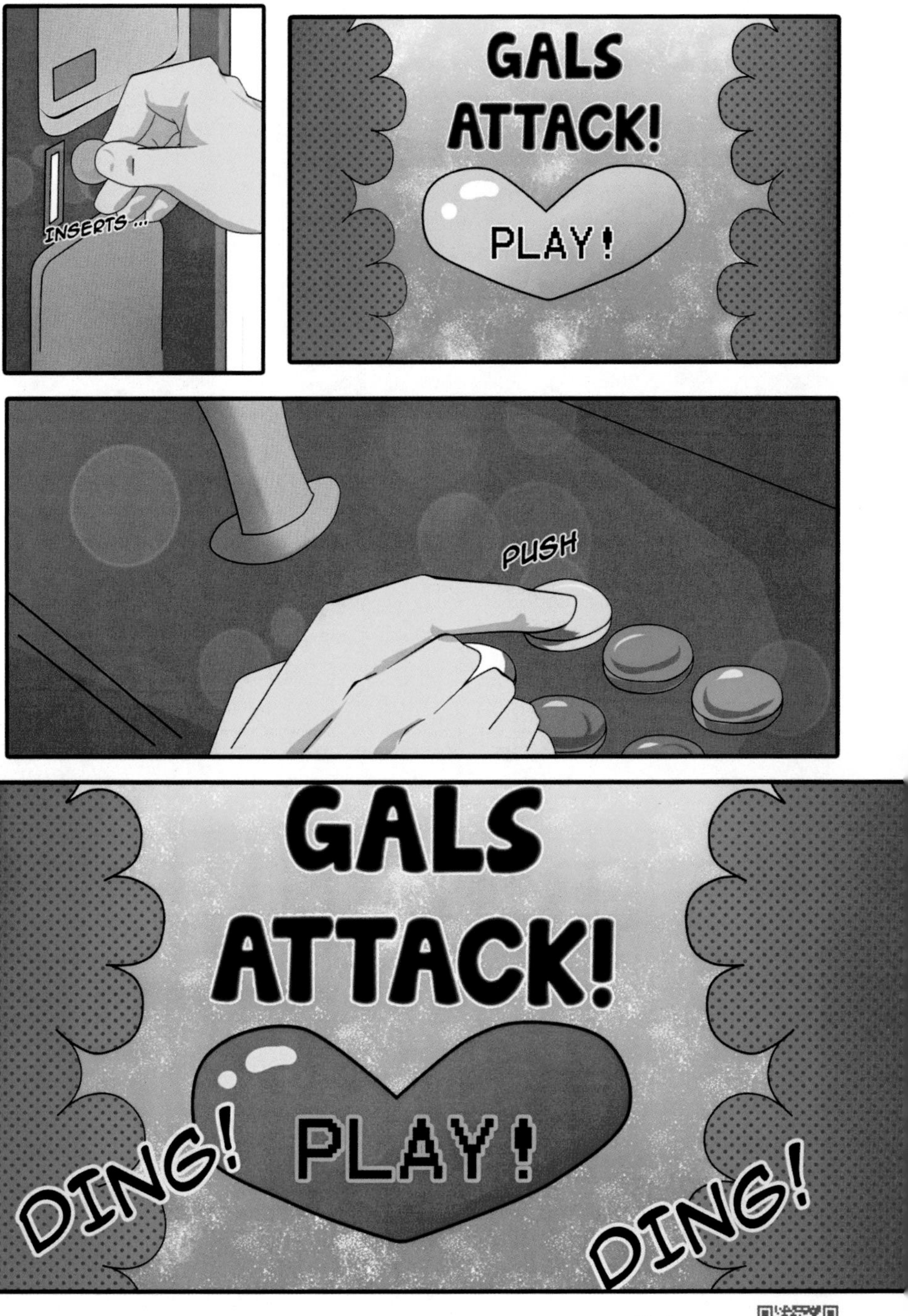
INSERTS ...
GALS ATTACK!
PLAY!
PUSH
GALS ATTACK!
DING!
PLAY!
DING!

Al Jarreau
Girls Know How

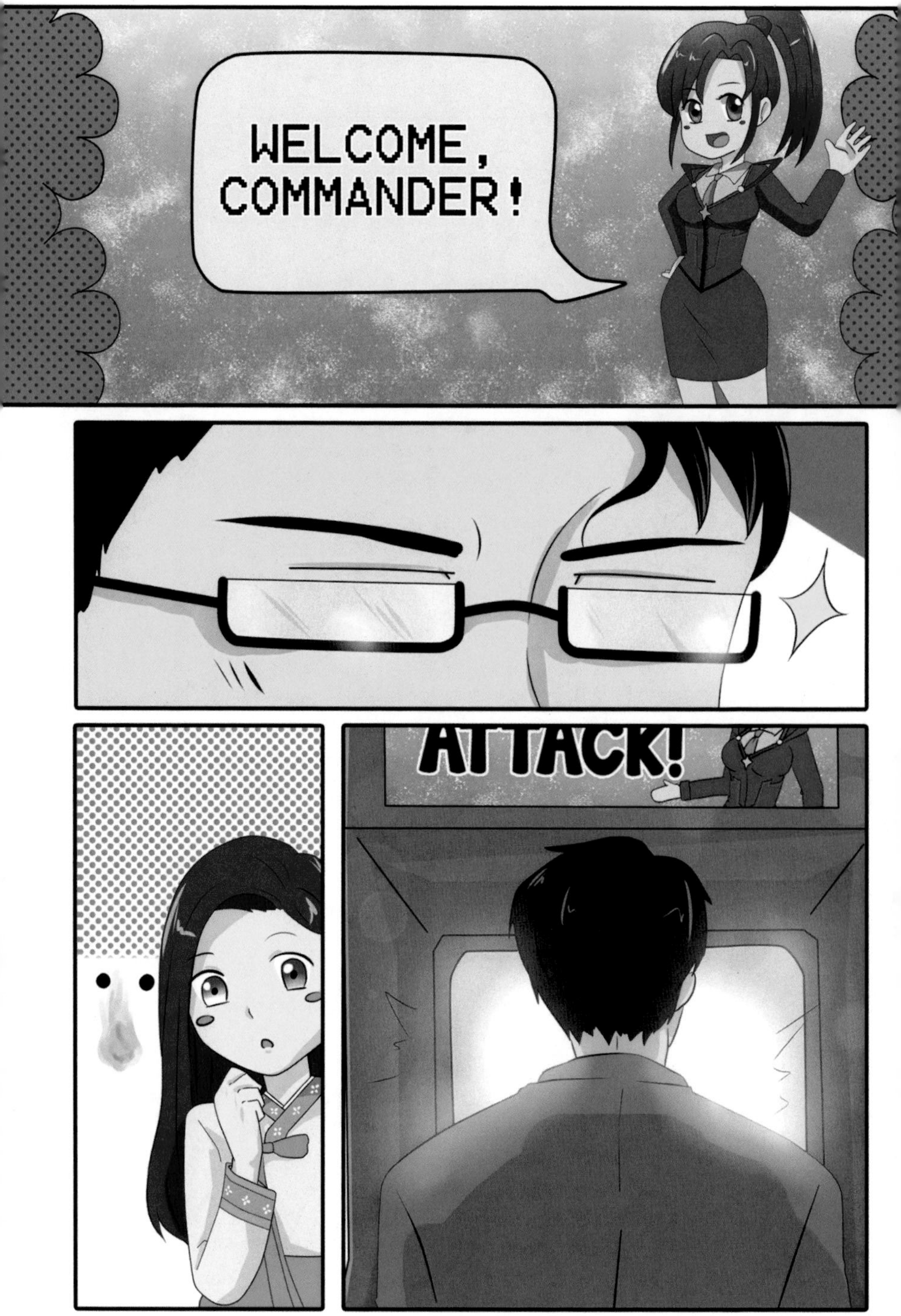
WELCOME, COMMANDER!
ATTACK!

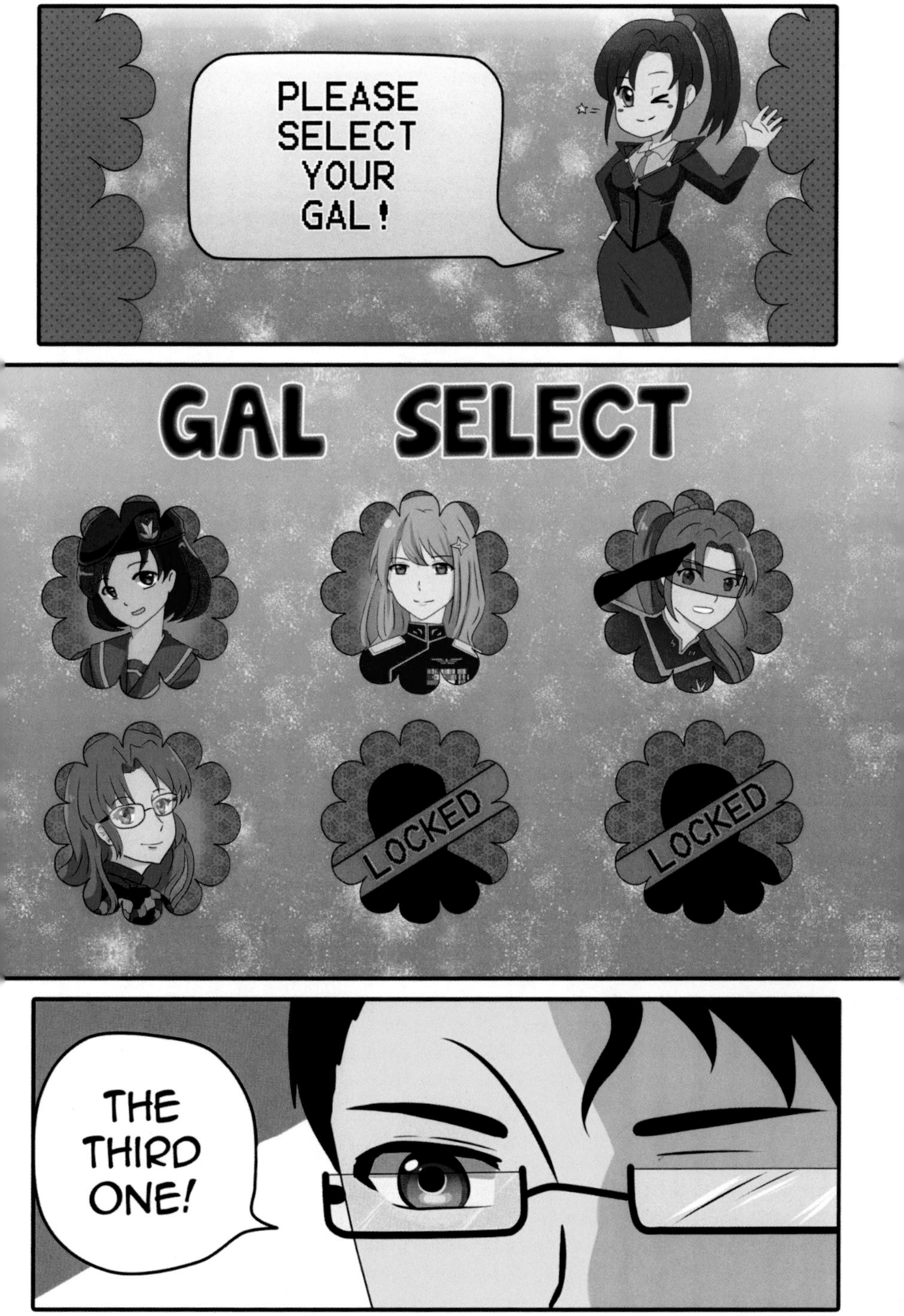
PLEASE SELECT YOUR GAL!
GAL SELECT
LOCKED
LOCKED
THE THIRD ONE!

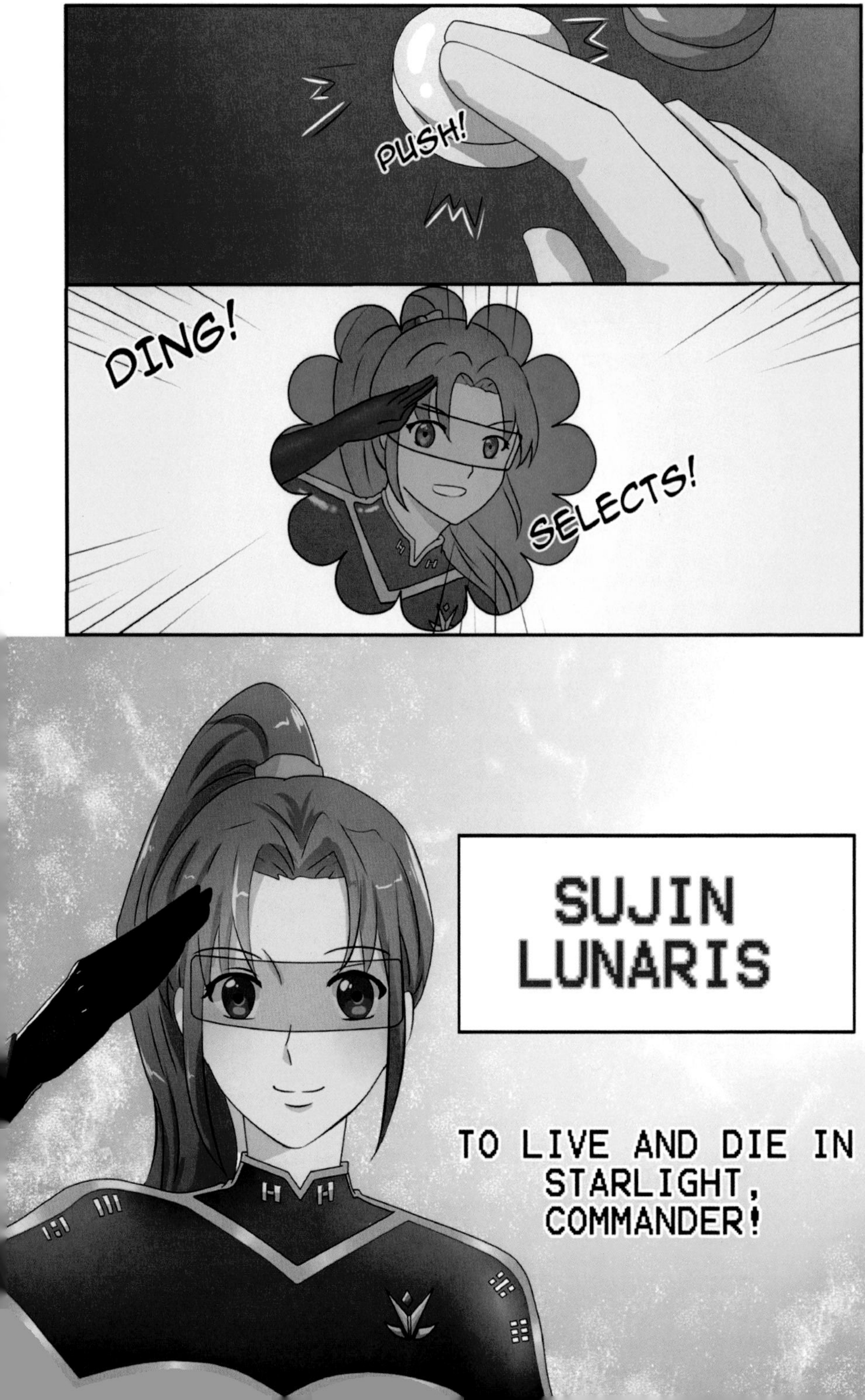
PUSH!
DING!
SELECTS!
SUJIN LUNARIS
TO LIVE AND DIE IN STARLIGHT, COMMANDER!

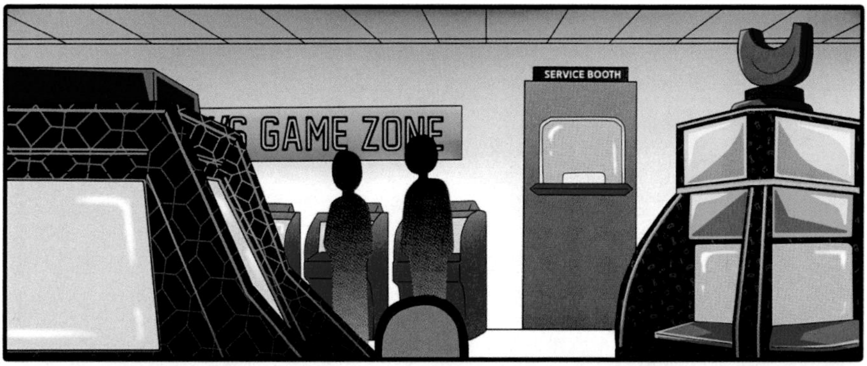
GAME ZONE
SERVICE BOOTH

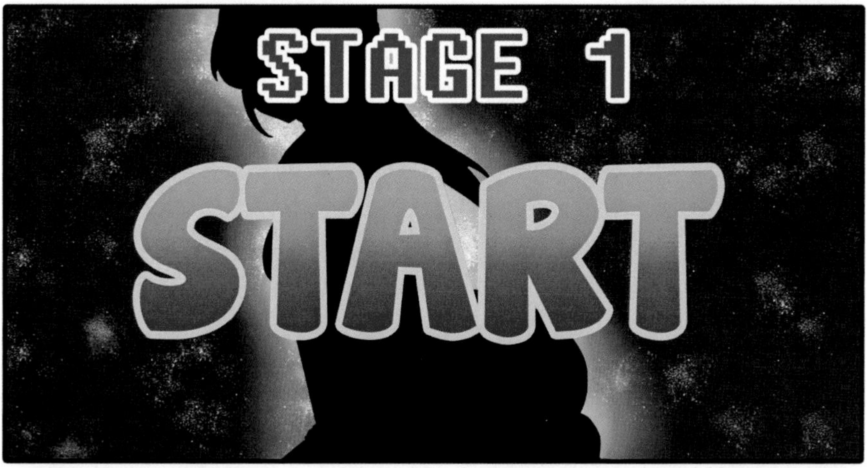
STAGE 1
START

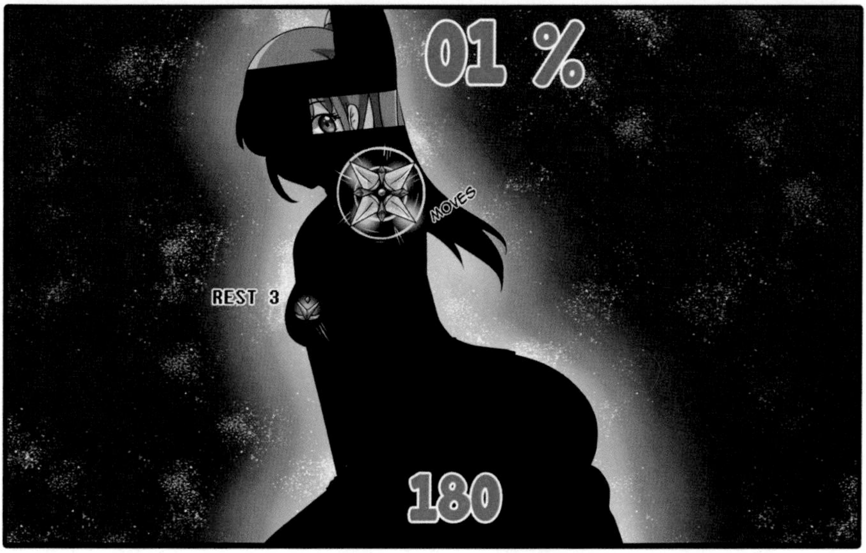
01 %
MOVES
REST 3
180

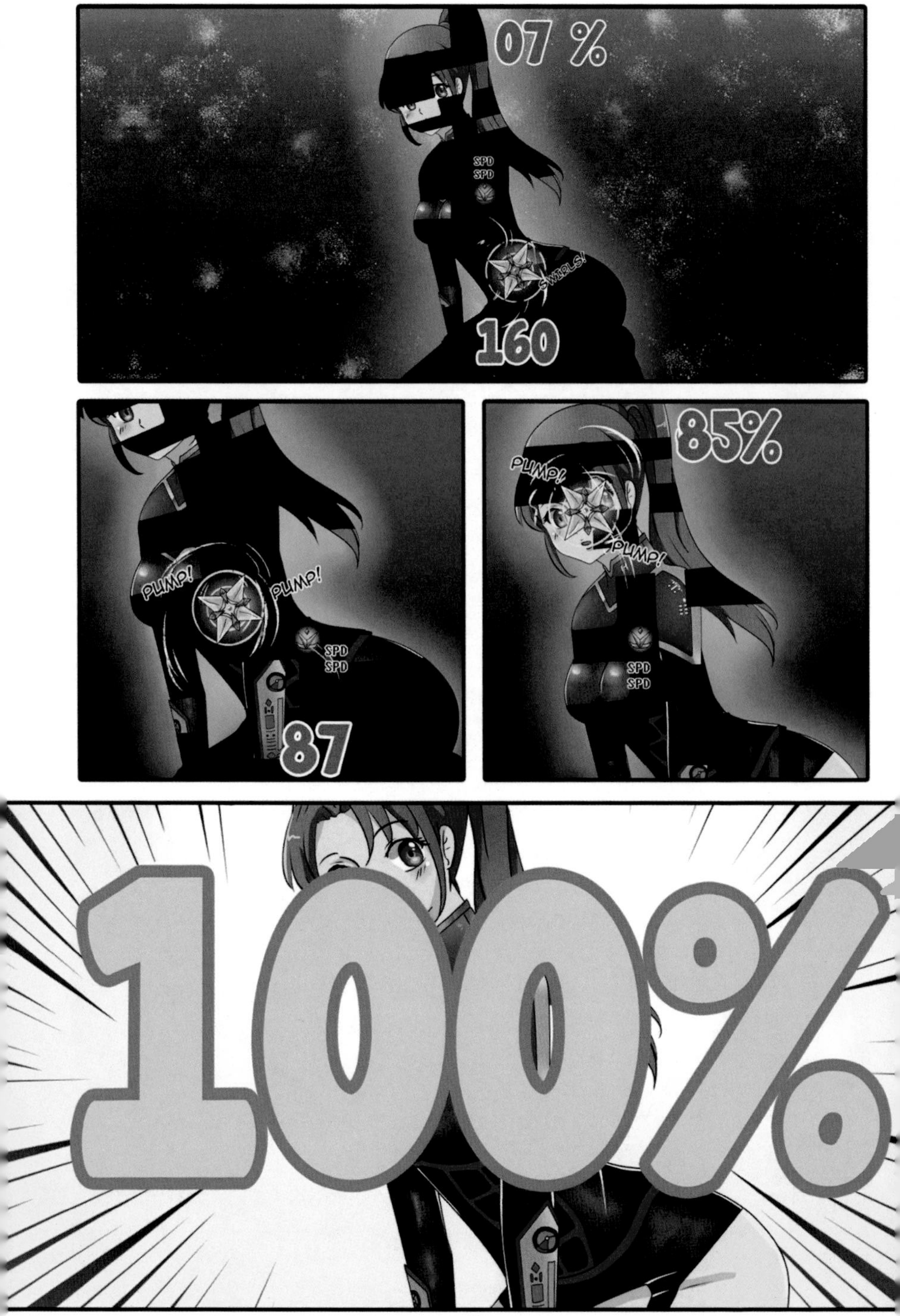
07 %
SPD
SPD
SWIRLS!
160
PUMP!
PUMP!
SPD
SPD
87
85%
PUMP!
PUMP!
SPD
SPD
100%

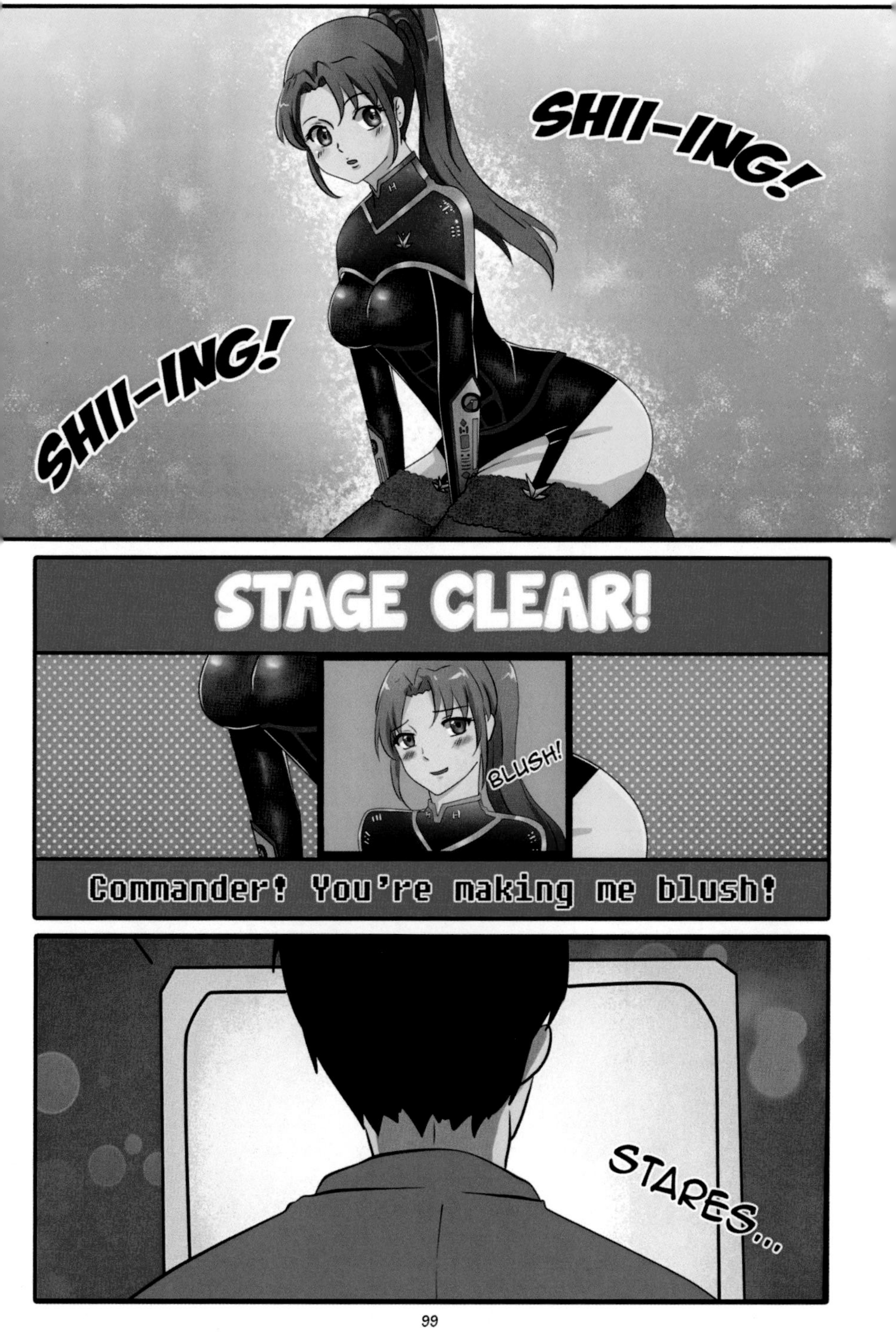
SHII-ING!
SHII-ING!
STAGE CLEAR!
BLUSH!
Commander! You're making me blush!
STARES...

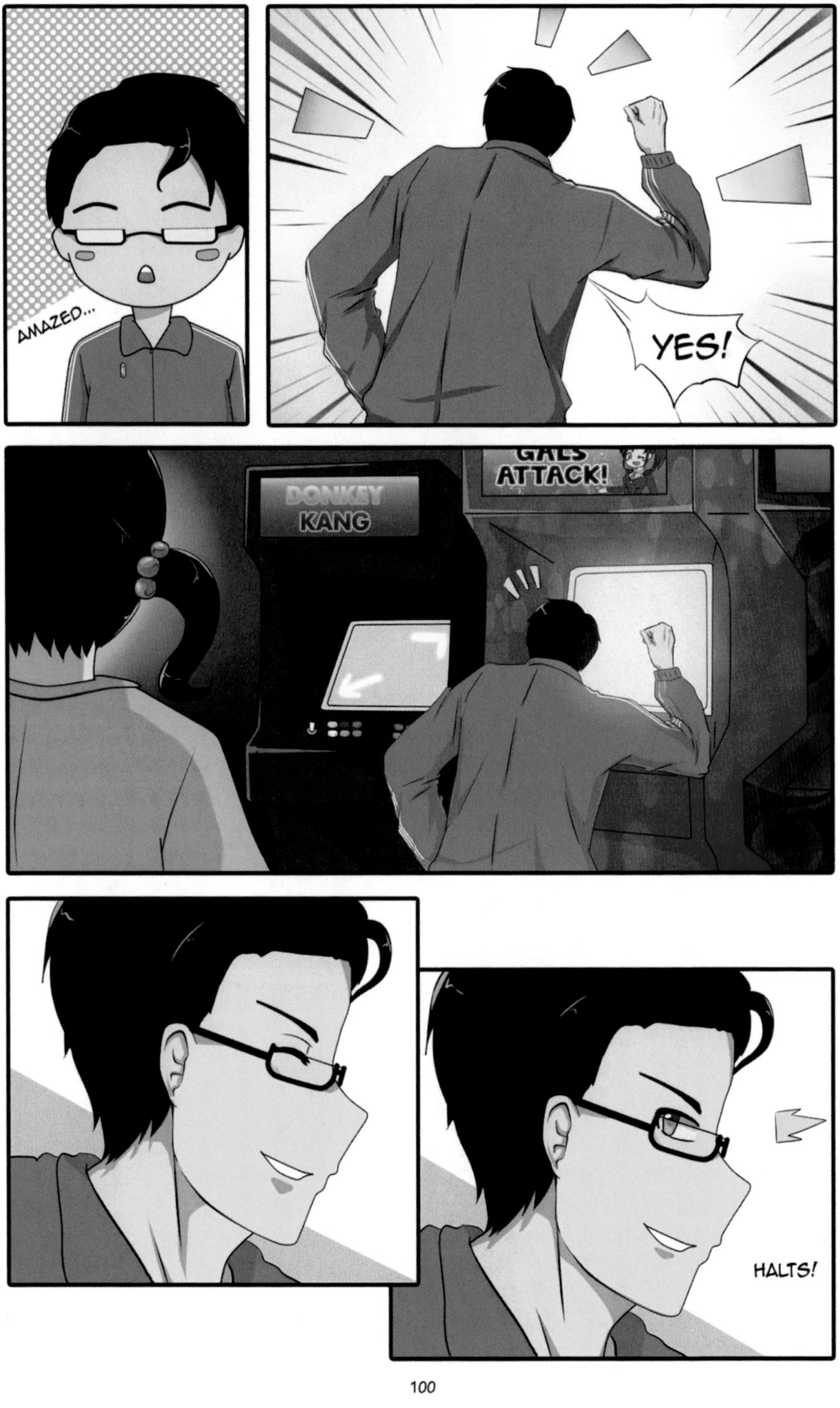
AMAZED...
YES!
GALS
ATTACK!
DONKEY
KANG
HALTS!

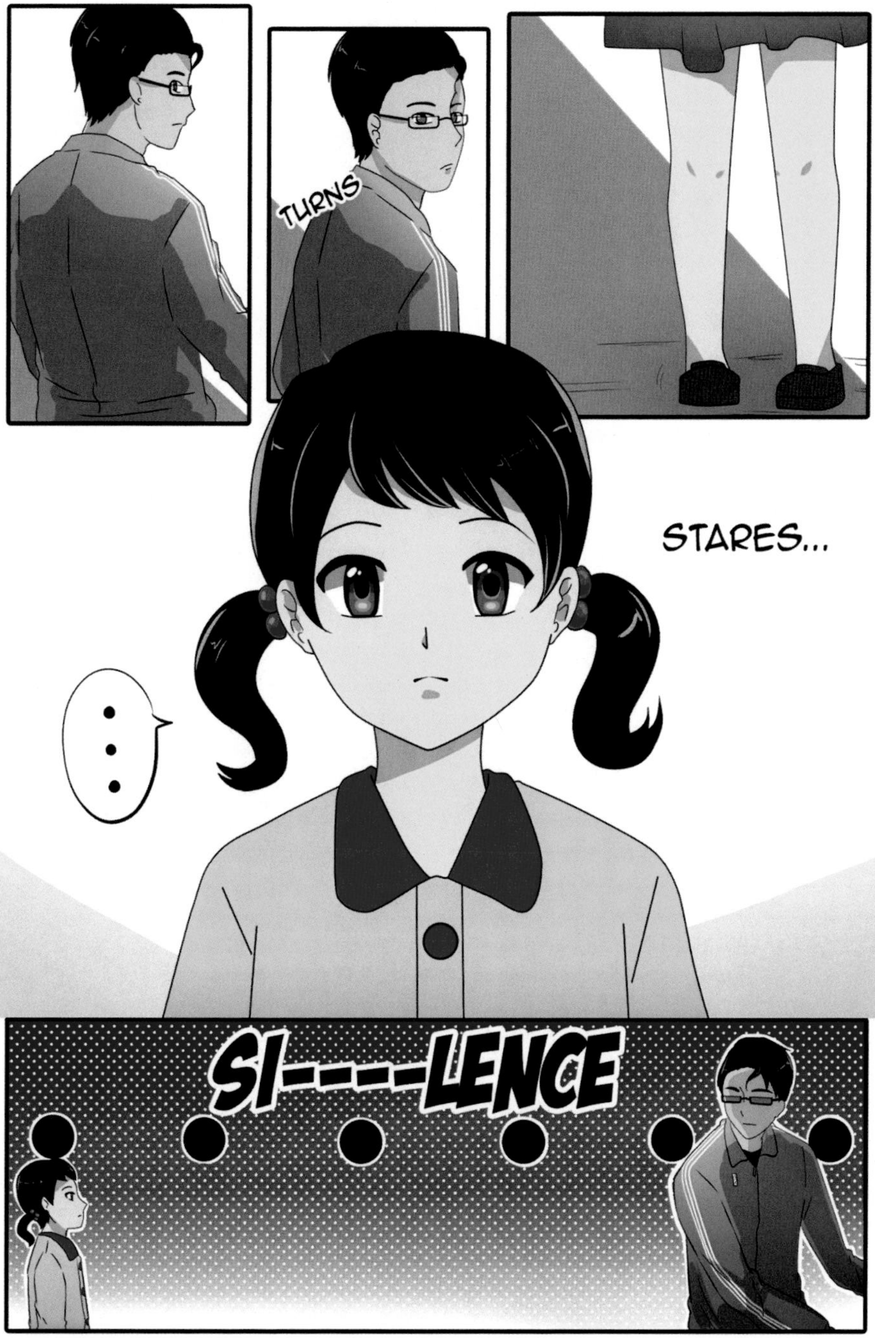
TURNS
STARES...
...
SI----LENCE

Al Jarreau
Girls Know How

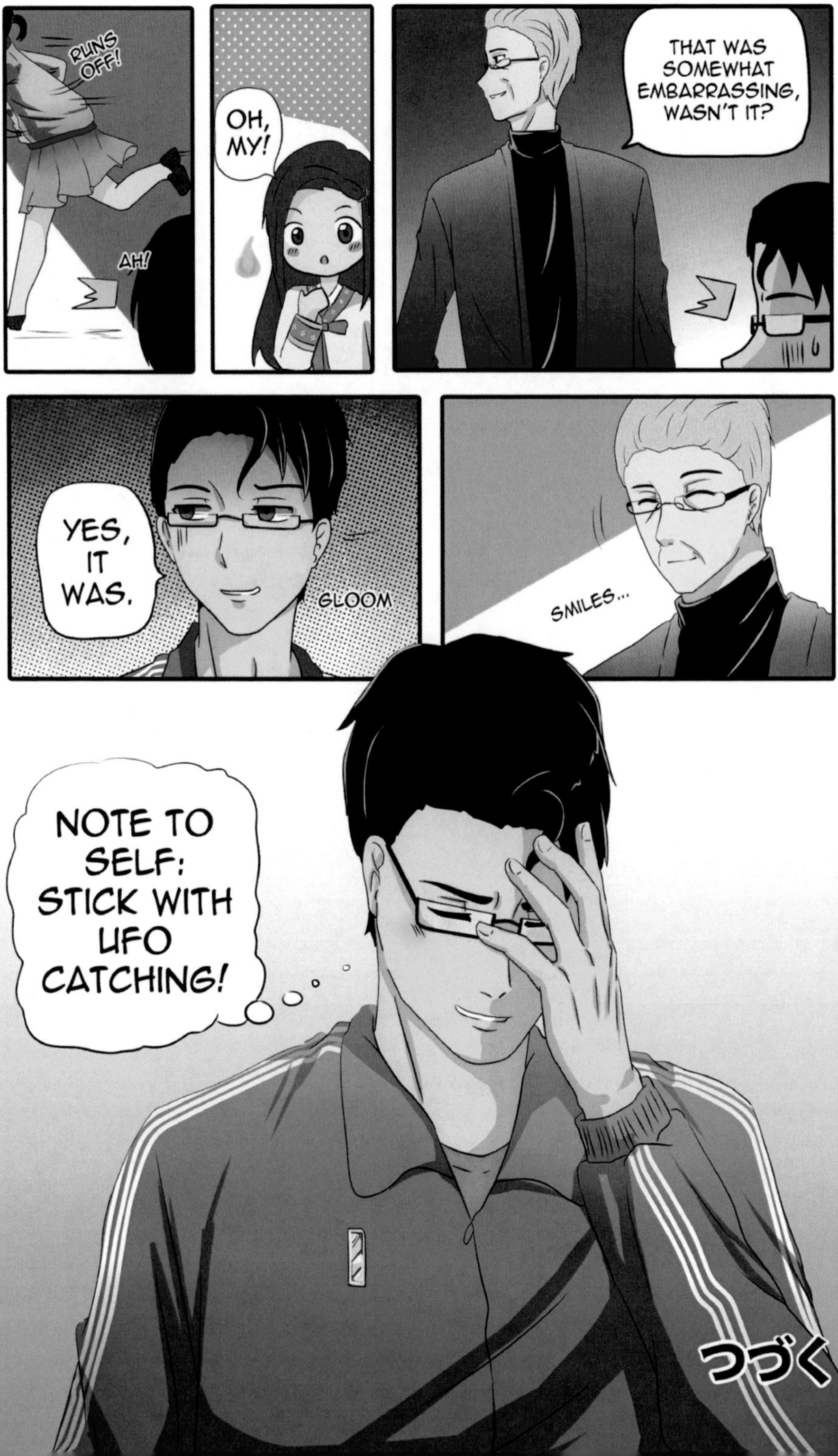
RUNS OFF!
AH!
OH, MY!
THAT WAS SOMEWHAT EMBARRASSING, WASN'T IT?
YES, IT WAS.
GLOOM
SMILES...
NOTE TO SELF: STICK WITH UFO CATCHING!
つづく

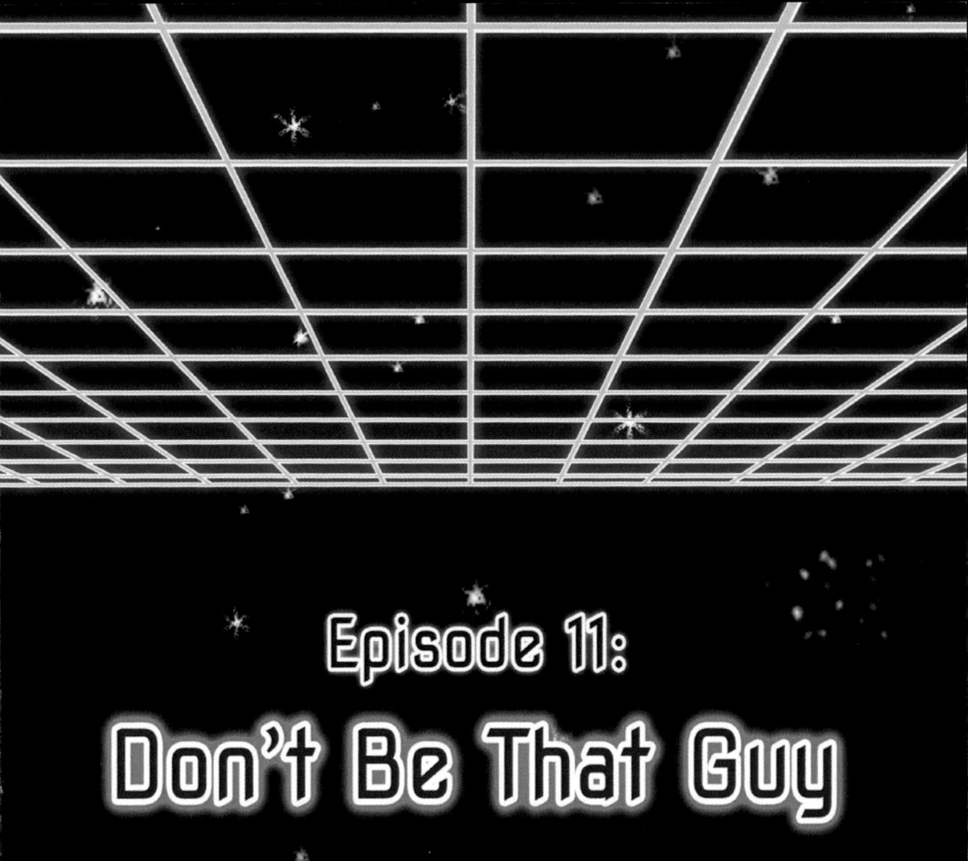

Episode 11:
Don't Be That Guy

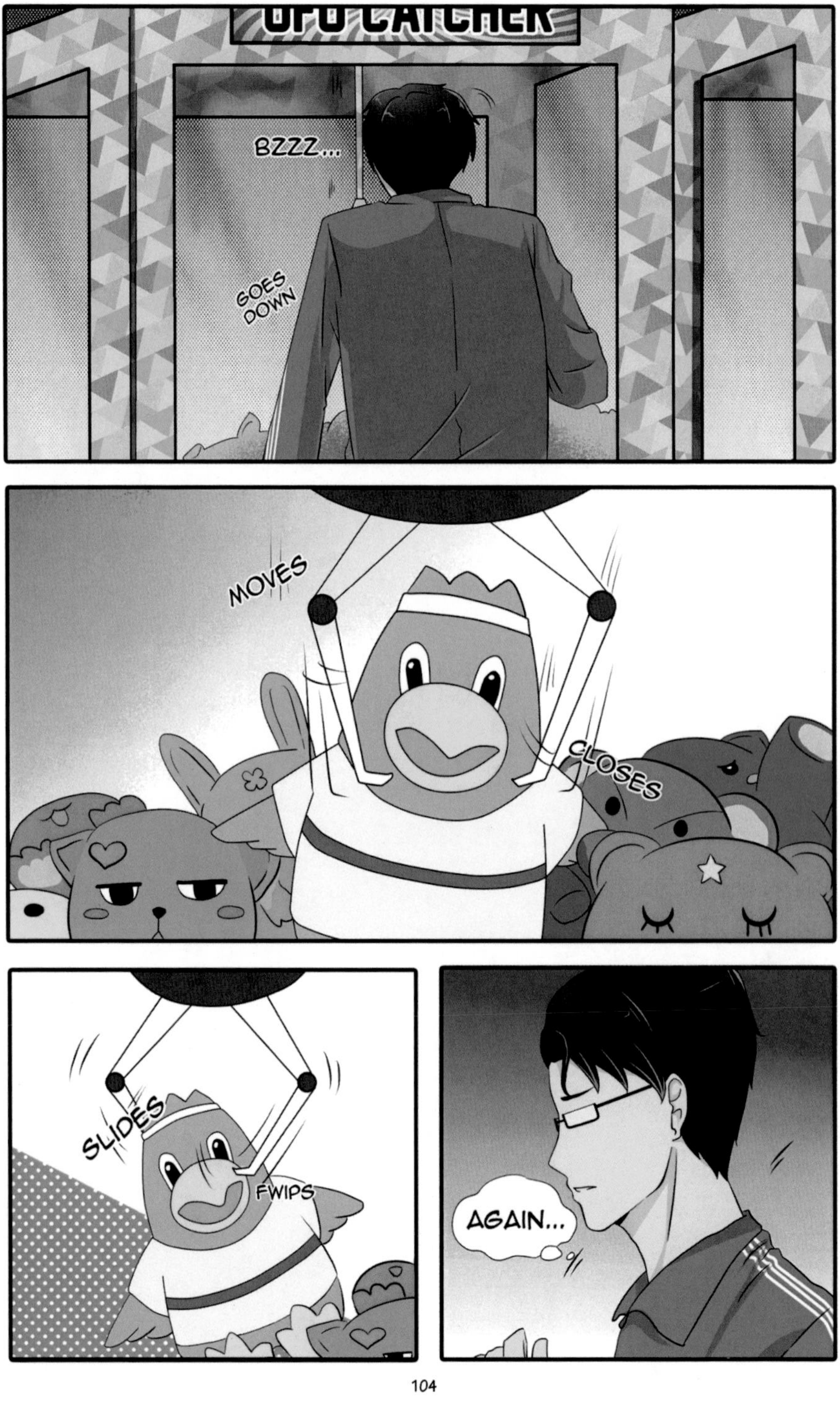
UFO CATCHER
BZZZ...
GOES DOWN
MOVES
CLOSES
SLIDES
FWIPS
AGAIN...

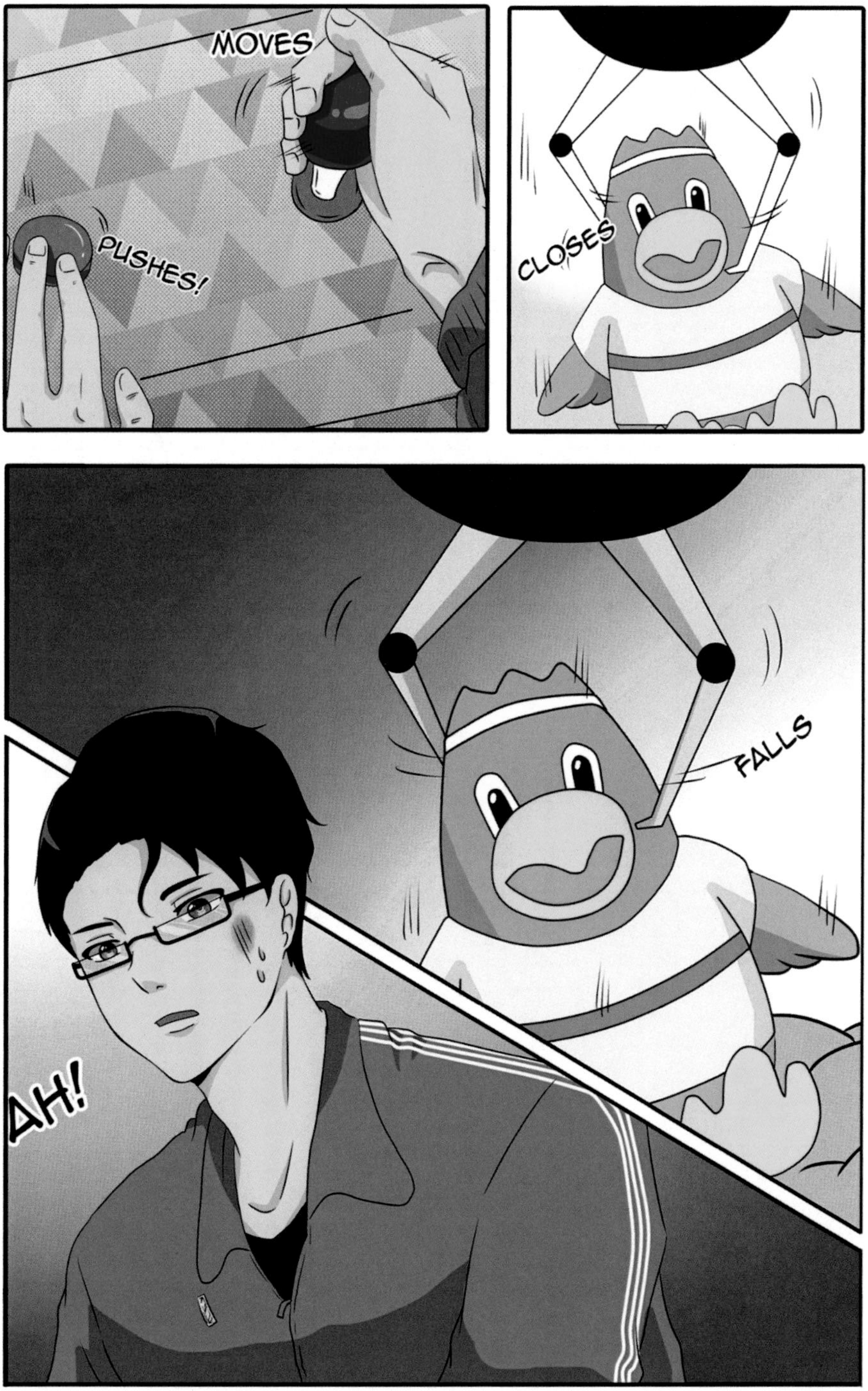
MOVES
PUSHES!
CLOSES
FALLS
AH!

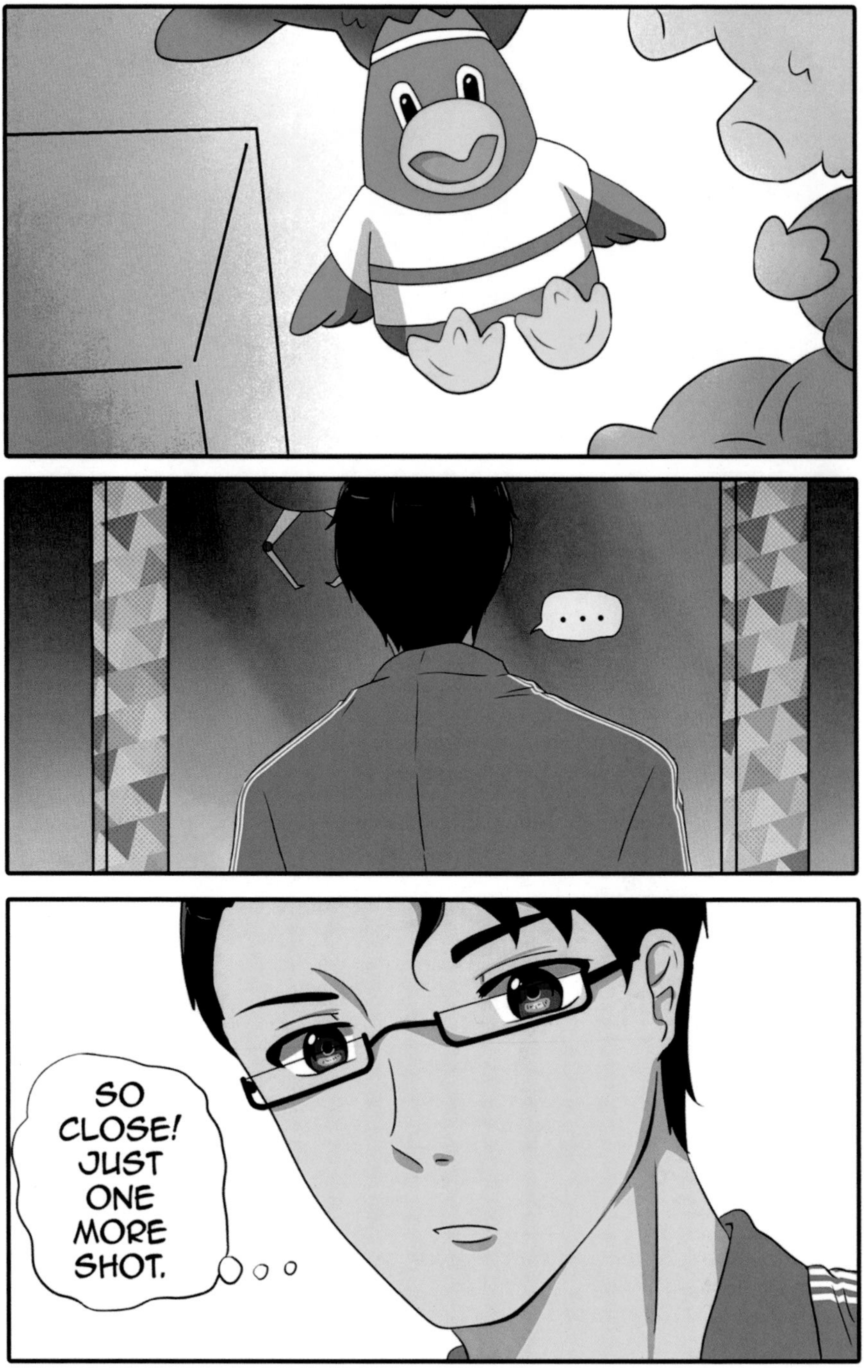
...
SO CLOSE! JUST ONE MORE SHOT.

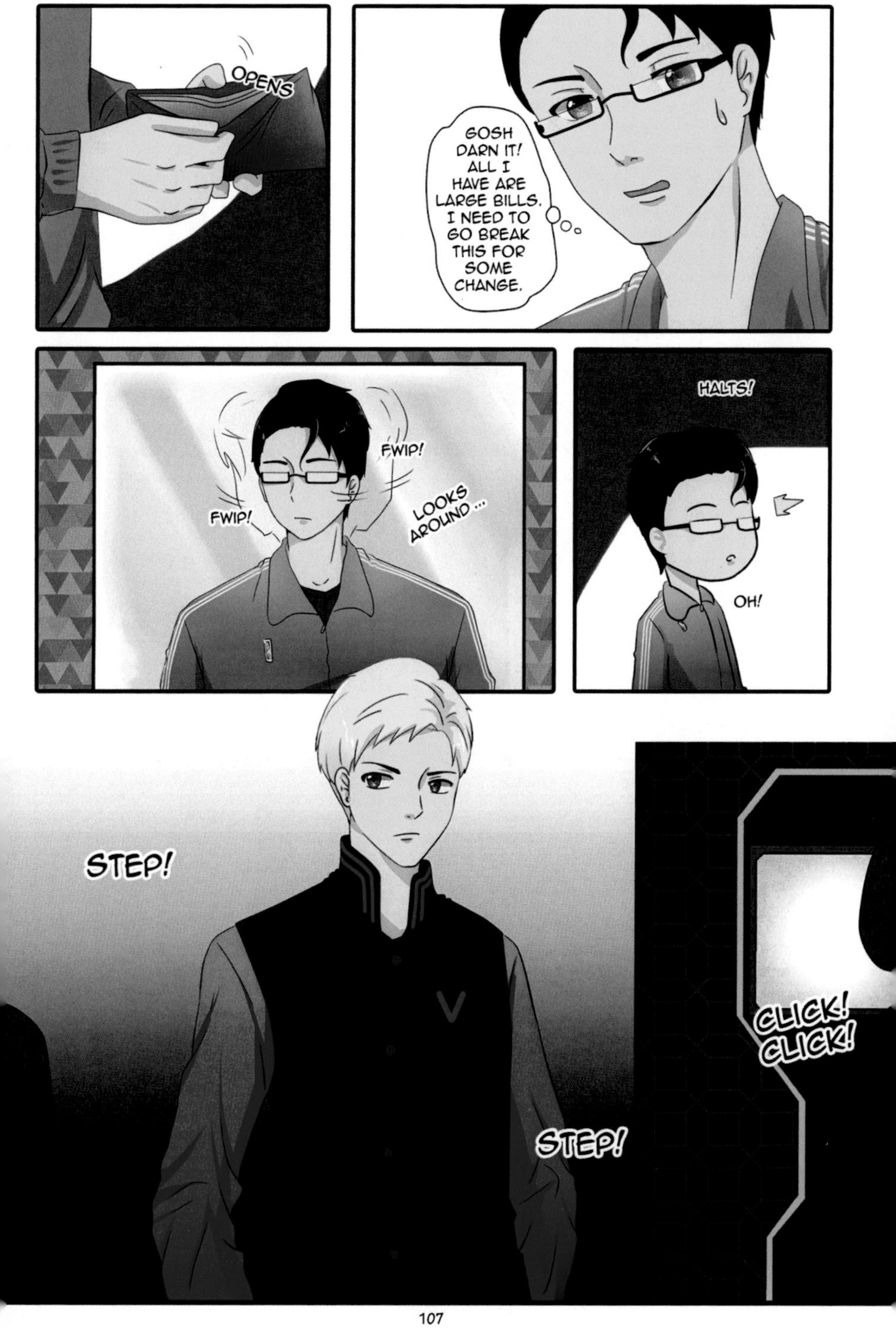
OPENS
GOSH DARN IT! ALL I HAVE ARE LARGE BILLS. I NEED TO GO BREAK THIS FOR SOME CHANGE.
FWIP!
FWIP!
LOOKS AROUND ...
HALTS!
OH!
STEP!
STEP!
CLICK! CLICK!

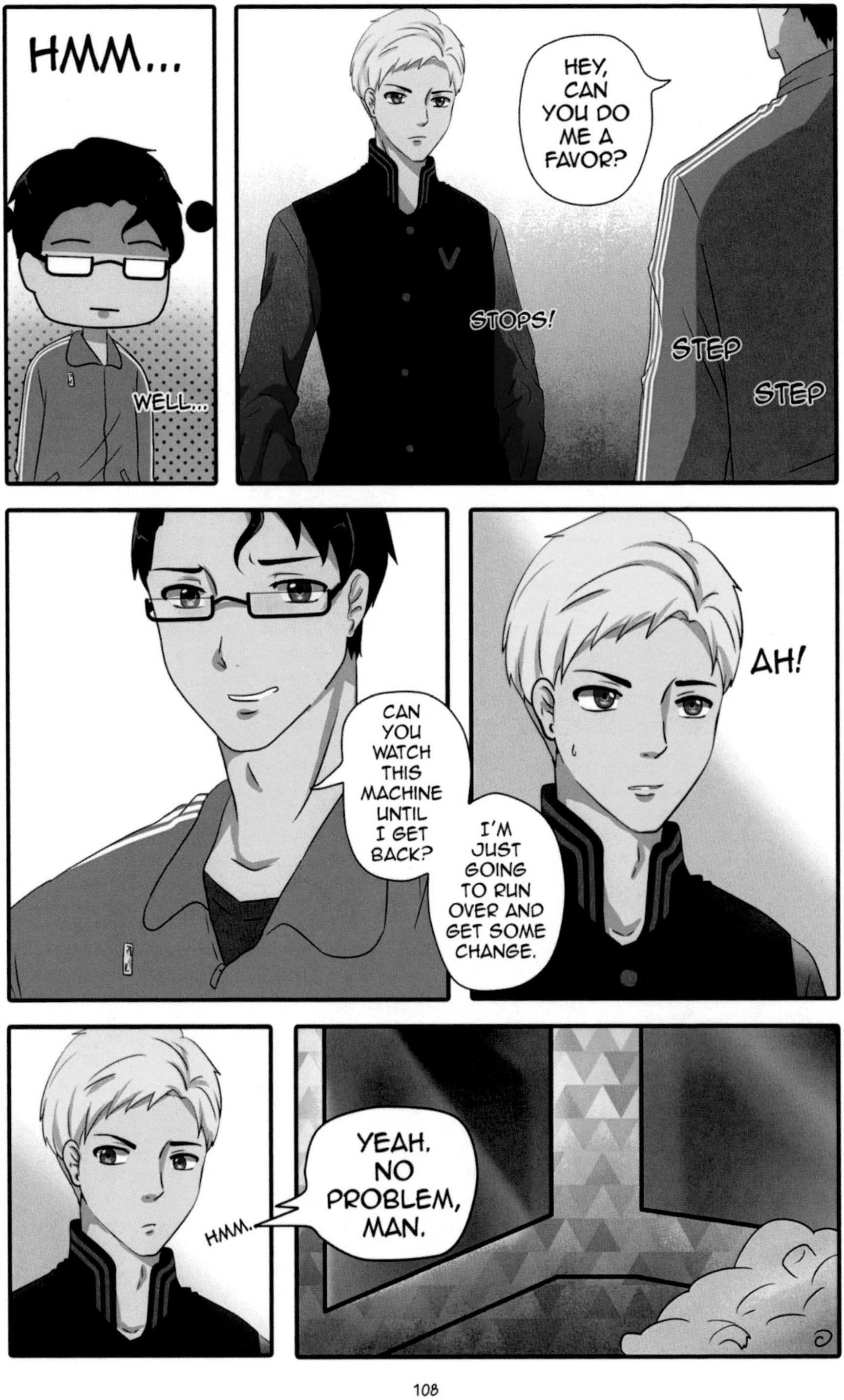
HMM...
WELL...
HEY, CAN YOU DO ME A FAVOR?
STOPS!
STEP
STEP
CAN YOU WATCH THIS MACHINE UNTIL I GET BACK?
I'M JUST GOING TO RUN OVER AND GET SOME CHANGE.
AH!
HMM.
YEAH. NO PROBLEM, MAN.

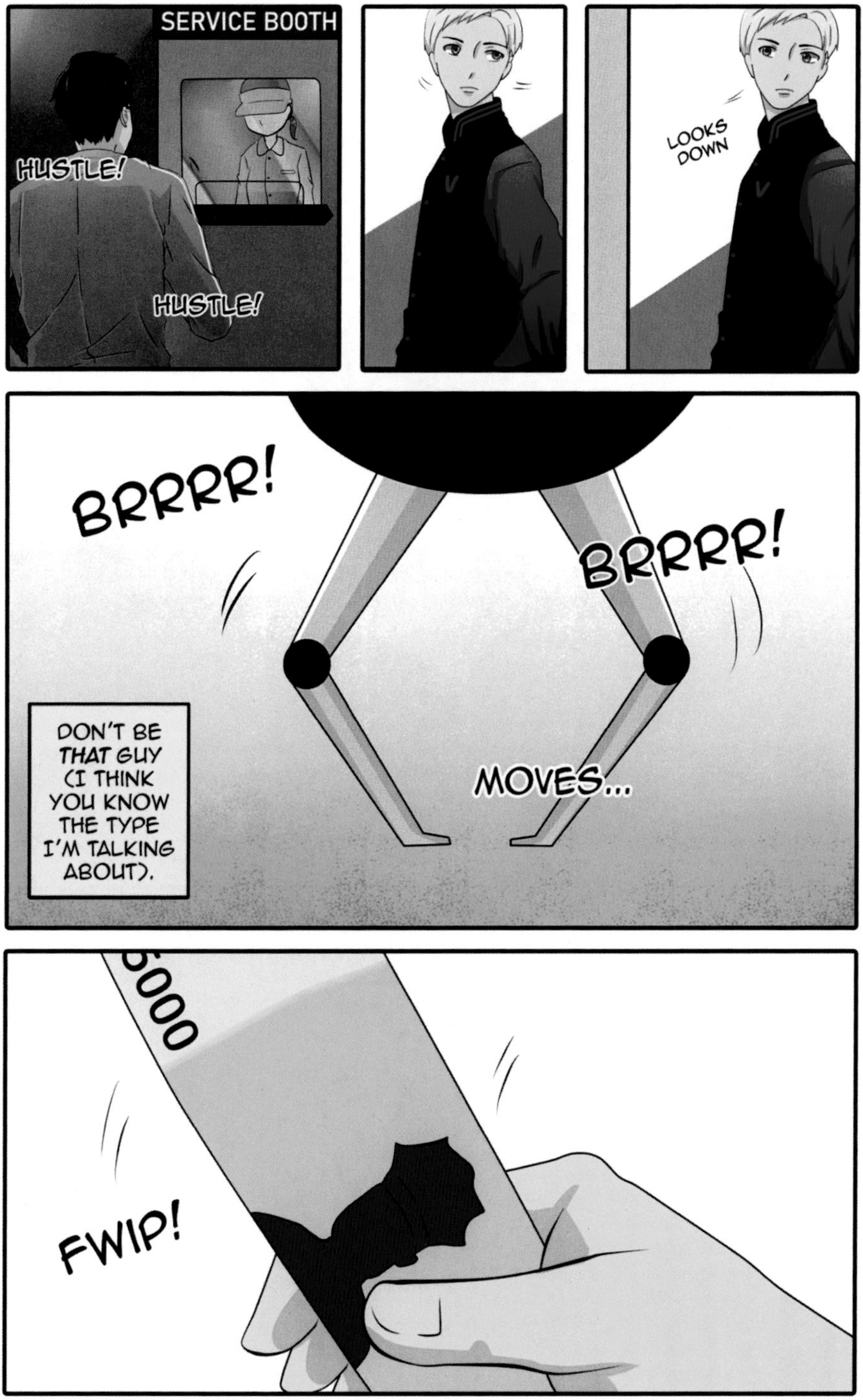
SERVICE BOOTH
HUSTLE!
HUSTLE!
LOOKS DOWN
BRRRR!
BRRRR!
DON'T BE THAT GUY (I THINK YOU KNOW THE TYPE I'M TALKING ABOUT).
MOVES...
5000
FWIP!

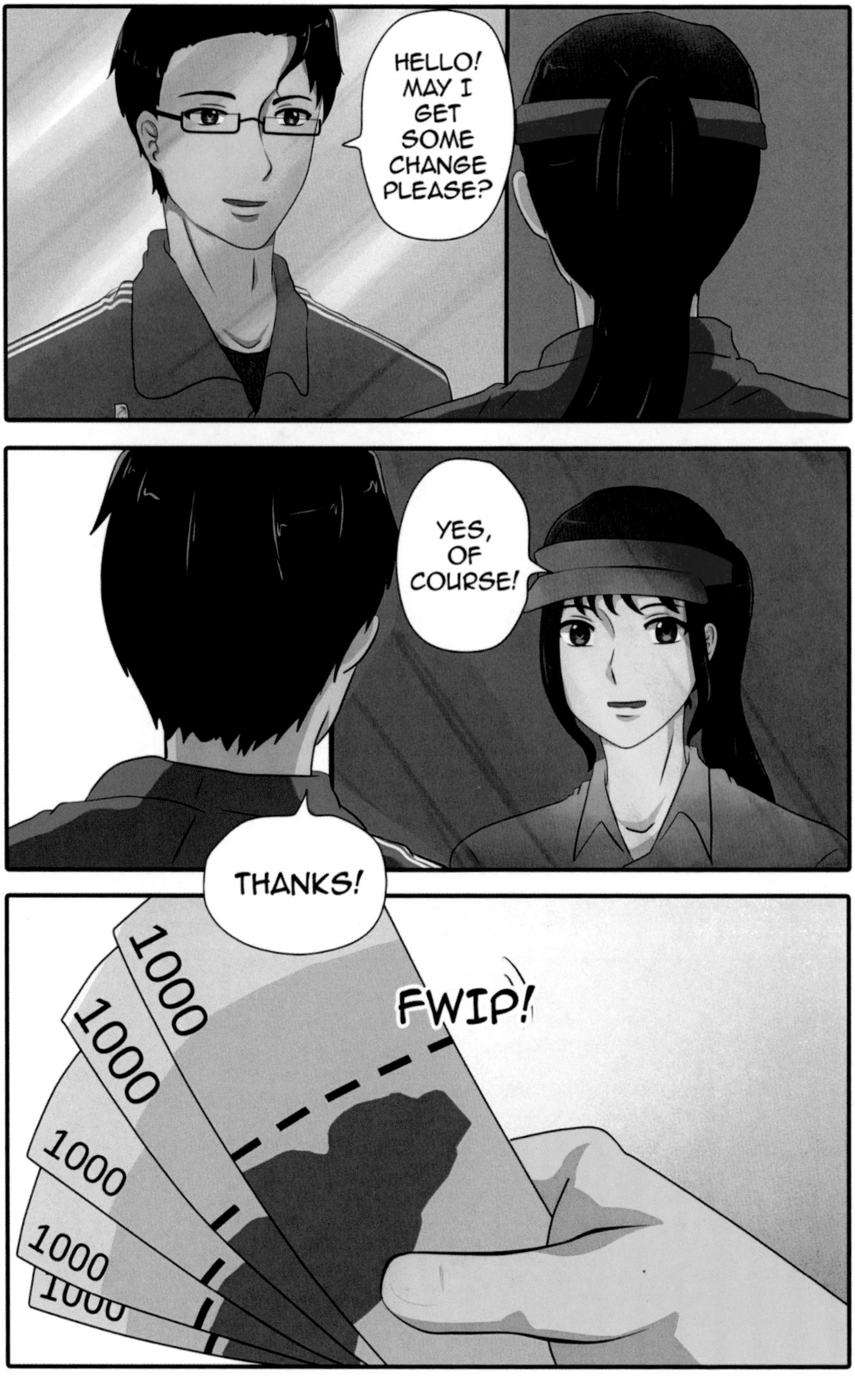
HELLO! MAY I GET SOME CHANGE PLEASE?
YES, OF COURSE!
THANKS!
1000
1000
1000
1000
FWIP!

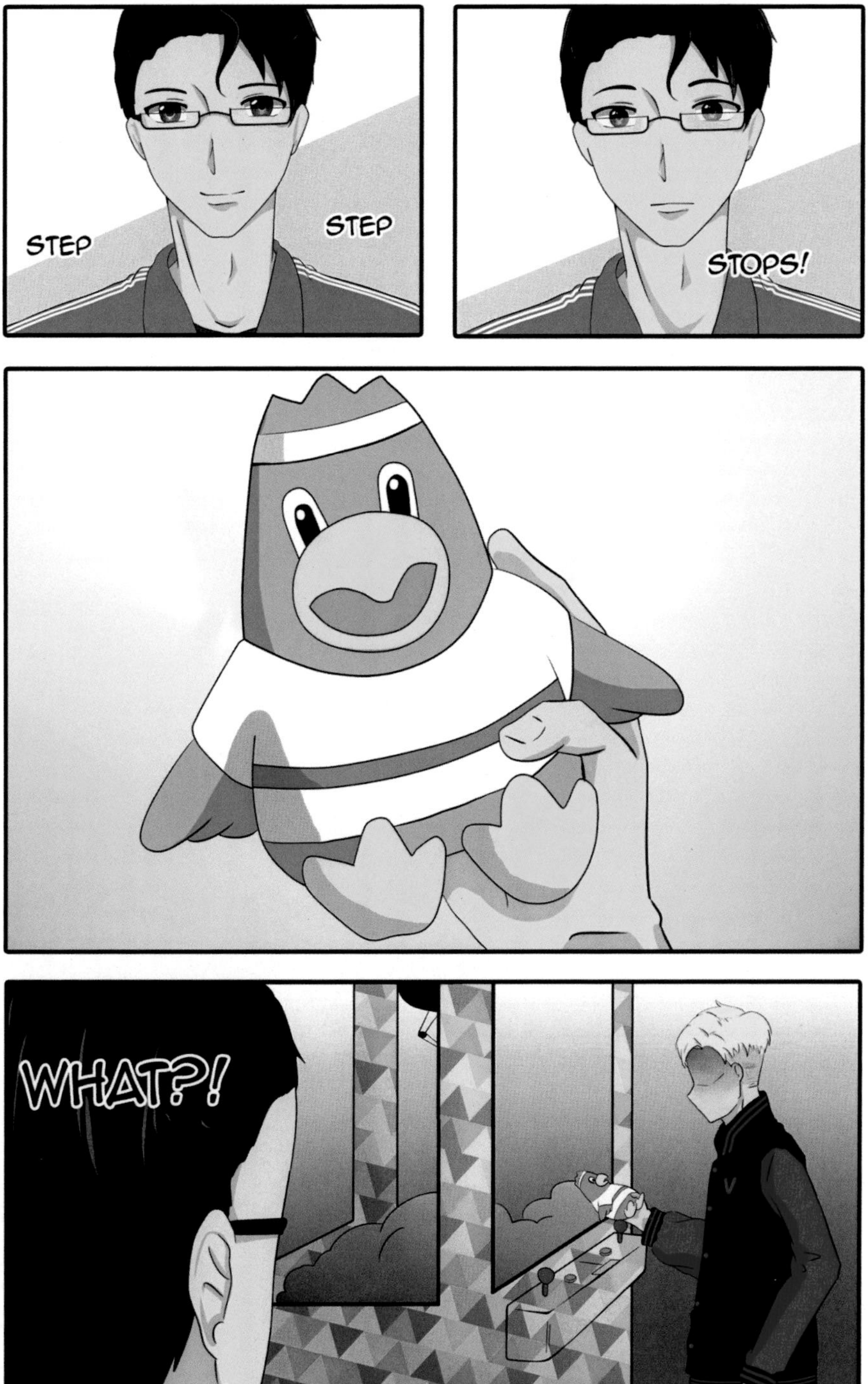
STEP
STEP
STOPS!
WHAT?!

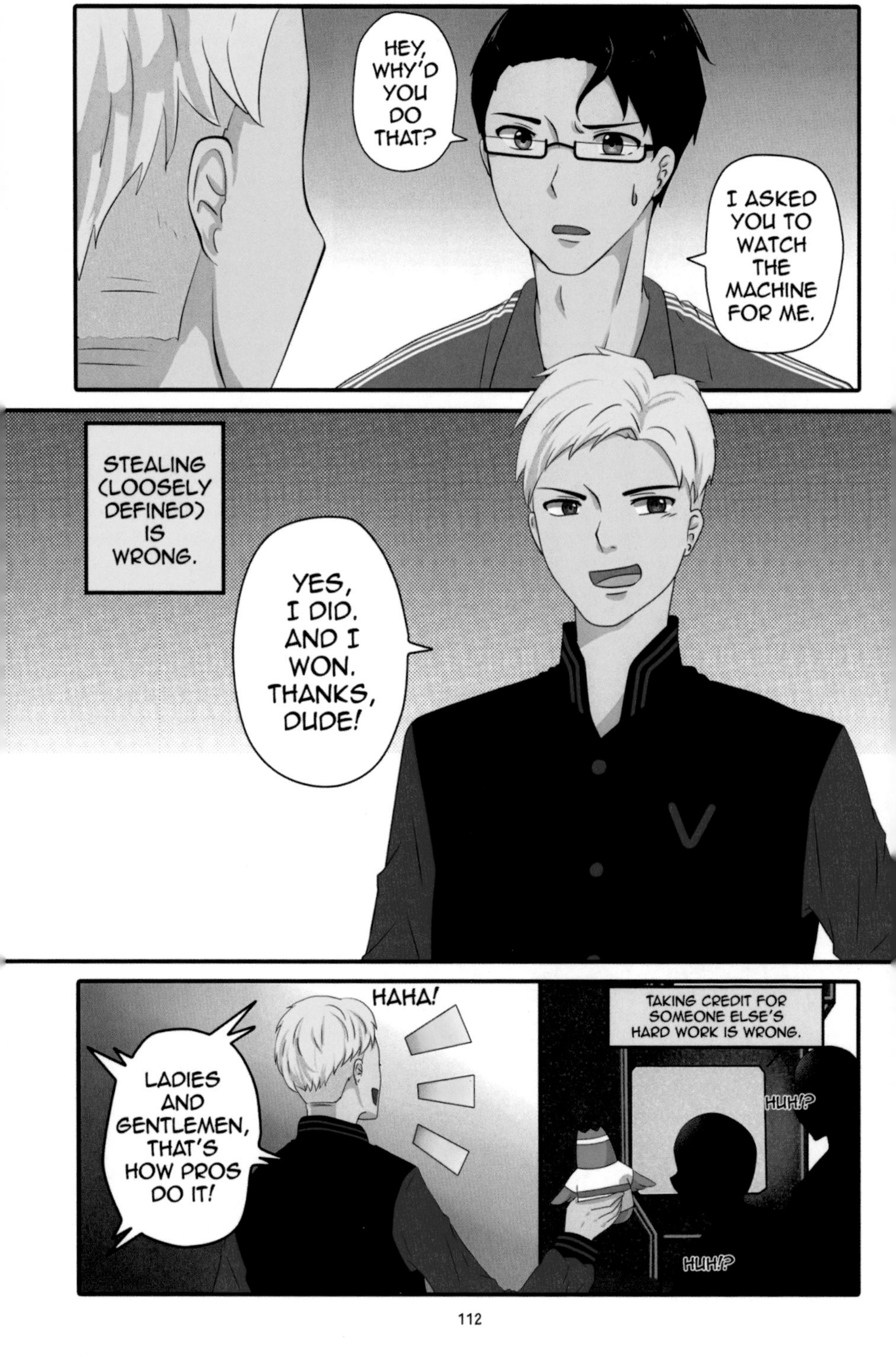
HEY, WHY'D YOU DO THAT?
I ASKED YOU TO WATCH THE MACHINE FOR ME.
STEALING (LOOSELY DEFINED) IS WRONG.
YES, I DID. AND I WON. THANKS, DUDE!
HAHA!
LADIES AND GENTLEMEN, THAT'S HOW PROS DO IT!
TAKING CREDIT FOR SOMEONE ELSE'S HARD WORK IS WRONG.
HUH!?
HUH!?

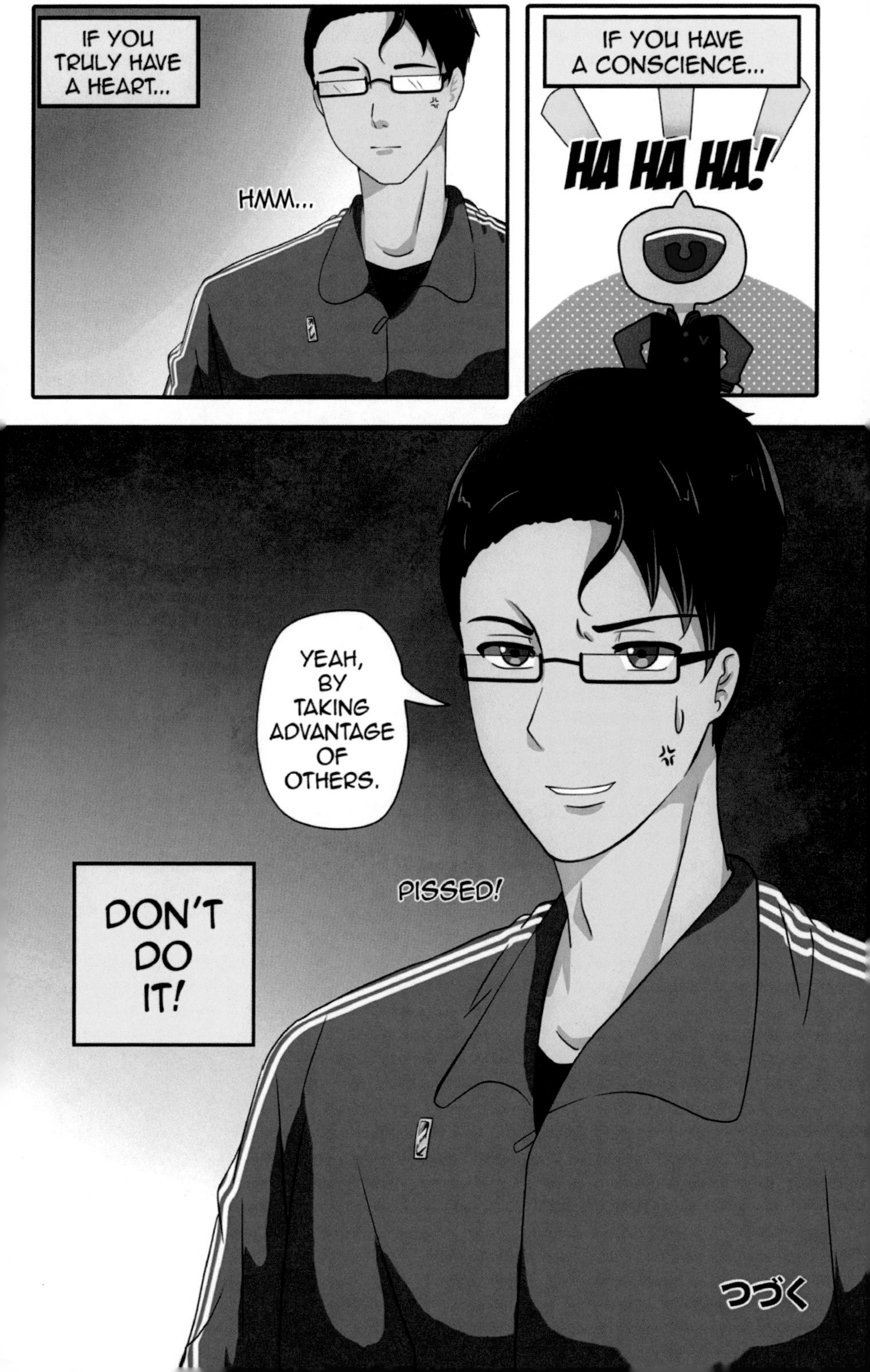
IF YOU TRULY HAVE A HEART...
HMM...
IF YOU HAVE A CONSCIENCE...
HA HA HA!
YEAH, BY TAKING ADVANTAGE OF OTHERS.
PISSED!
DON'T DO IT!
つづく

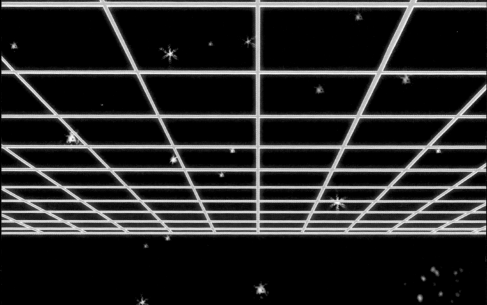

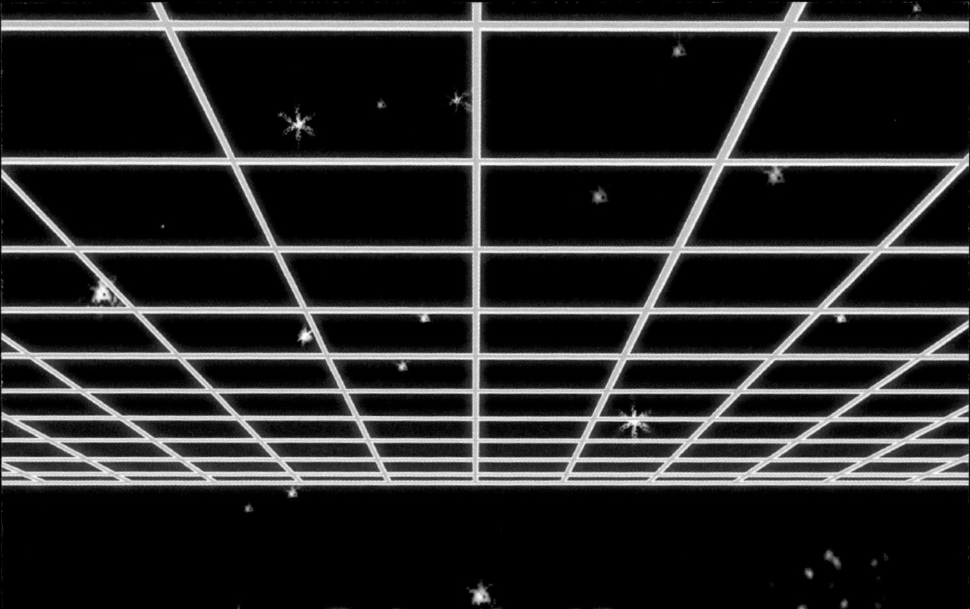

Episode 12:

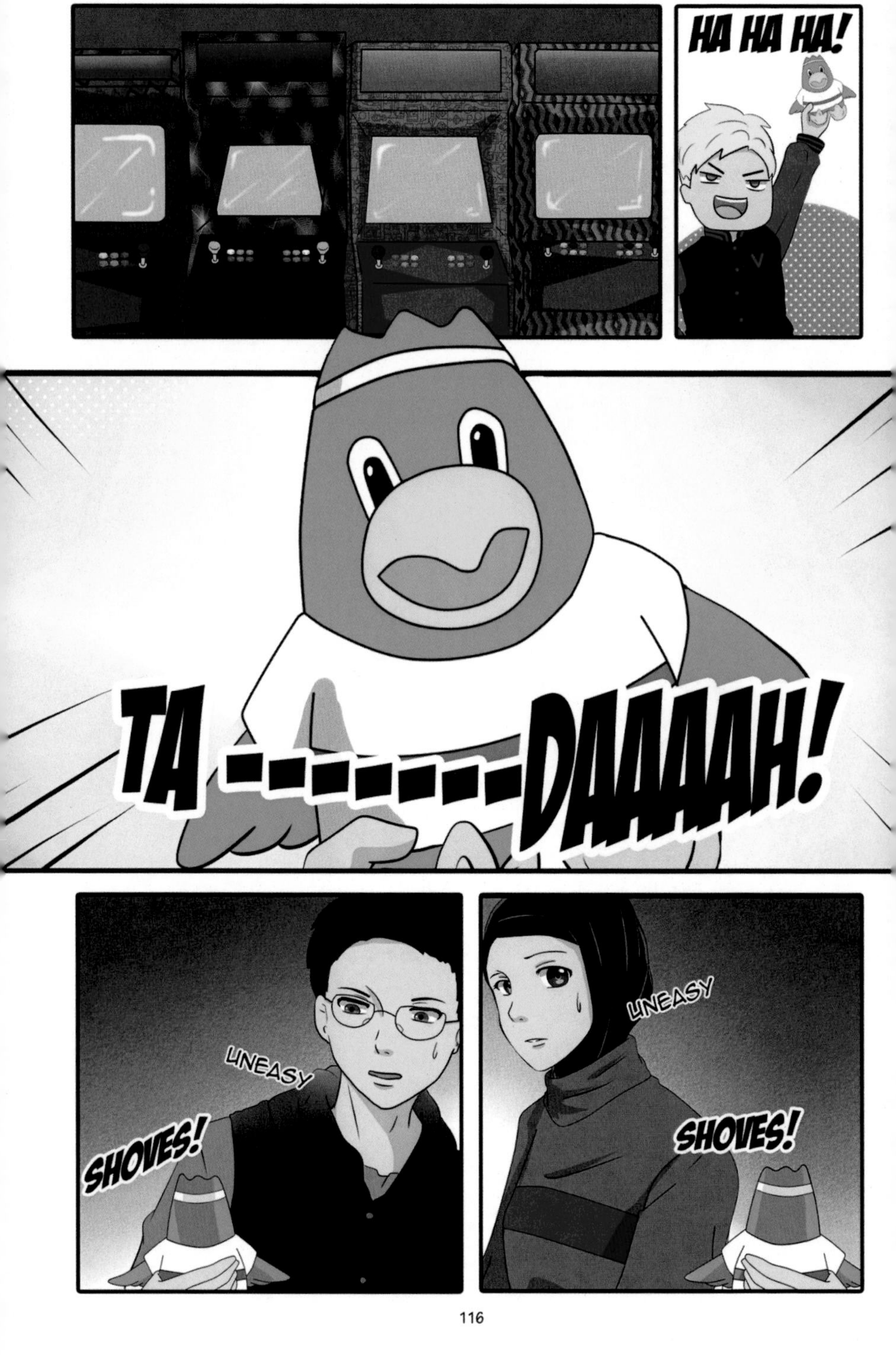
HA HA HA!
TA --------DAAAAAH!
UNEASY
SHOVES!
UNEASY
SHOVES!

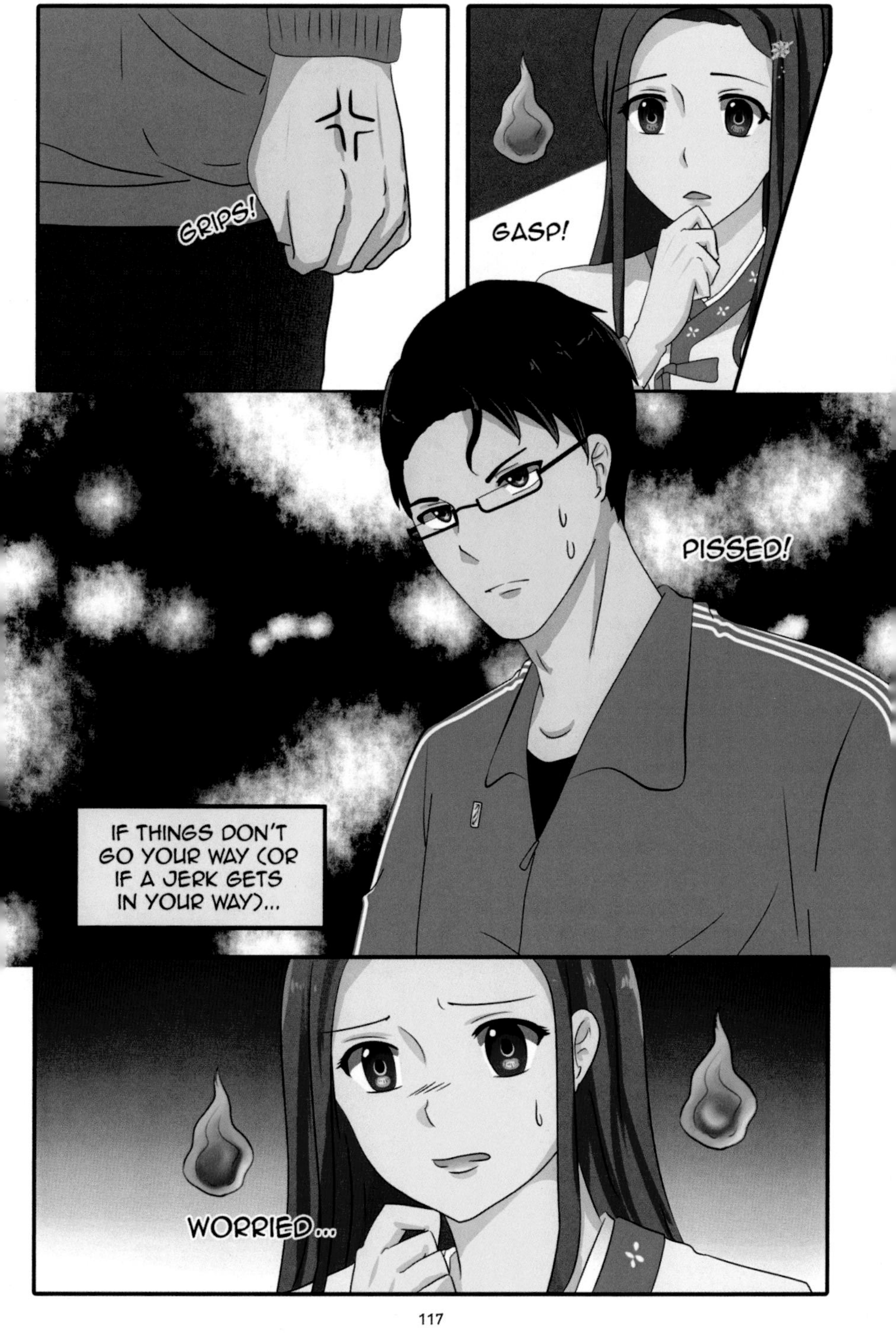
GRIPS!
GASP!
PISSED!
IF THINGS DON'T GO YOUR WAY (OR IF A JERK GETS IN YOUR WAY)...
WORRIED...

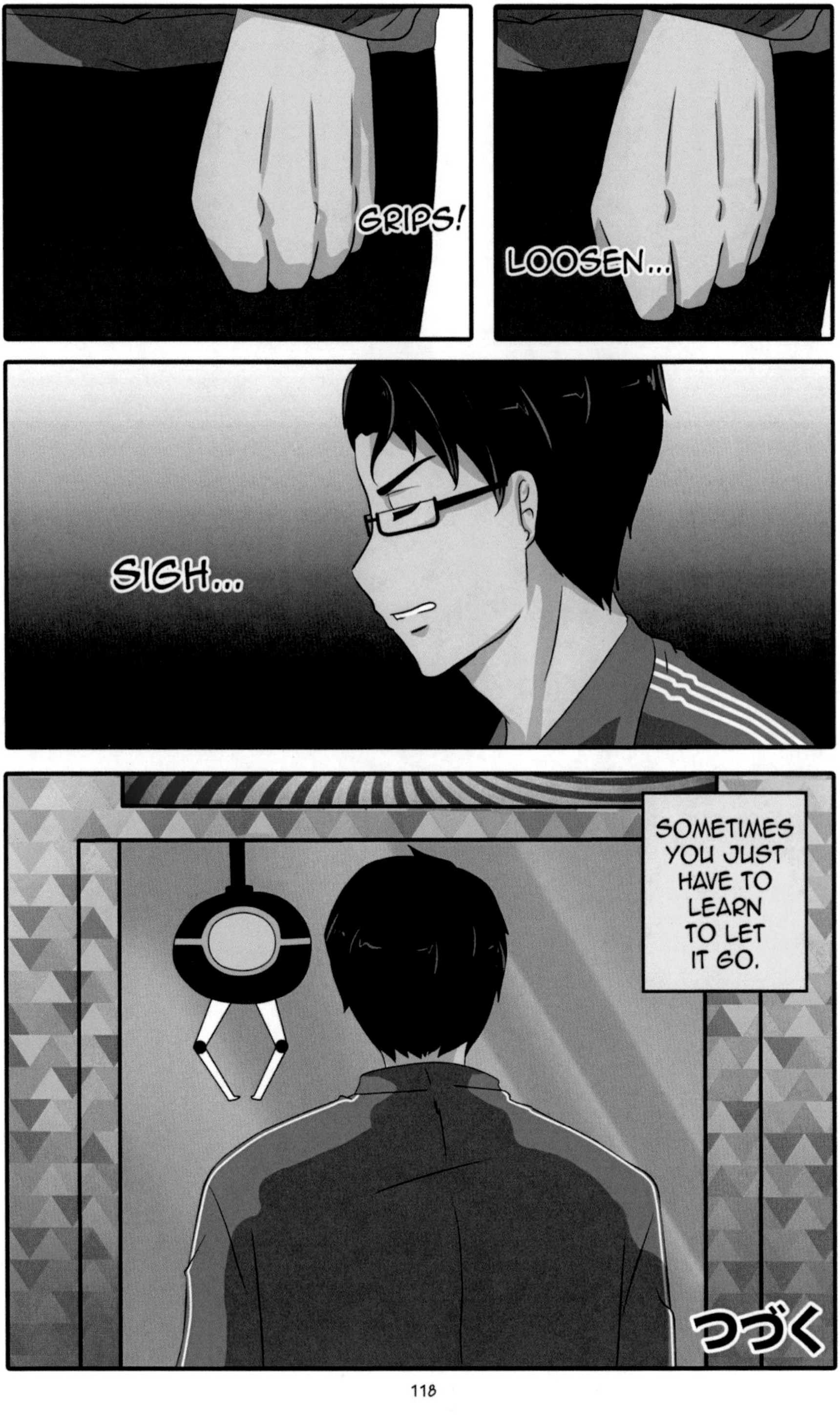
GRIPS!
LOOSEN...
SIGH...
SOMETIMES YOU JUST HAVE TO LEARN TO LET IT GO.
つづく

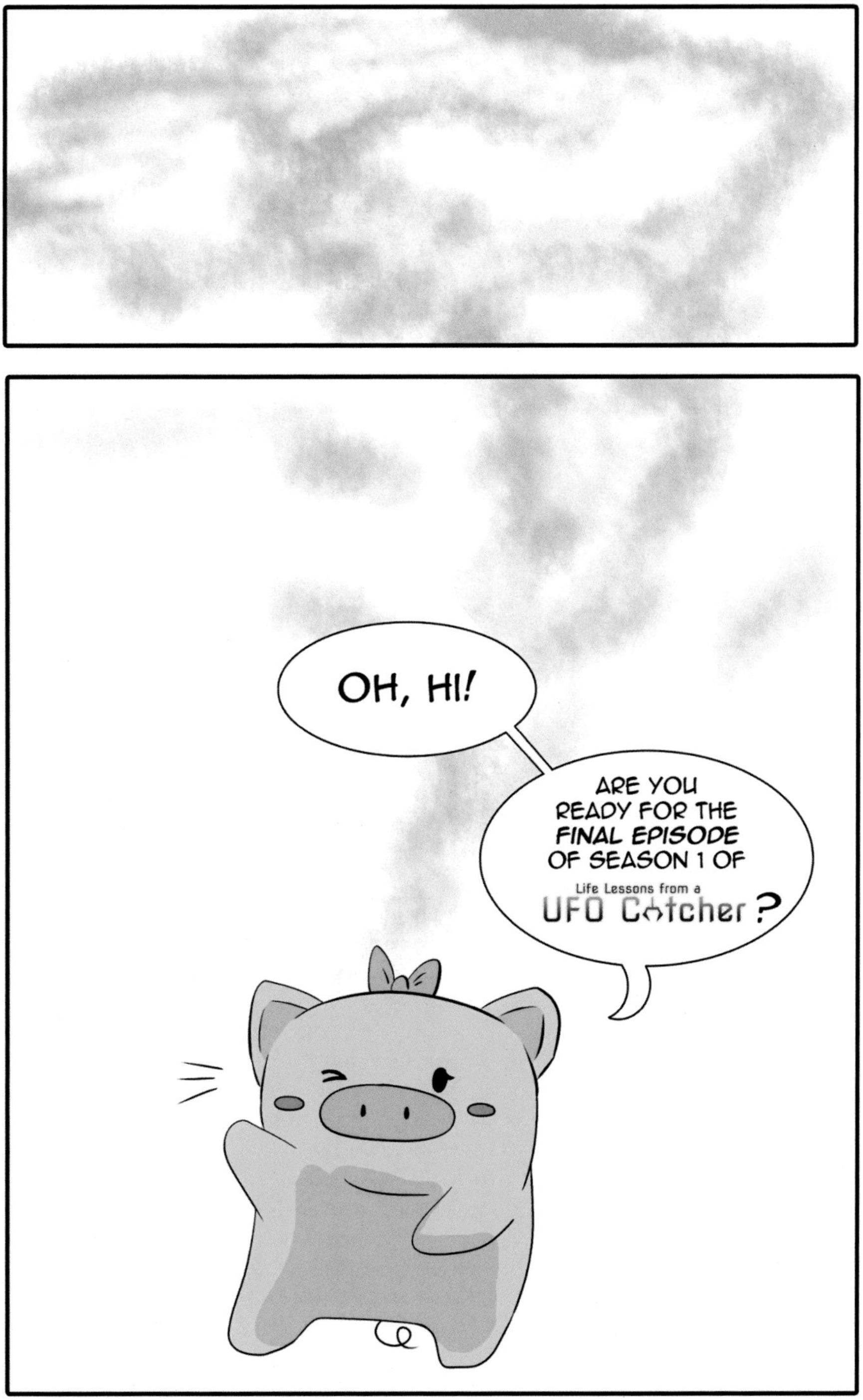
OH, HI!
ARE YOU READY FOR THE FINAL EPISODE OF SEASON 1 OF
Life Lessons from a UFO Catcher?

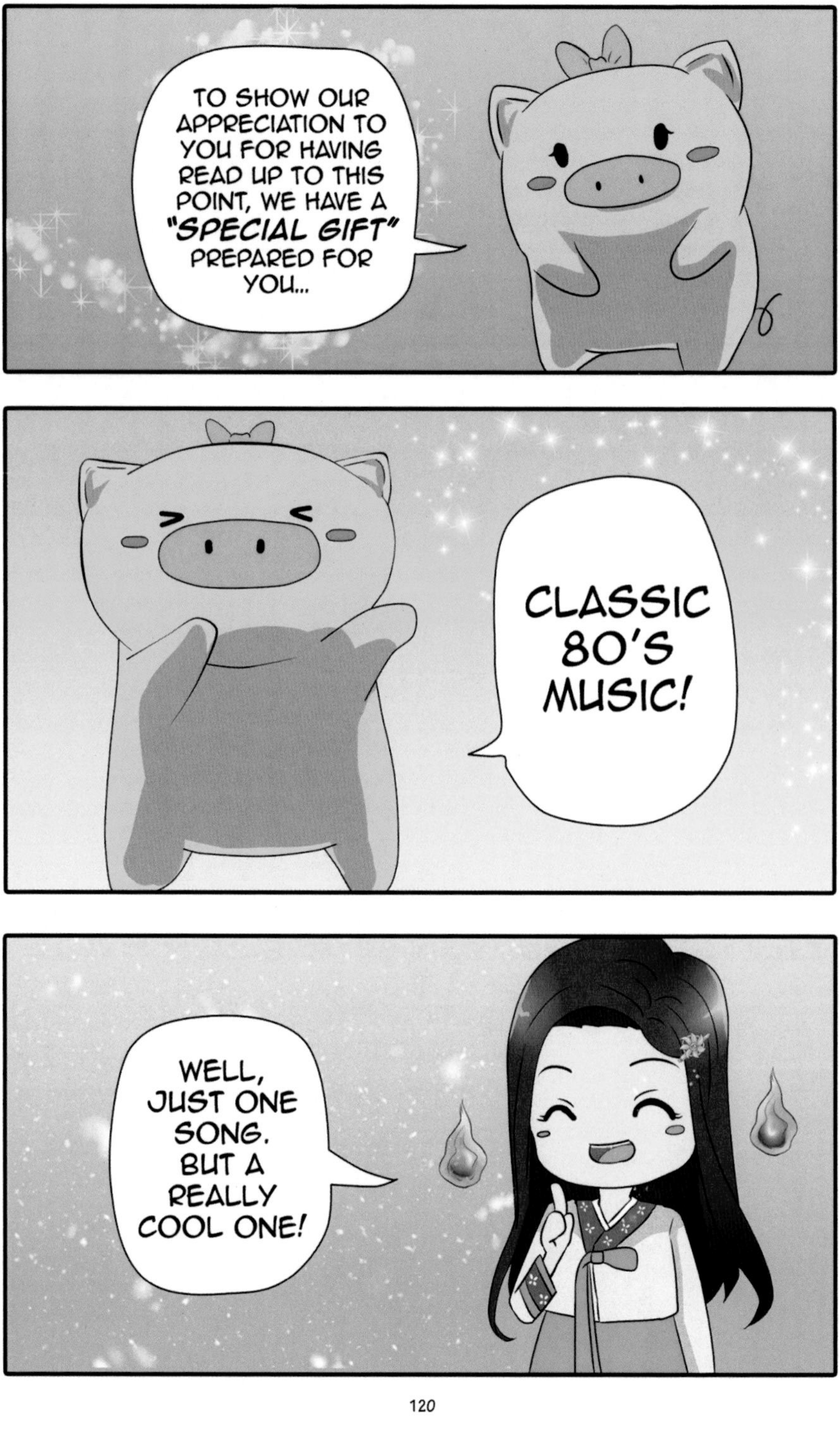
TO SHOW OUR APPRECIATION TO YOU FOR HAVING READ UP TO THIS POINT, WE HAVE A "SPECIAL GIFT" PREPARED FOR YOU...
CLASSIC 80'S MUSIC!
WELL, JUST ONE SONG. BUT A REALLY COOL ONE!

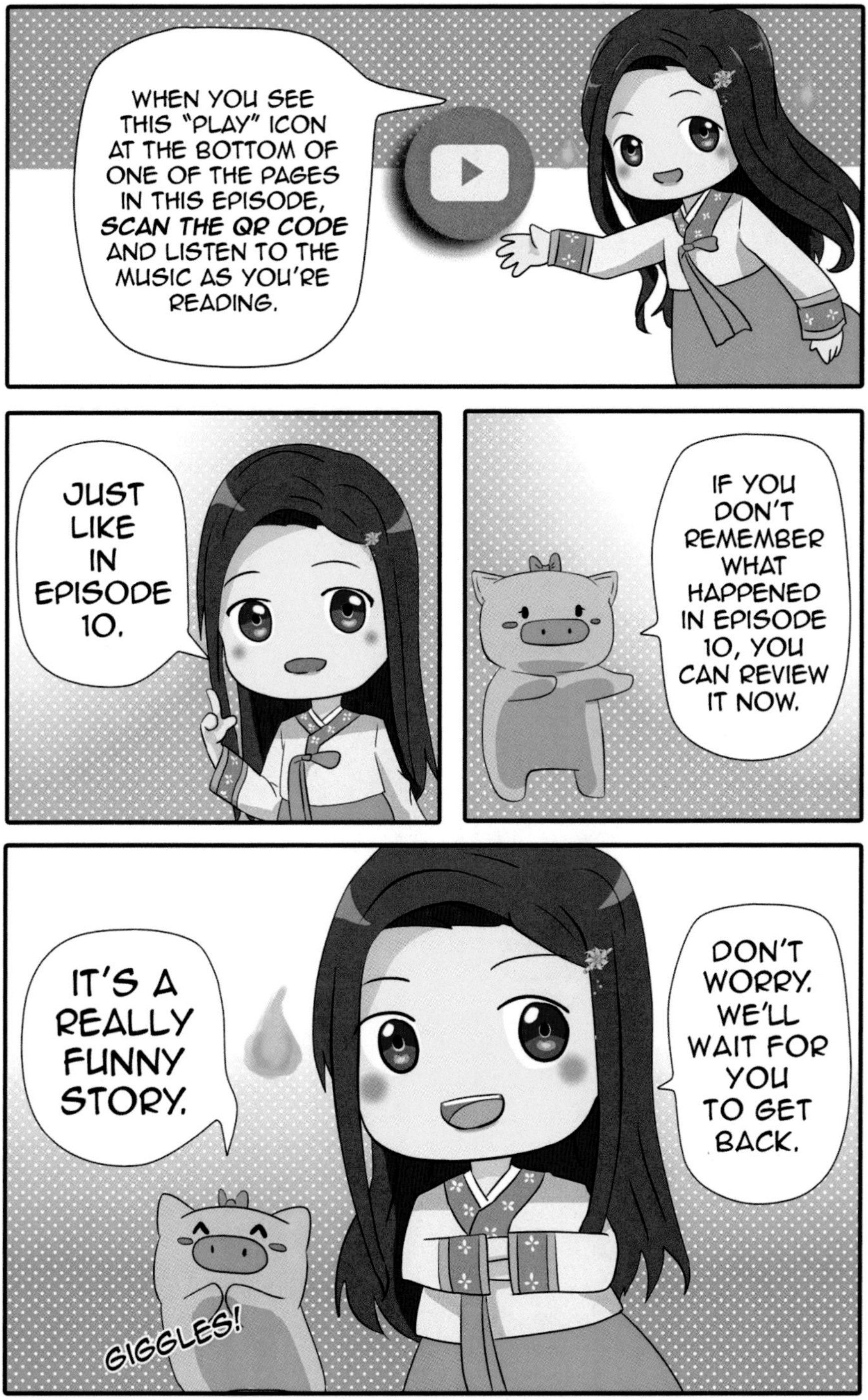
WHEN YOU SEE THIS "PLAY" ICON AT THE BOTTOM OF ONE OF THE PAGES IN THIS EPISODE, SCAN THE QR CODE AND LISTEN TO THE MUSIC AS YOU'RE READING.
JUST LIKE IN EPISODE 10.
IF YOU DON'T REMEMBER WHAT HAPPENED IN EPISODE 10, YOU CAN REVIEW IT NOW.
DON'T WORRY. WE'LL WAIT FOR YOU TO GET BACK.
IT'S A REALLY FUNNY STORY.
GIGGLES!

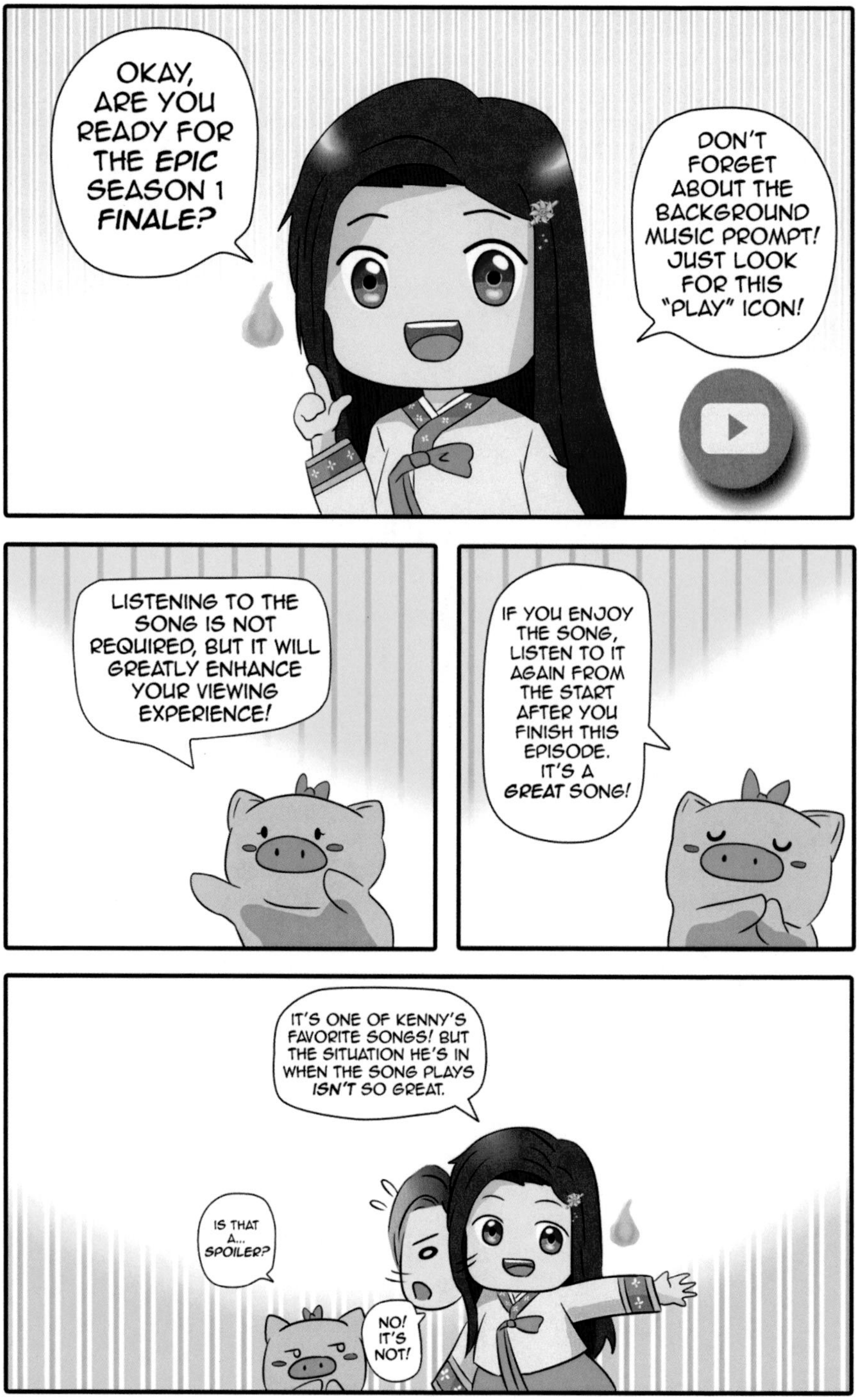
OKAY, ARE YOU READY FOR THE EPIC SEASON 1 FINALE?
DON'T FORGET ABOUT THE BACKGROUND MUSIC PROMPT! JUST LOOK FOR THIS "PLAY" ICON!
LISTENING TO THE SONG IS NOT REQUIRED, BUT IT WILL GREATLY ENHANCE YOUR VIEWING EXPERIENCE!
IF YOU ENJOY THE SONG, LISTEN TO IT AGAIN FROM THE START AFTER YOU FINISH THIS EPISODE. IT'S A GREAT SONG!
IT'S ONE OF KENNY'S FAVORITE SONGS! BUT THE SITUATION HE'S IN WHEN THE SONG PLAYS ISN'T SO GREAT.
IS THAT A... SPOILER?
NO! IT'S NOT!

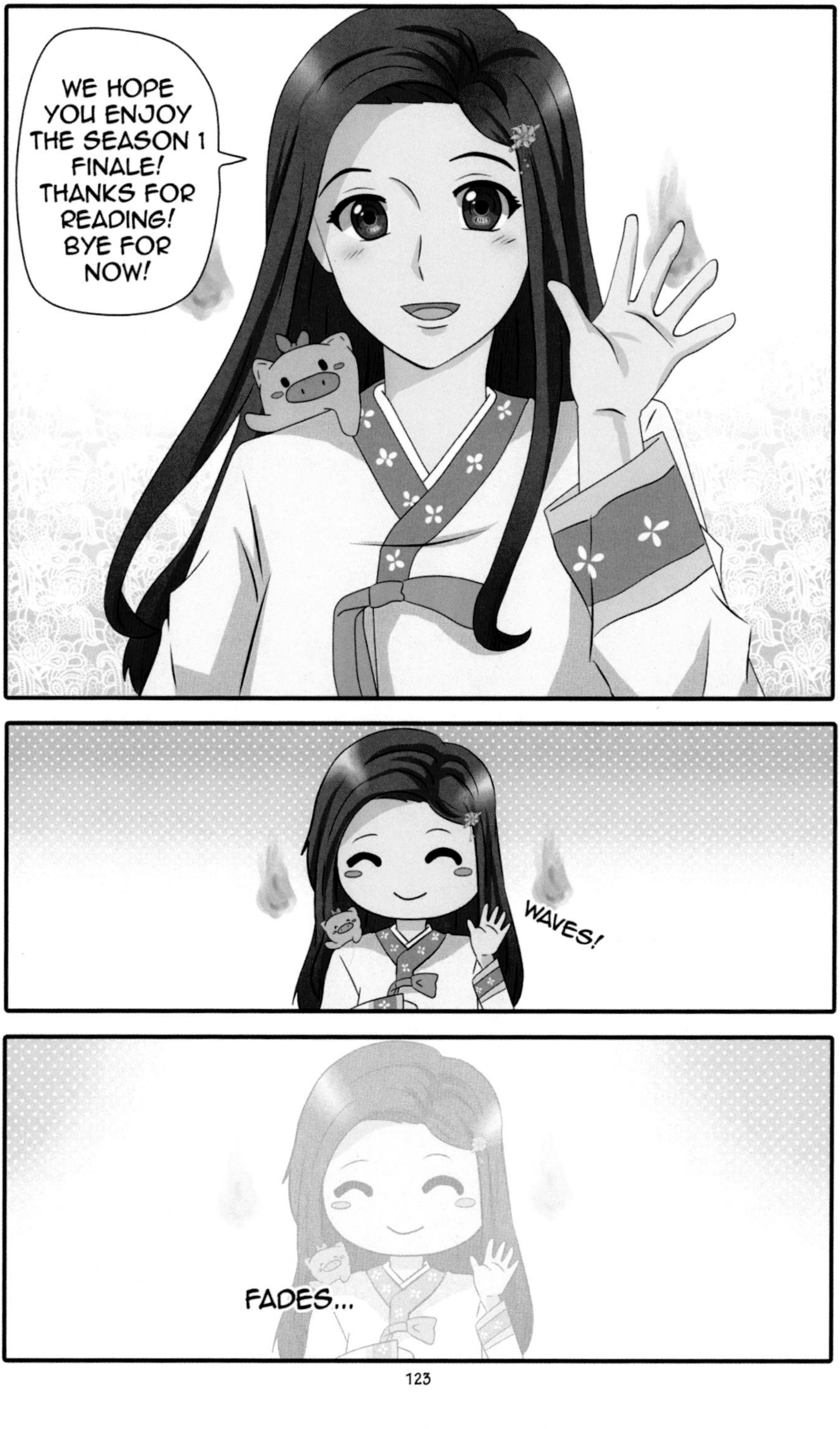
WE HOPE YOU ENJOY THE SEASON 1 FINALE! THANKS FOR READING! BYE FOR NOW!
WAVES!
FADES...

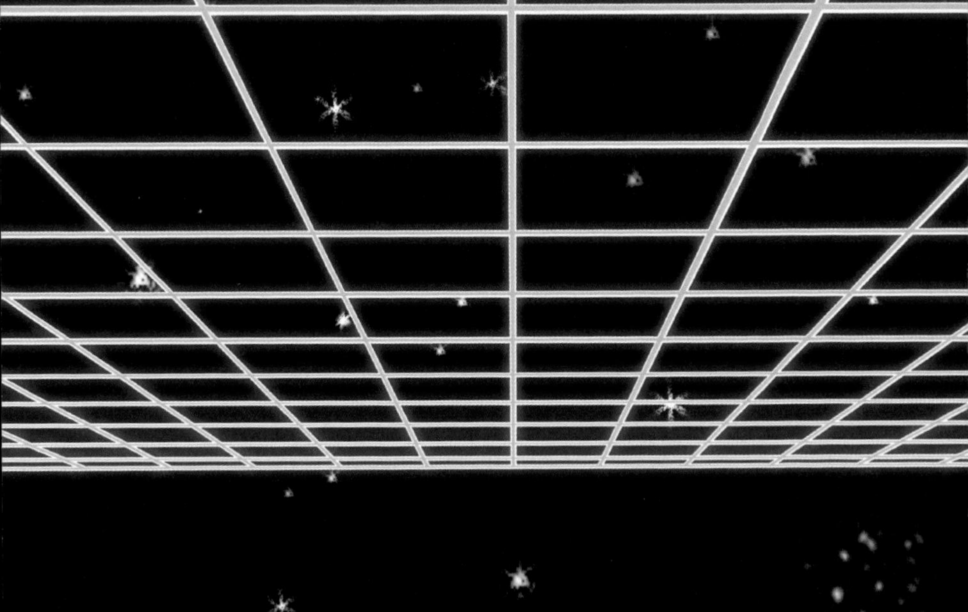

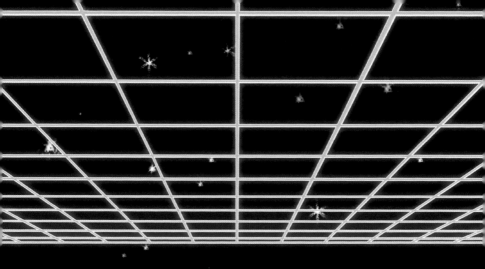

Episode 13:

What Have I Done To Deserve This?

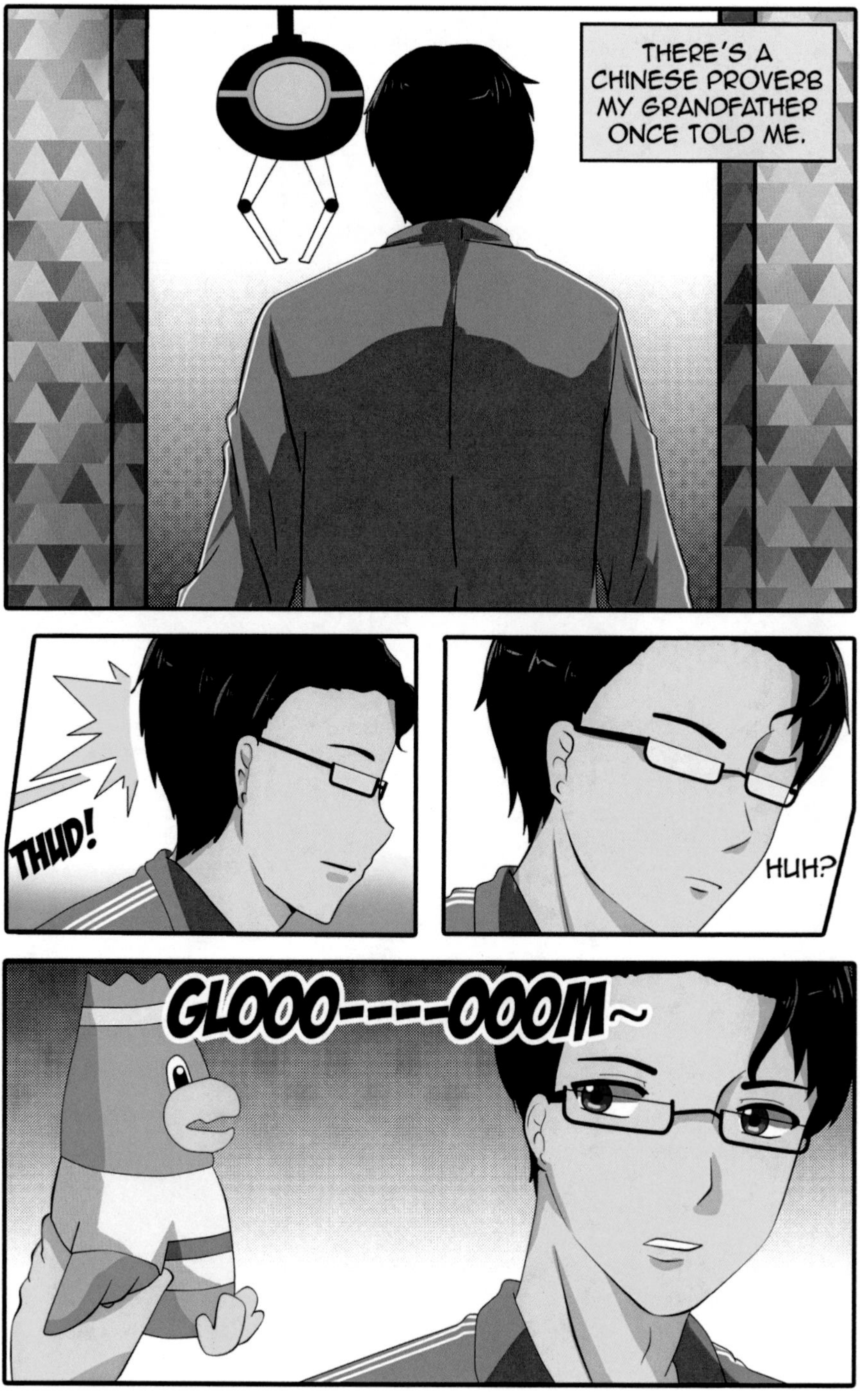
THERE'S A CHINESE PROVERB MY GRANDFATHER ONCE TOLD ME.
THUD!
HUH?
GLOOO----OOOM~

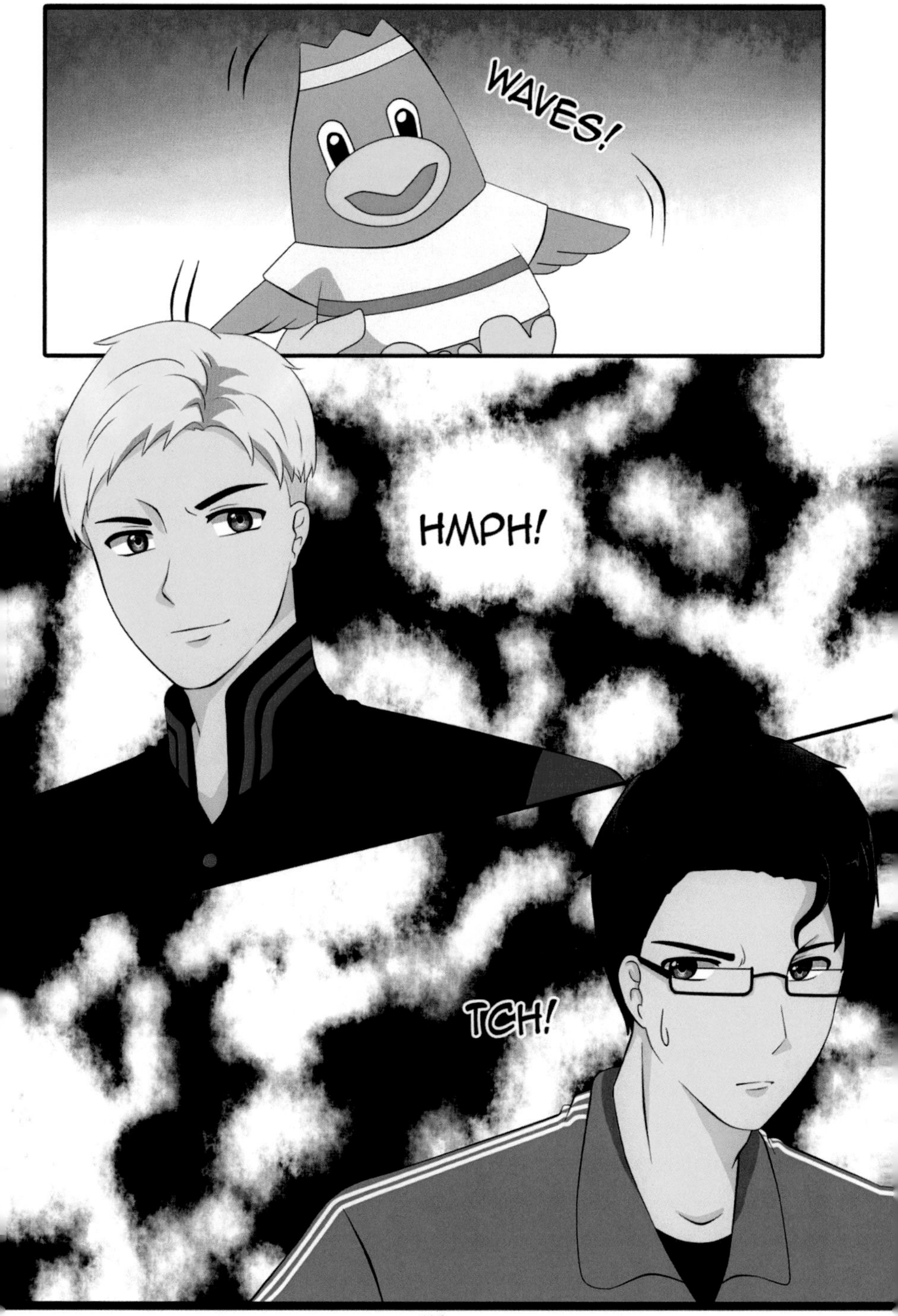
WAVES!
HMPH!
TCH!

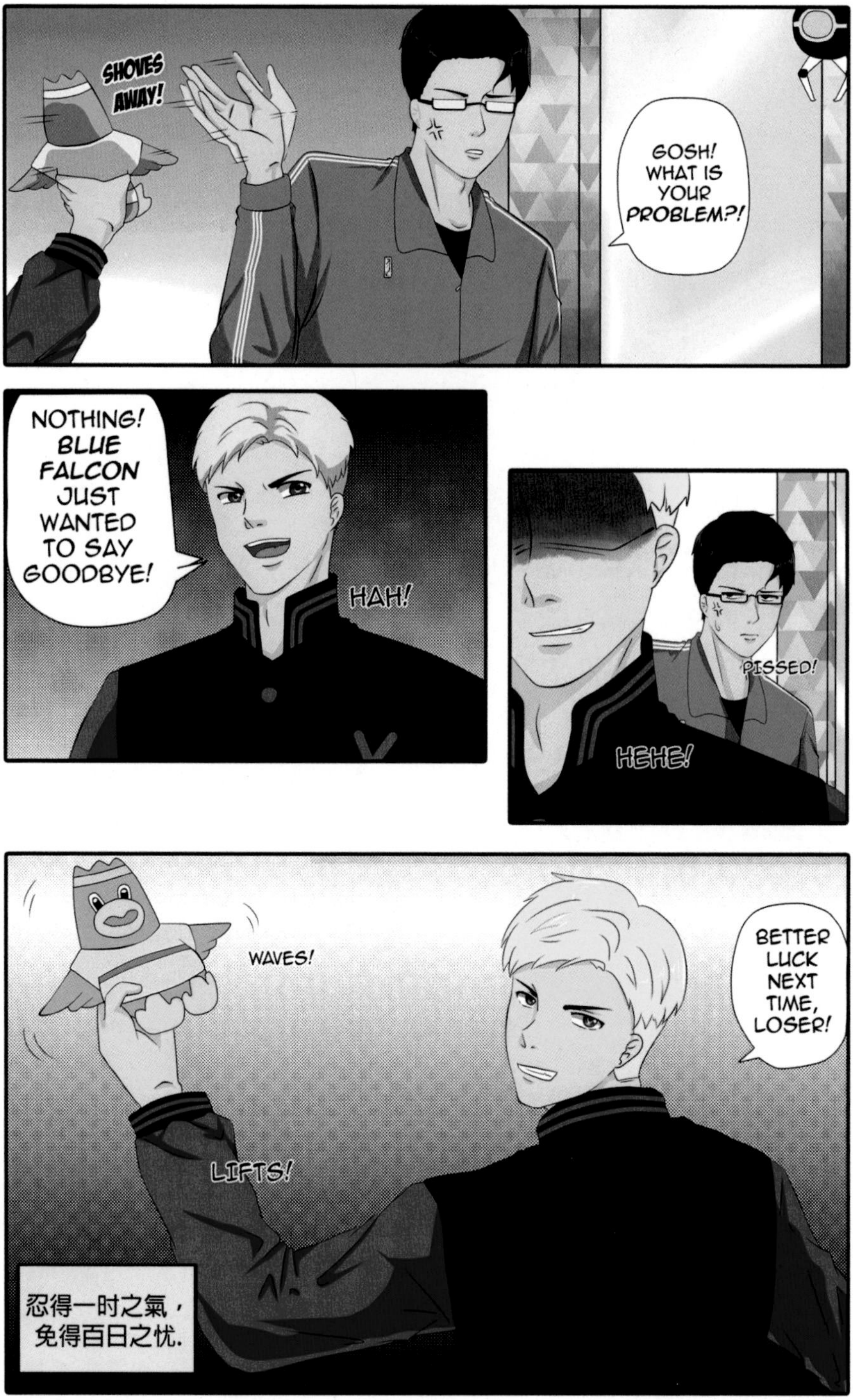
SHOVES AWAY!
GOSH! WHAT IS YOUR PROBLEM?!
NOTHING! BLUE FALCON JUST WANTED TO SAY GOODBYE!
HAH!
PISSED!
HEHE!
WAVES!
BETTER LUCK NEXT TIME, LOSER!
LIFTS!
忍得一时之氣，
免得百日之忧.

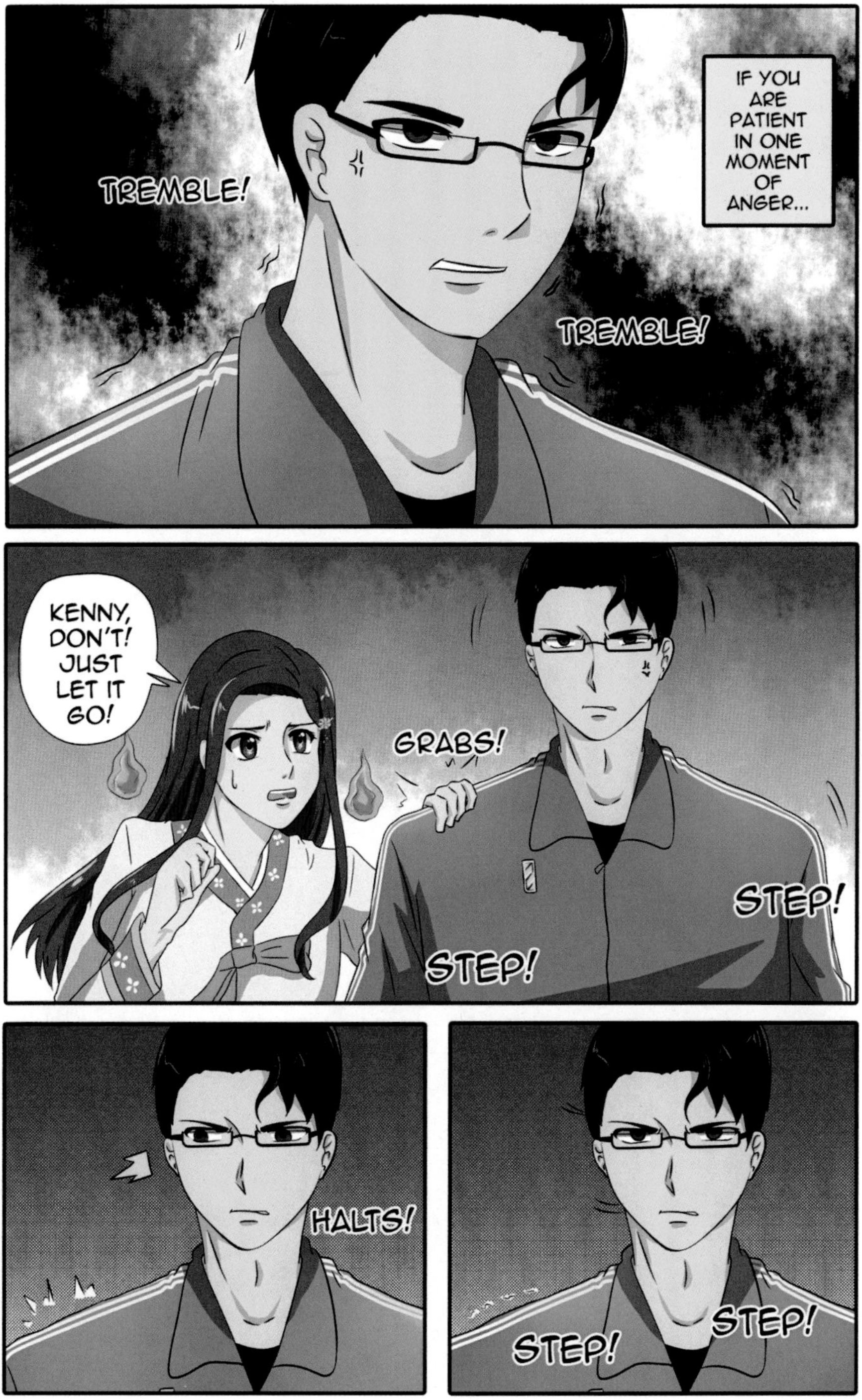
IF YOU ARE PATIENT IN ONE MOMENT OF ANGER...
TREMBLE!
TREMBLE!
KENNY, DON'T! JUST LET IT GO!
GRABS!
STEP!
STEP!
HALTS!
STEP!
STEP!

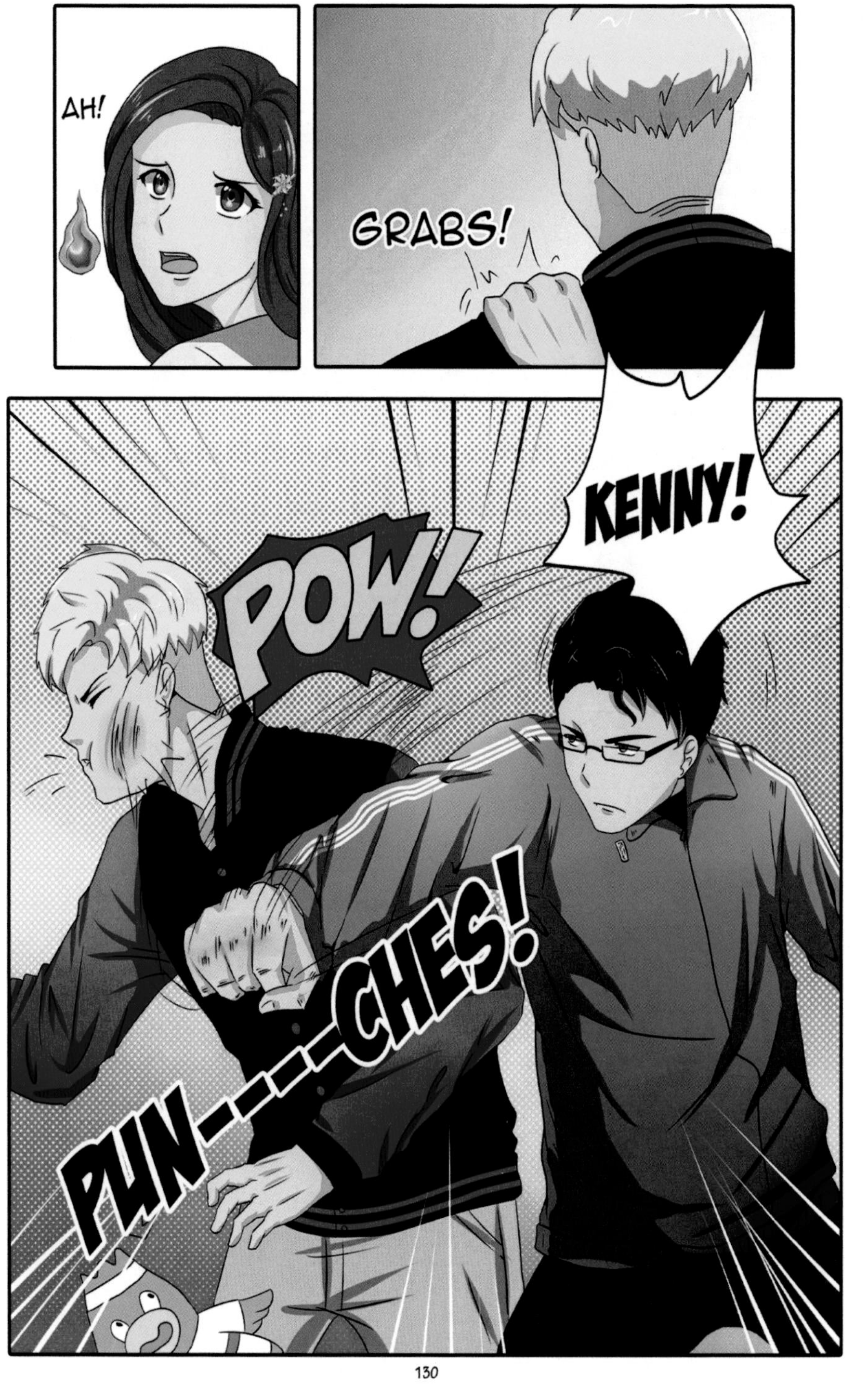
AH!
GRABS!
KENNY!
POW!
PUN-----CHES!

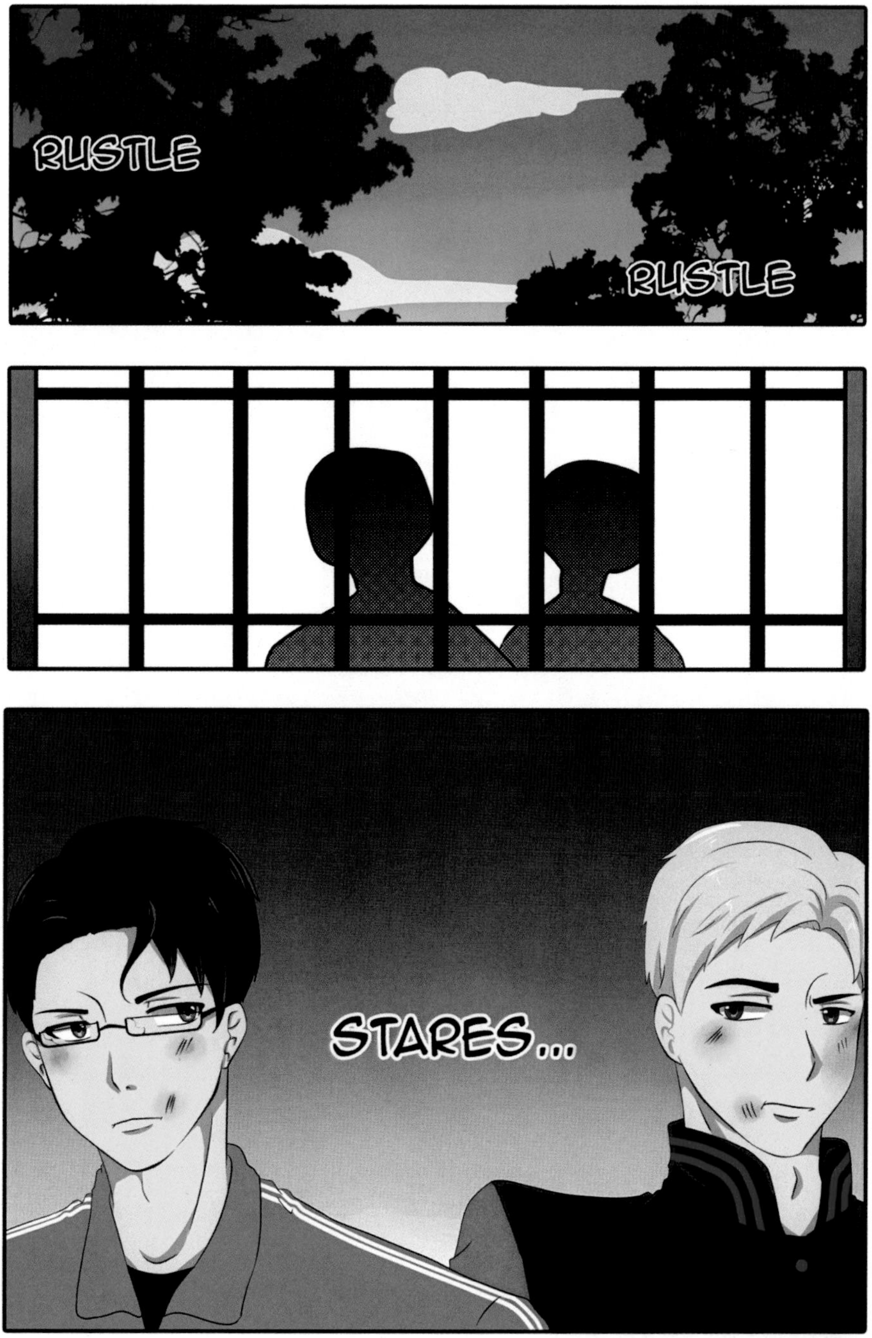
RUSTLE
RUSTLE
STARES...

Pet Shop Boys
What Have I Done to Deserve This?

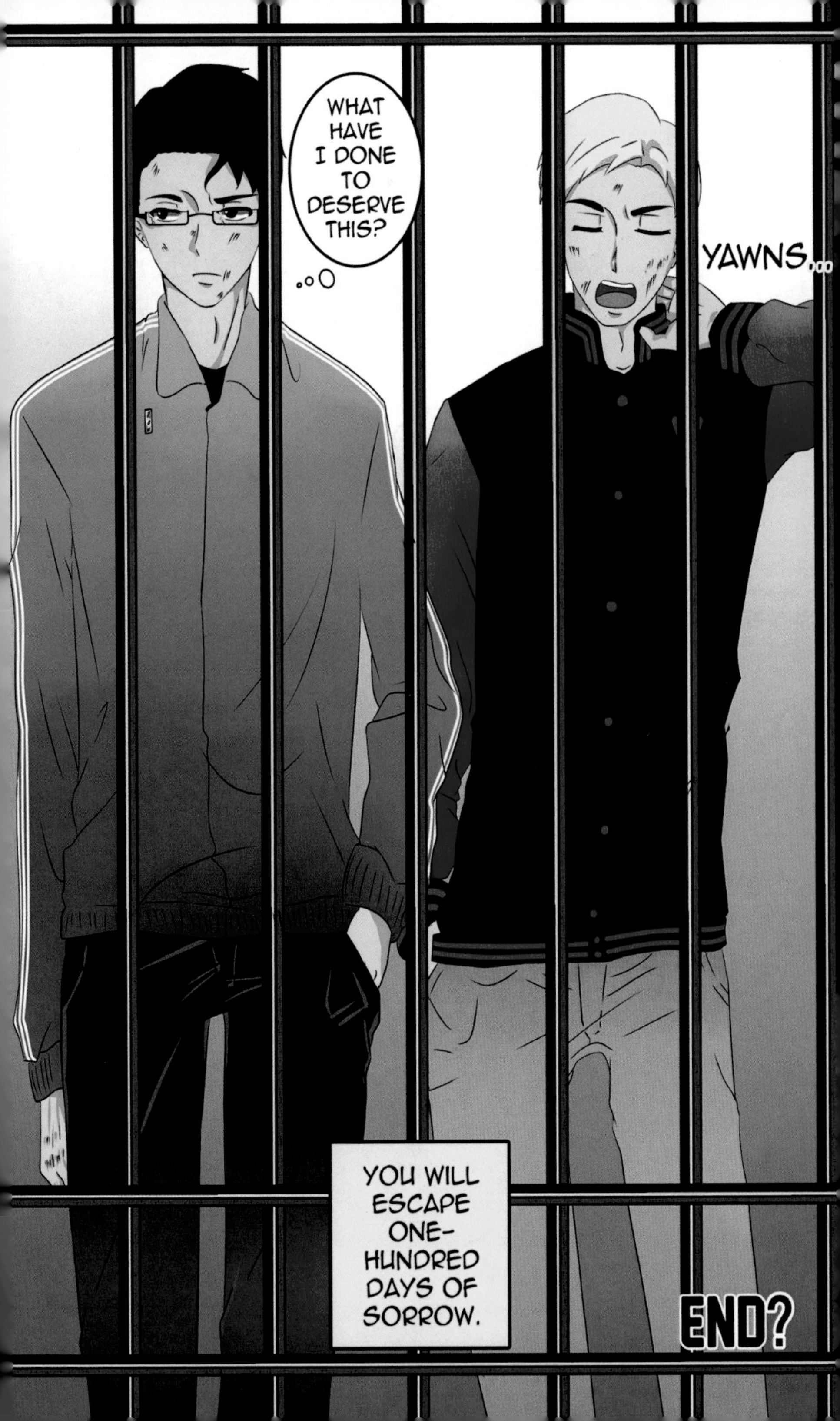
YAWNS...
WHAT HAVE I DONE TO DESERVE THIS?
YOU WILL ESCAPE ONE-HUNDRED DAYS OF SORROW.
END?

Epilogue:
Some Lessons Are Learned the Hard Way

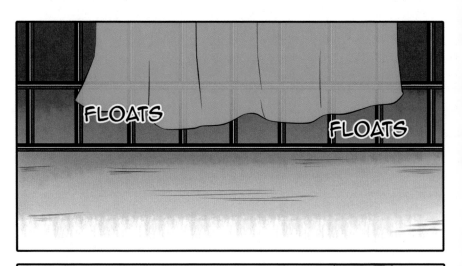

FLOATS

FLOATS

SOME LESSONS IN LIFE ARE LEARNED THE HARD WAY... ESPECIALLY IF YOU'RE A HOTHEAD.

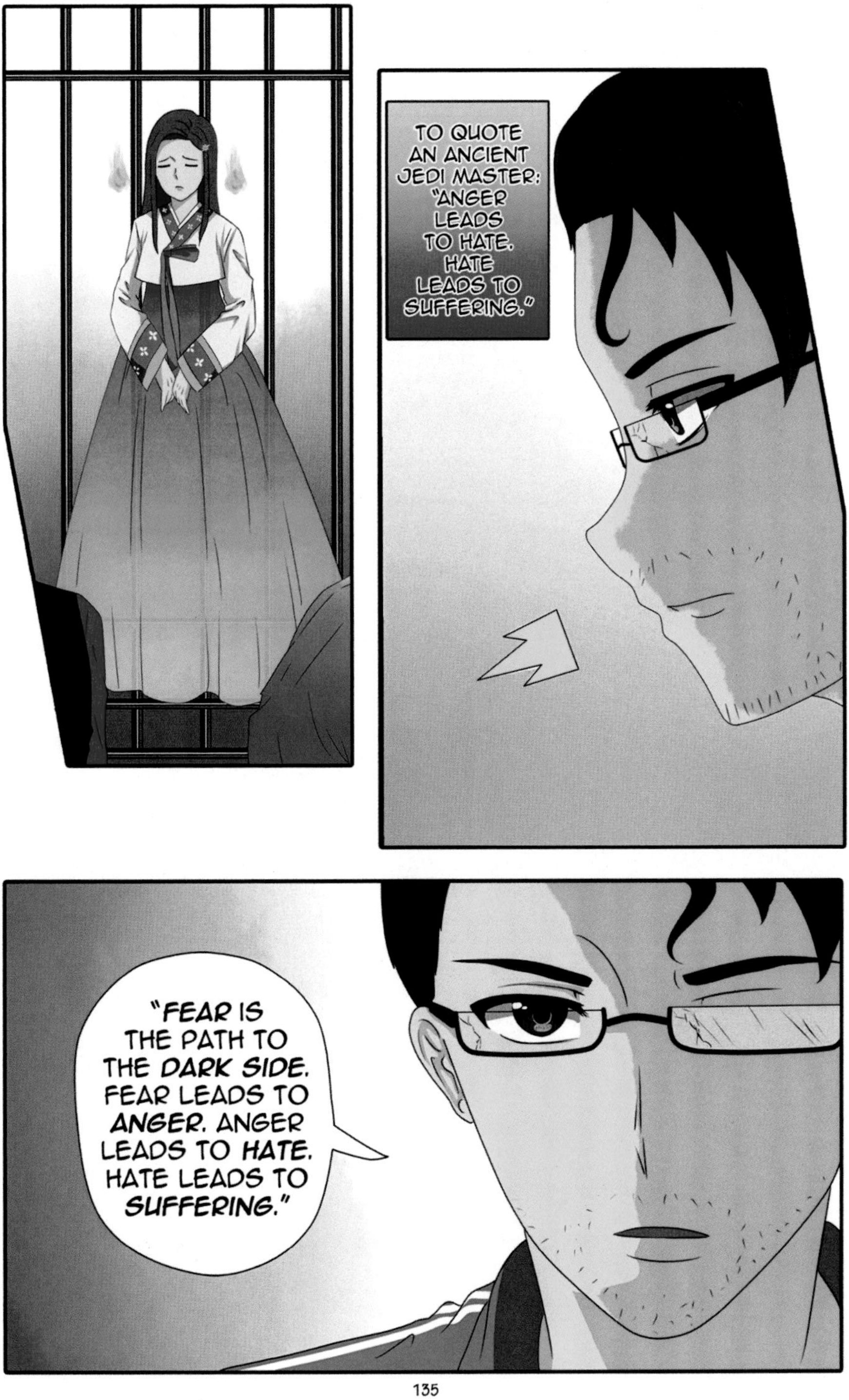
TO QUOTE AN ANCIENT JEDI MASTER: "ANGER LEADS TO HATE. HATE LEADS TO SUFFERING."
"FEAR IS THE PATH TO THE DARK SIDE. FEAR LEADS TO ANGER. ANGER LEADS TO HATE. HATE LEADS TO SUFFERING."

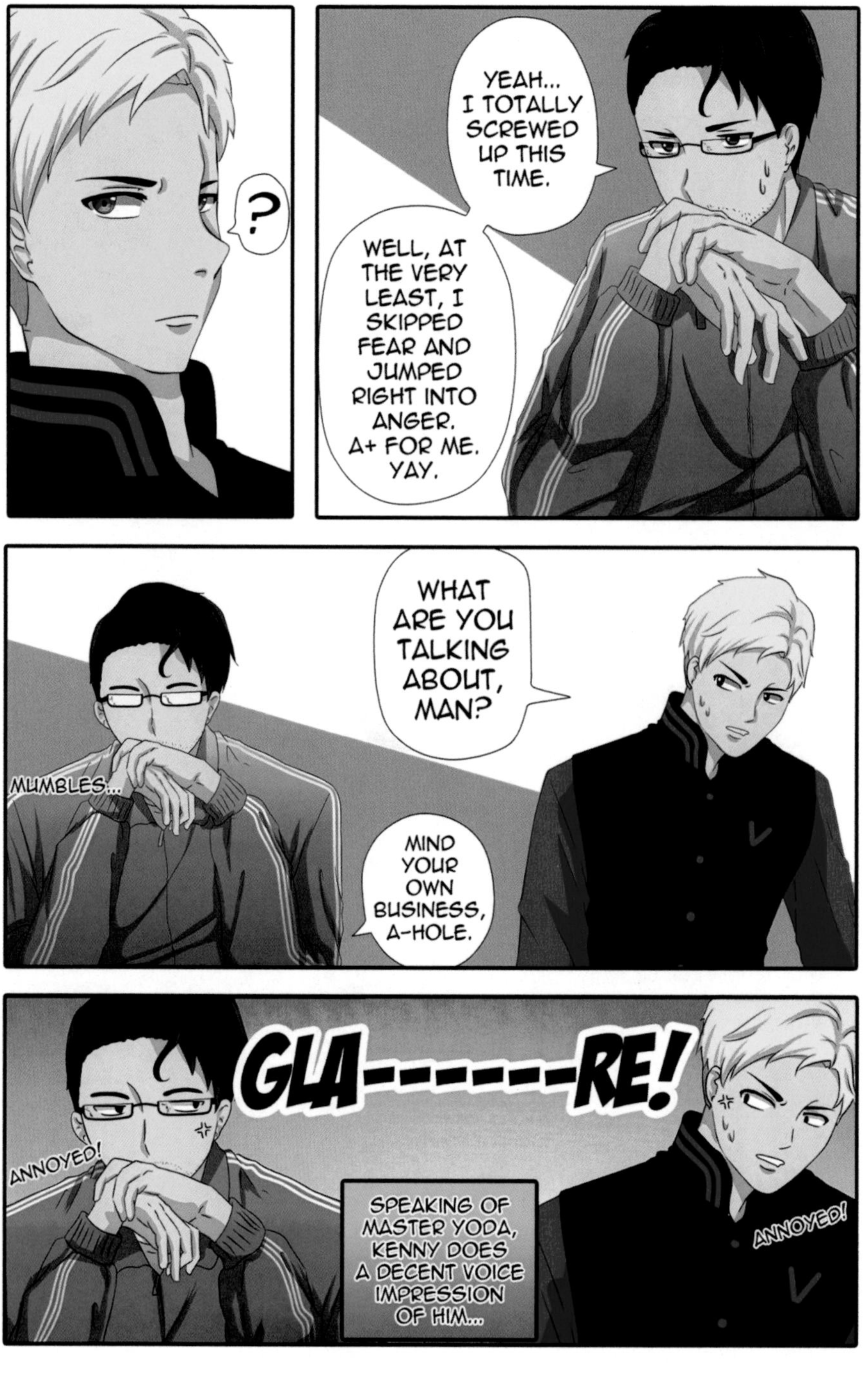
?
YEAH... I TOTALLY SCREWED UP THIS TIME.
WELL, AT THE VERY LEAST, I SKIPPED FEAR AND JUMPED RIGHT INTO ANGER. A+ FOR ME. YAY.
WHAT ARE YOU TALKING ABOUT, MAN?
MUMBLES...
MIND YOUR OWN BUSINESS, A-HOLE.
GLA-------RE!
ANNOYED!
ANNOYED!
SPEAKING OF MASTER YODA, KENNY DOES A DECENT VOICE IMPRESSION OF HIM...

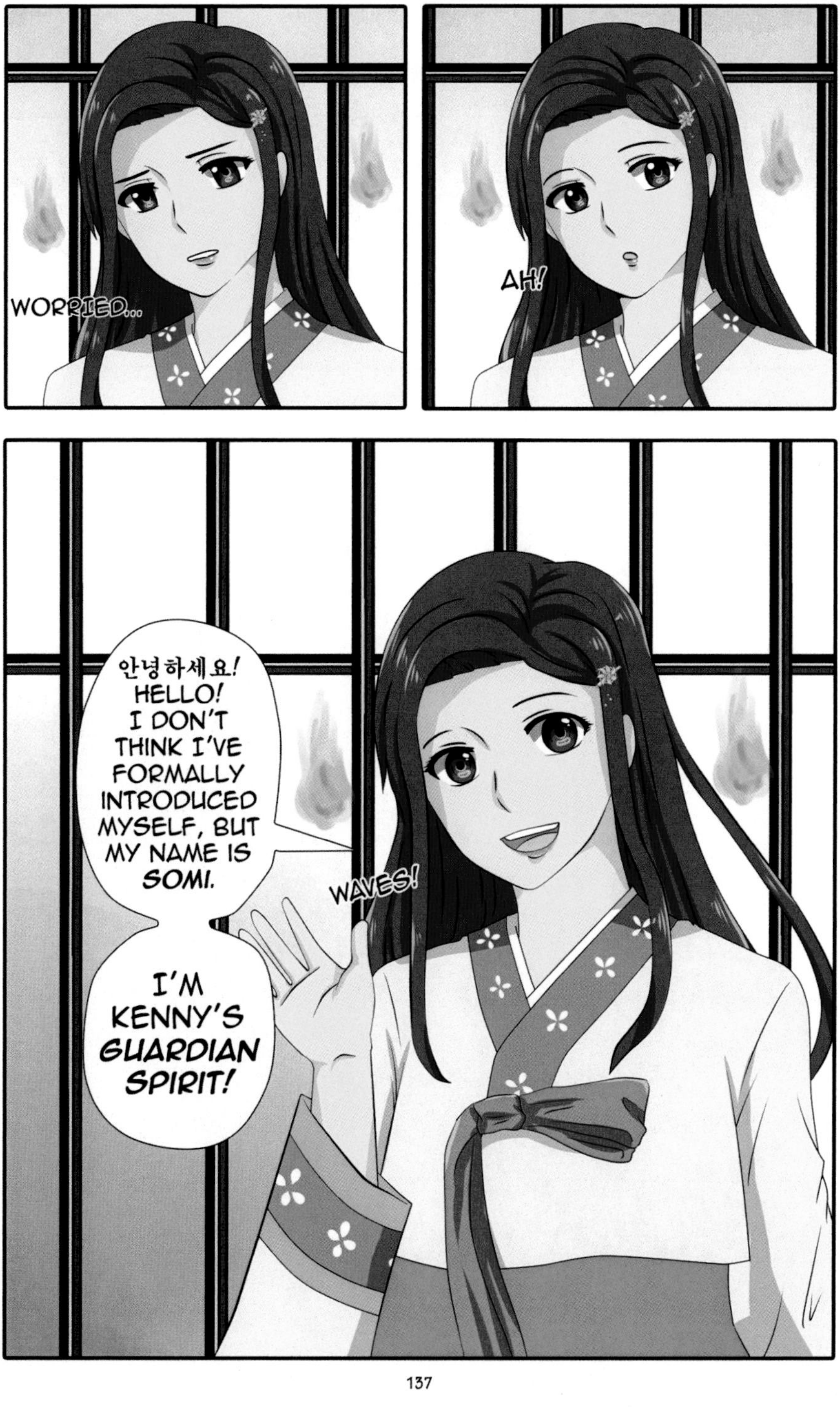
WORRIED...
AH!
안녕하세요! HELLO! I DON'T THINK I'VE FORMALLY INTRODUCED MYSELF, BUT MY NAME IS SOMI.
WAVES!
I'M KENNY'S GUARDIAN SPIRIT!

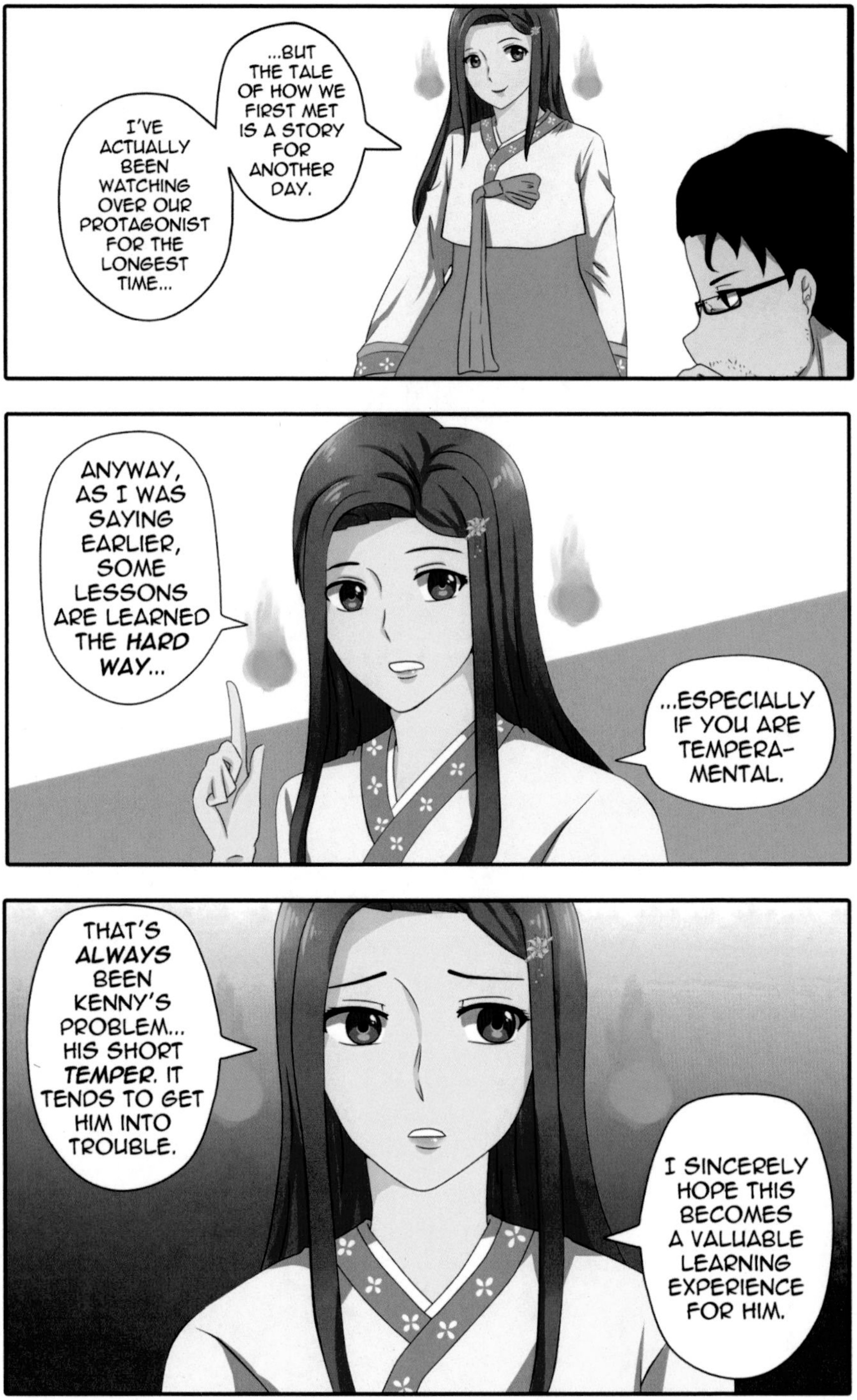
...BUT THE TALE OF HOW WE FIRST MET IS A STORY FOR ANOTHER DAY.
I'VE ACTUALLY BEEN WATCHING OVER OUR PROTAGONIST FOR THE LONGEST TIME...
ANYWAY, AS I WAS SAYING EARLIER, SOME LESSONS ARE LEARNED THE HARD WAY...
...ESPECIALLY IF YOU ARE TEMPERA-MENTAL.
THAT'S ALWAYS BEEN KENNY'S PROBLEM... HIS SHORT TEMPER. IT TENDS TO GET HIM INTO TROUBLE.
I SINCERELY HOPE THIS BECOMES A VALUABLE LEARNING EXPERIENCE FOR HIM.

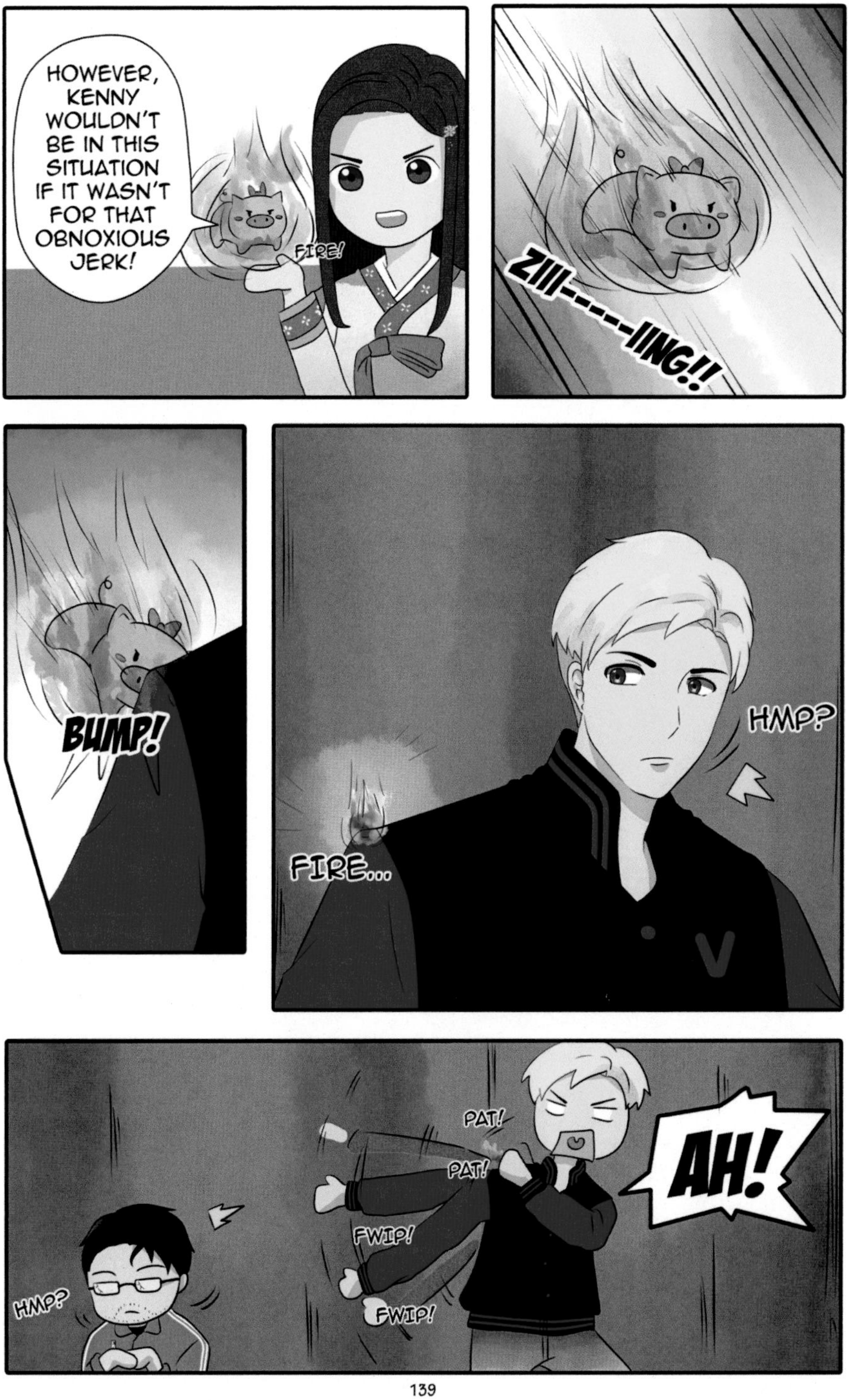
HOWEVER, KENNY WOULDN'T BE IN THIS SITUATION IF IT WASN'T FOR THAT OBNOXIOUS JERK!
FIRE!
ZIII------IING!!
BUMP!
HMP?
FIRE...
PAT!
PAT!
AH!
FWIP!
FWIP!
HMP?

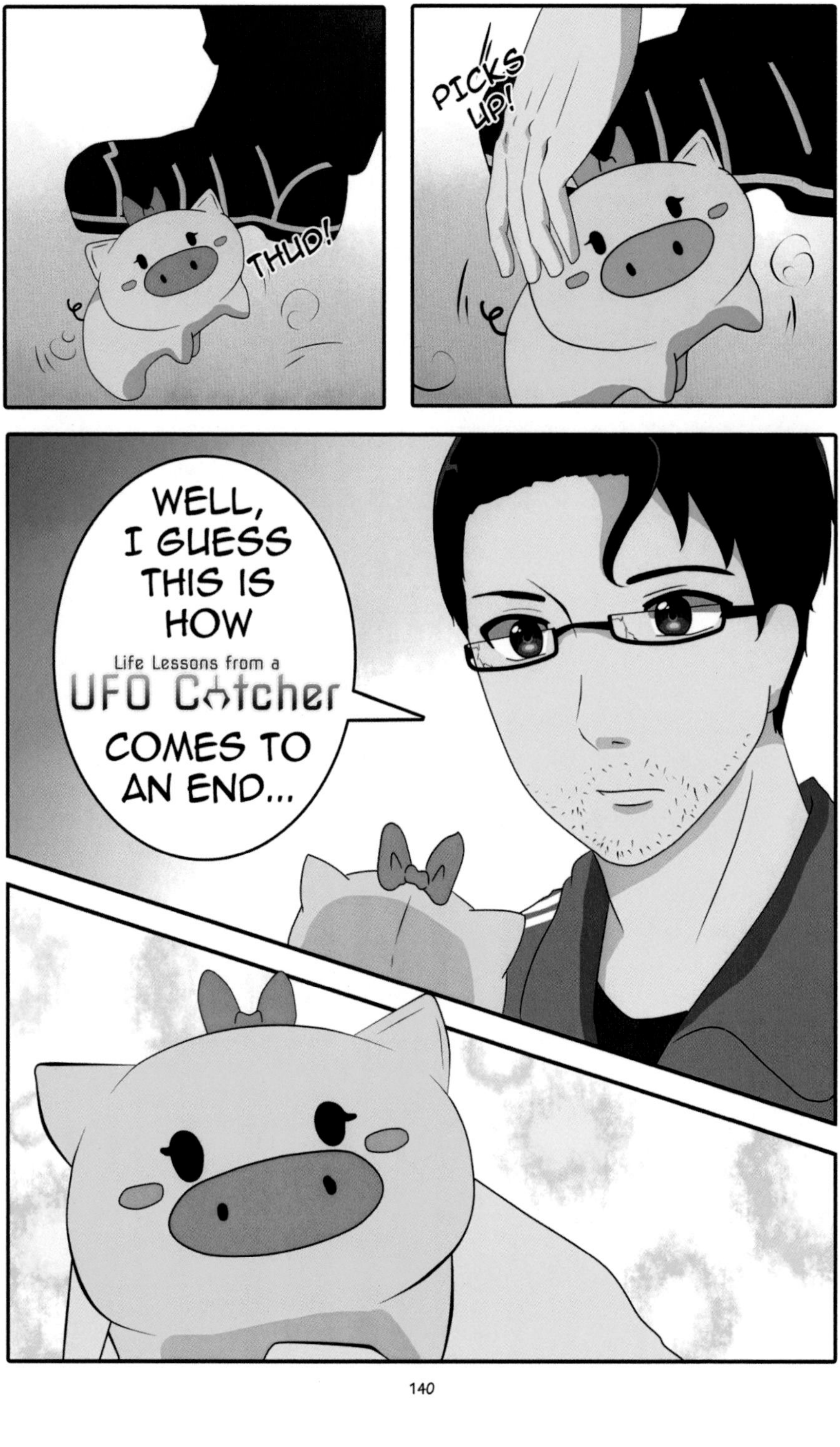
THUD!
PICKS UP!
WELL, I GUESS THIS IS HOW
Life Lessons from a UFO Catcher
COMES TO AN END...

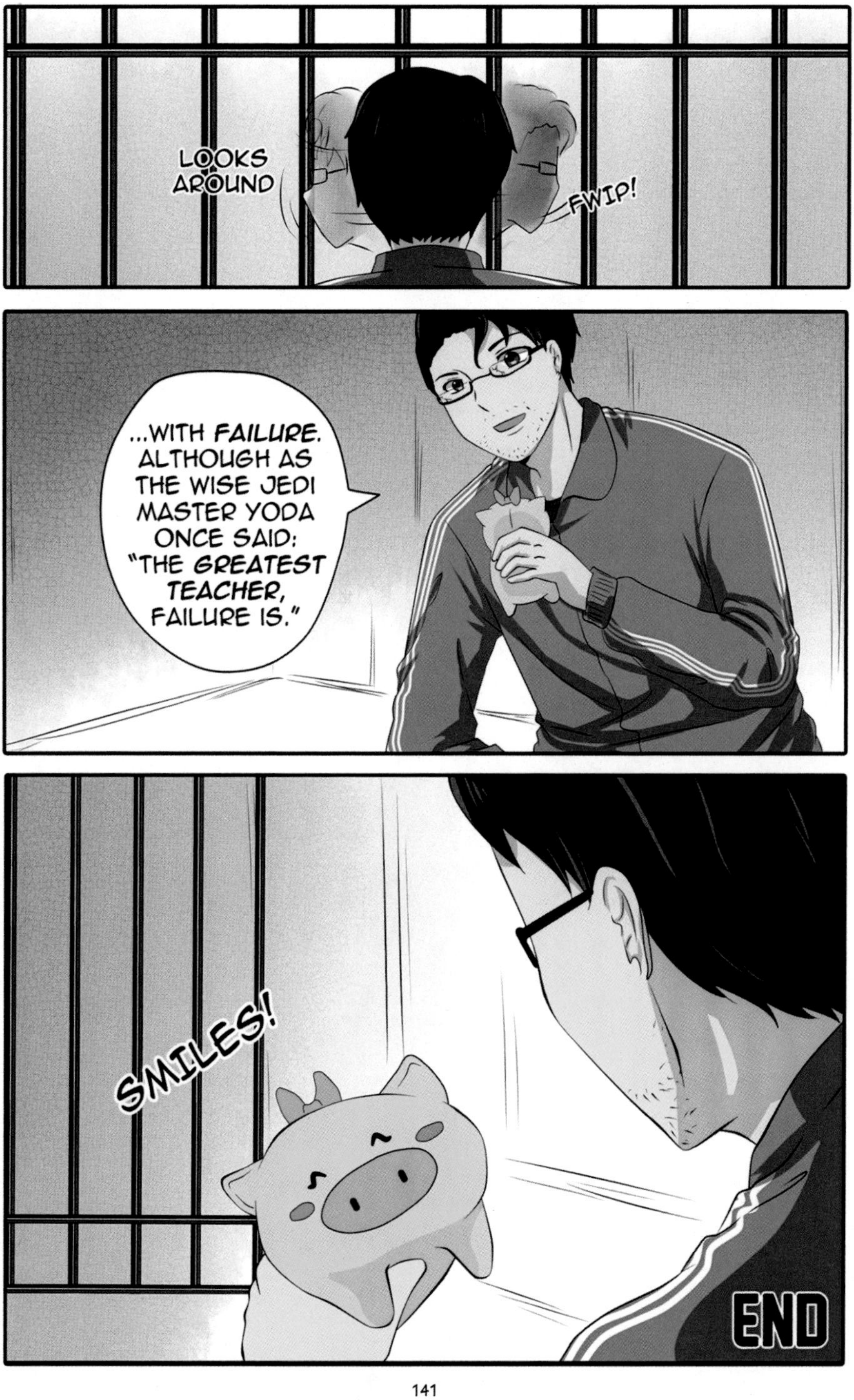
LOOKS AROUND
FWIP!
...WITH FAILURE. ALTHOUGH AS THE WISE JEDI MASTER YODA ONCE SAID: "THE GREATEST TEACHER, FAILURE IS."
SMILES!
END

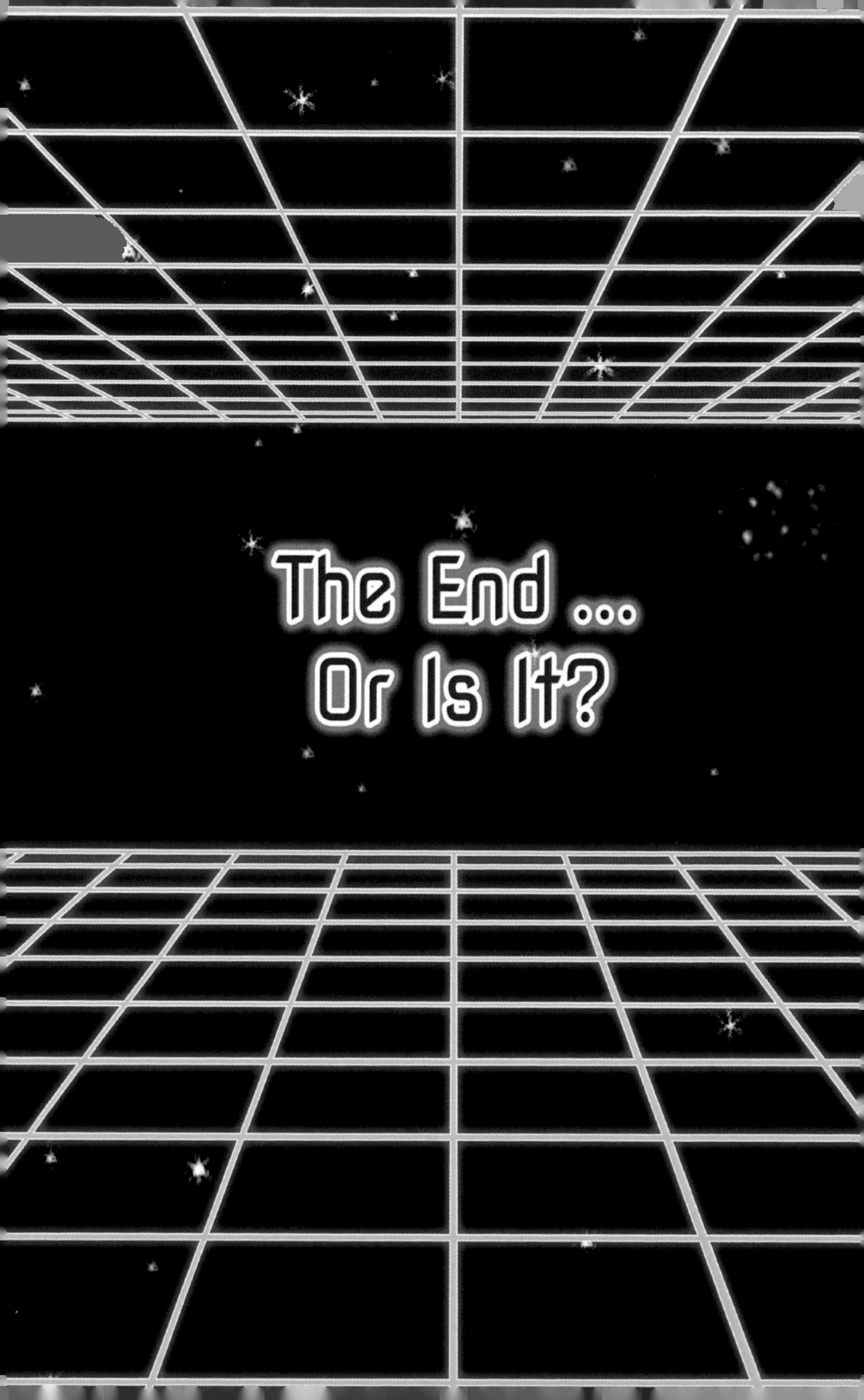
The End ...
Or Is It?

Kenny

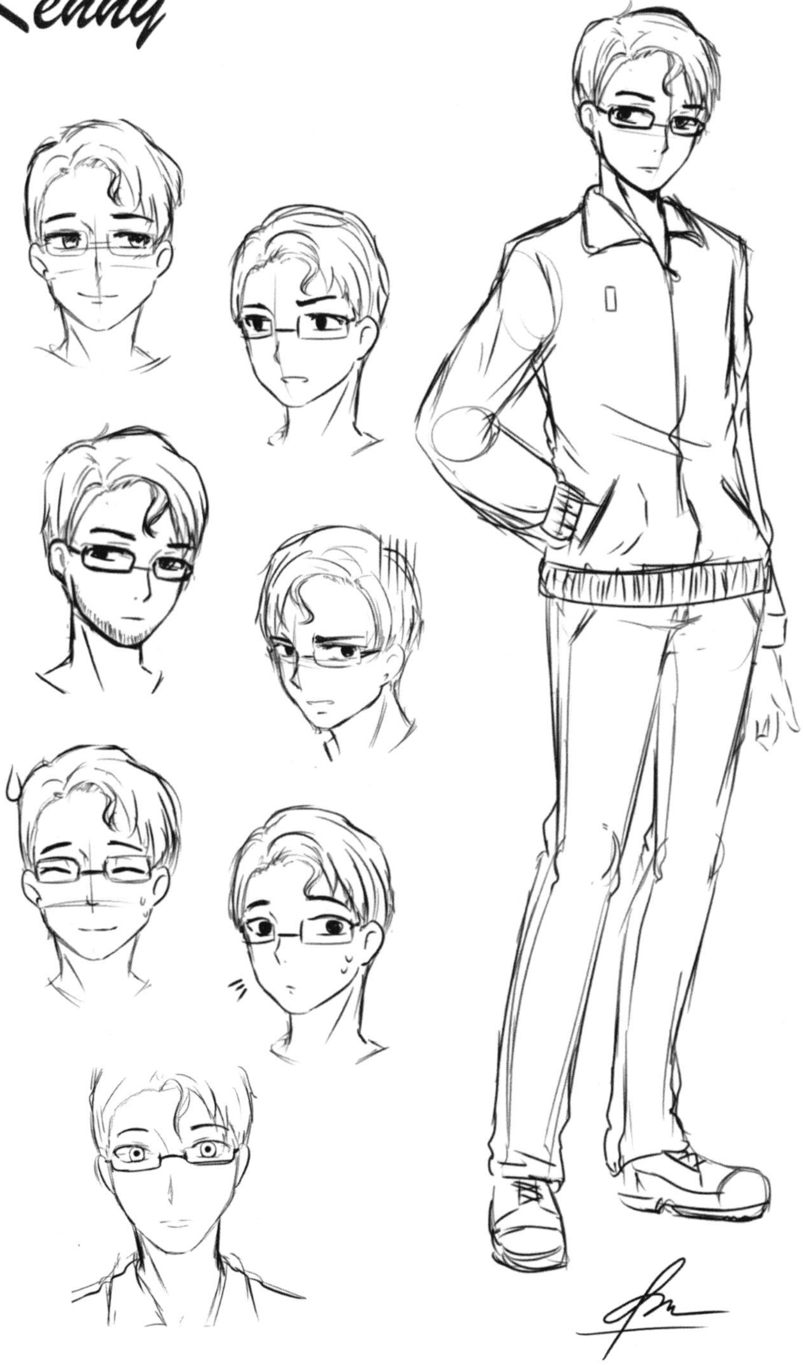

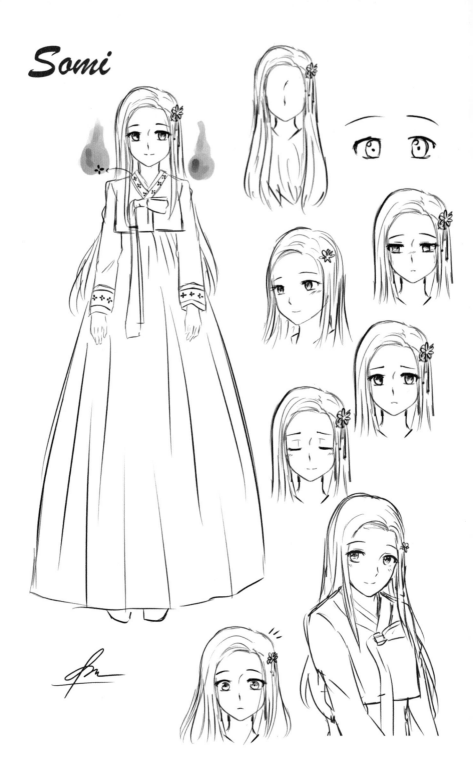

Somi

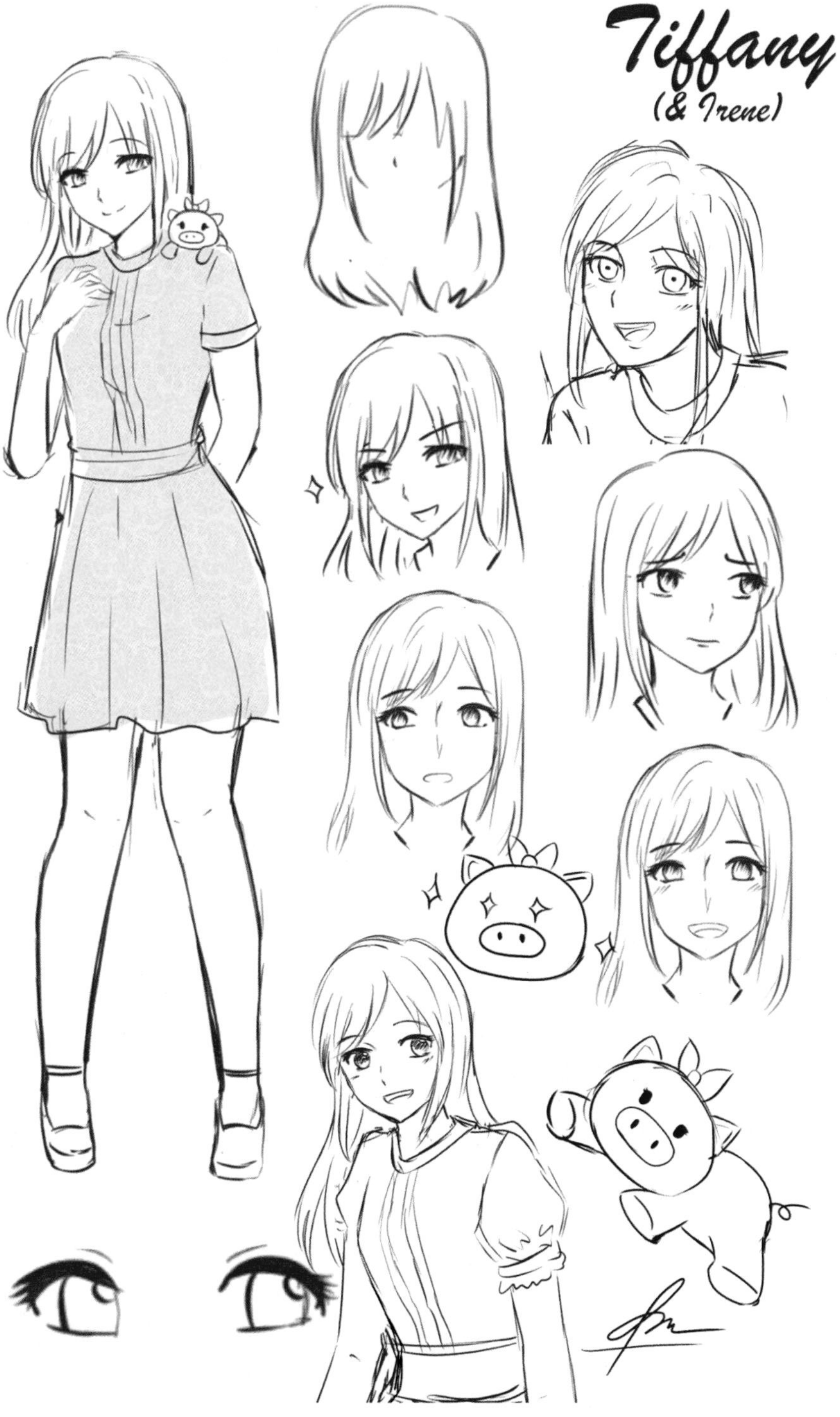
Tiffany
(& Irene)

Killian

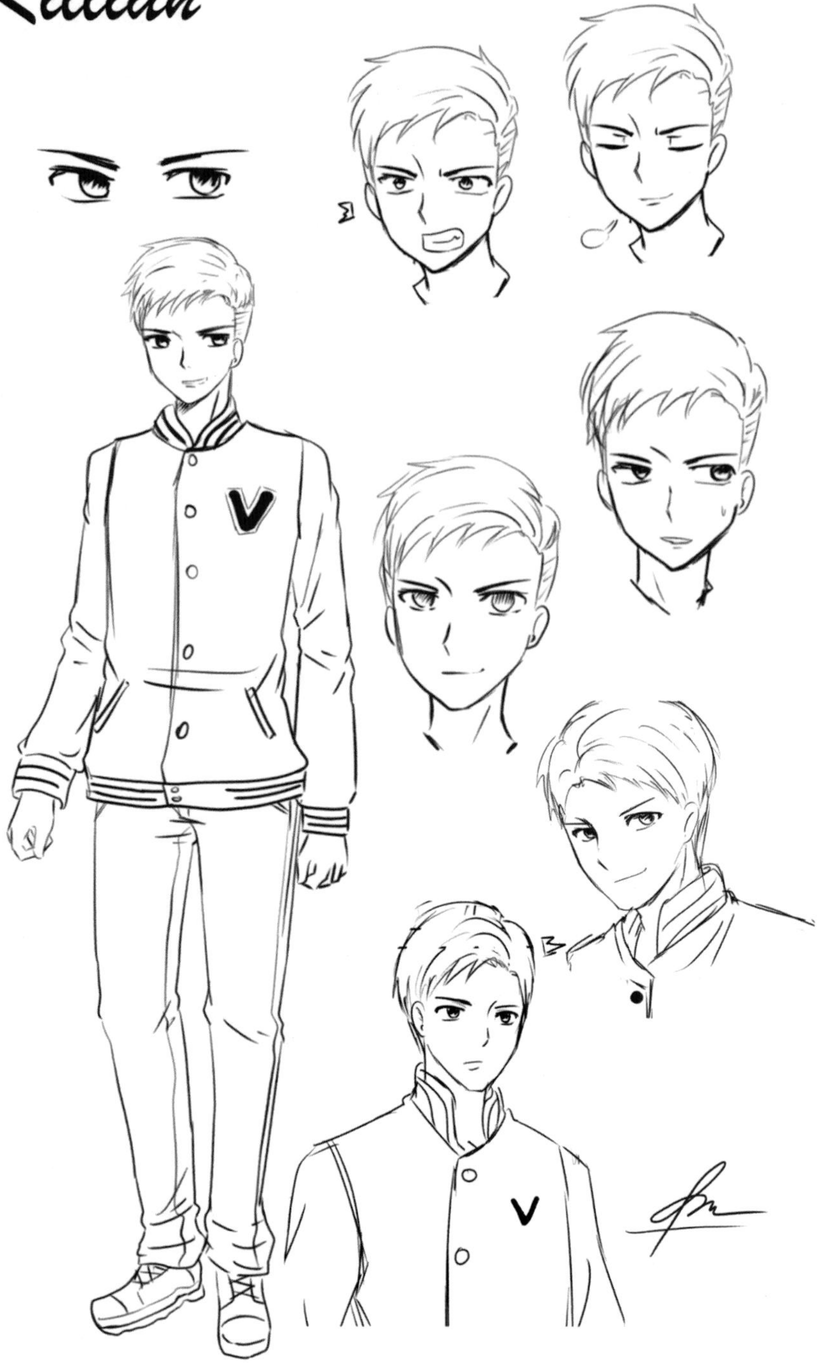

Dr. Gerry

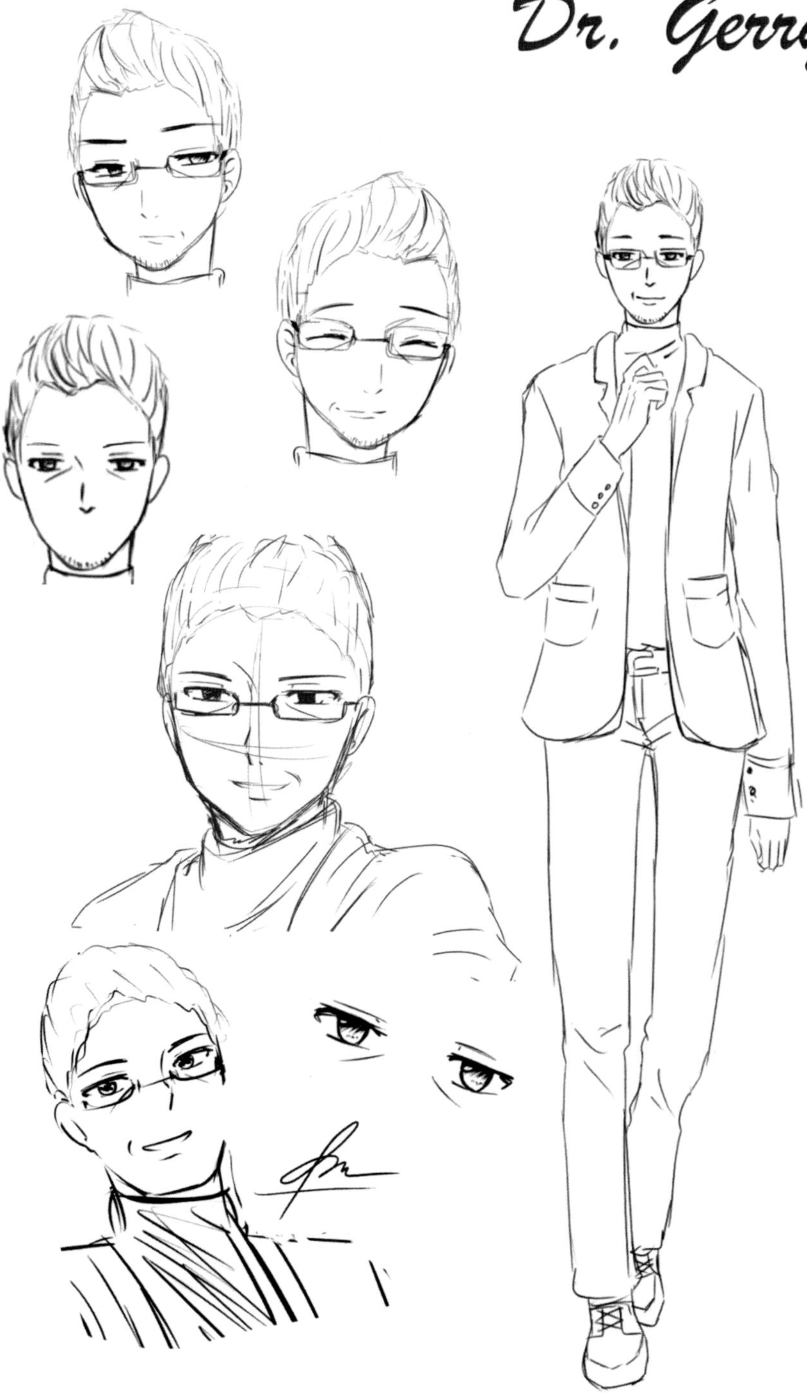

Life Lessons from a UFO Catcher²

An Autobiographical Manga

Story by Kenny Loui, Ph.D.

Art by Yamawe

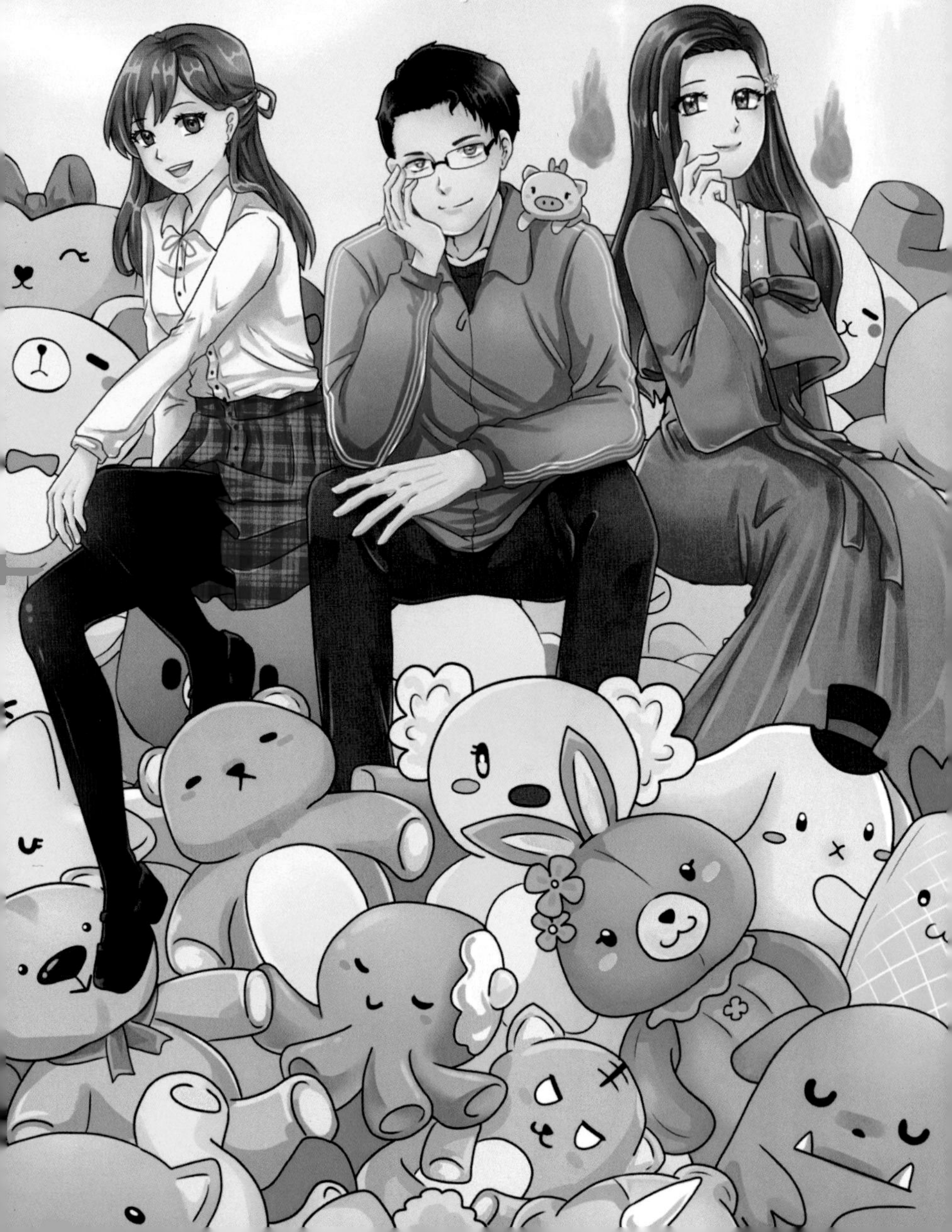

OUR UFO-CATCHING ADVENTURES TOGETHER *DON'T* HAVE TO END HERE!

WEBTOON CANVAS

SCAN THE QR CODE TO READ *SEASON 2* NOW!

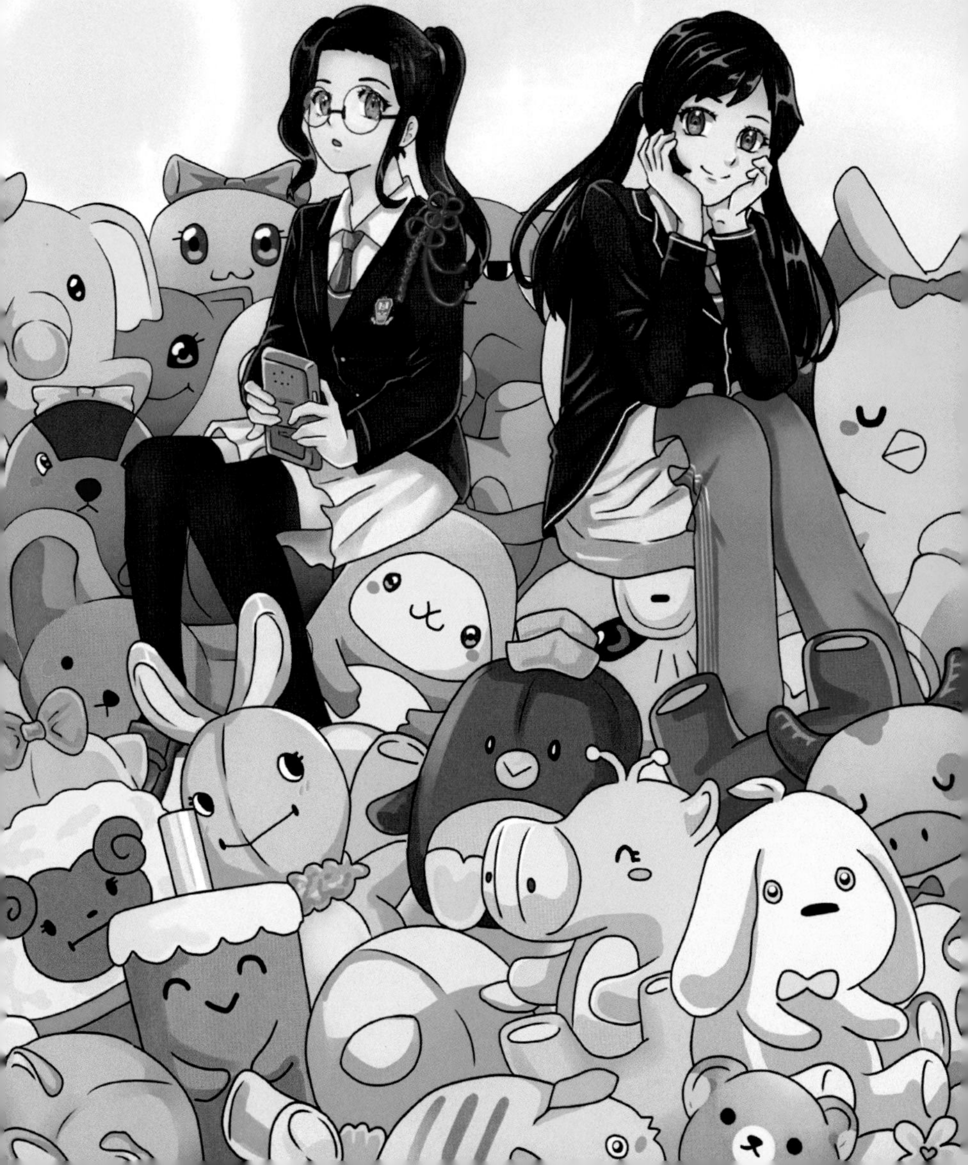

CREATORS

AUTHOR

KENNY LOUI is a doctor (of philosophy), college professor, Civil Air Patrol officer, lifelong otaku, and professional third wheel. His hobbies include reading, writing, stargazing, and liberating cute and cuddly plushies trapped inside arcade crane games. He has been "UFO catching" since 2007 and has a rescue count of over 700 plush dolls, figures, and random thingamabobs.

YAMAWE is a self-taught artist from the Philippines whose style draws inspiration from Japanese anime and manga. She holds a Bachelor of Information Technology and has been working as a freelance digital artist since 2014.

ARTIST